THE
INSIDER

A Volume in the Series
JOURNALISM AND DEMOCRACY

Edited by
KATHY ROBERTS FORDE
AND
SID BEDINGFIELD

THE INSIDER

How the *Kiplinger Newsletter*
Bridged Washington
and Wall Street

ROB WELLS

University of Massachusetts Press
AMHERST AND BOSTON

Copyright © 2022 by University of Massachusetts Press
All rights reserved
Printed in the United States of America

ISBN 978-1-62534-703-9 (paper); 704-6 (hardcover)

Designed by Sally Nichols
Set in Old Standard and Minion Pro
Printed and bound by Books International, Inc.

Cover design by Derek Thornton, Notch Design

Library of Congress Cataloging-in-Publication Data

Names: Wells, Rob, author.
Title: The insider : how the Kiplinger newsletter bridged Washington and Wall Street / Rob Wells.
Description: Amherst : University of Massachusetts Press, [2022] | Series: Journalism and democracy | Includes bibliographical references and index.
Identifiers: LCCN 2022022433 (print) | LCCN 2022022434 (ebook) | ISBN 9781625347046 (hardcover) | ISBN 9781625347039 (paperback) | ISBN 9781613769812 (ebook) | ISBN 9781613769829 (ebook)
Subjects: LCSH: Kiplinger, W. M. (Willard Monroe), 1891–1967. | Kiplinger Washington Letter. | Journalists—United States—Biography. | Journalism—Political aspects—United States. | Press and politics—United States—History—20th century. | New Deal, 1933–1939—Press coverage. | United States—Economic conditions—1918–1945. | United States—Economic policy—1933–1945. | United States—Politics and government—1933–1945.
Classification: LCC PN4874.K548 W45 2022 (print) | LCC PN4874.K548 (ebook) | DDC 070.92—dc23/eng/20220706
LC record available at https://lccn.loc.gov/2022022433
LC ebook record available at https://lccn.loc.gov/2022022434

British Library Cataloguing-in-Publication Data
A catalog record for this book is available from the British Library.

Portions of the introduction and chapters 2 and 3 were previously published as " 'Serve It Up Hot and Brief': The Journalistic Innovations and Influence of Willard M. Kiplinger," *American Journalism* 38, no. 2 (2021): 177–201. Copyright © 2021 American Journalism Historians Association, available online: http://www.tandfonline.com/10.1080/08821127.2021.1912982.

To Jack and Virginia Wells:

Thank you.

Contents

Acknowledgments ix

INTRODUCTION 1

CHAPTER 1
"Pound My Beat and My Typewriter" 31

CHAPTER 2
A Bridge between Wall Street and Washington .. 66

CHAPTER 3
A Two-Way Street 88

CHAPTER 4
Fetching Information and Guidance 112

CHAPTER 5
A Battle with "Economic Royalists" 139

CHAPTER 6
"They SEEM Reasonable" 166

CHAPTER 7
The Promise of Independent Journalism 198

Notes 207

Index 241

Acknowledgments

I am grateful for the many friends and colleagues who helped me at various stages in the production of this book. My wife, Deborah St. Coeur, provided constant support, listening patiently and with great interest to my many discoveries as the research unfolded from the summer of 2019. Our dinner table conversations helped me frame and comprehend the book's argument. A big thank-you to my editor and mentor, Kathy Roberts-Forde, who envisioned how this story could be situated in the broader history of journalism and democracy. My friend David Sicilia suggested a huge stack of books to consume on economic and business history in the New Deal, as did Michael Pierce. Both Sicilia and Pierce provided outstanding comments on early drafts. Pallavi Guha and Steve Sakson offered helpful comments and questions. I was very fortunate that my former editor at Bloomberg News, Mark Willen, was between his own book projects and had time to make some highly insightful edits. It was a real treat to work with him again.

An earlier version of this research was published in the Spring 2021 issue of *American Journalism*. Thank you to Ford Risley, the former editor, and Pamela Walck, his successor, for their support for that article and to the anonymous reviewers who provided constructive comments. This research was supported by the American Journalism Historians Association, which awarded me the McKerns Grant to help defray travel and other archival research expenses. I was extremely lucky to have a talented graduate student, Matthew Moore, as a research assistant on this project. He helped categorize thousands of documents using various software tools that allowed me to see the forest from the trees, and then to better understand the nature of the trees. The University of Arkansas has been a big supporter of my work, with special thanks to Larry Foley, chair of the School of Journalism and Strategic Media, and Robin Roggio of the Mullins Library, who worked magic in obtaining obscure documents and books from all over the country. Thank you to Lucy Dalglish at the University of Maryland Philip Merrill College of Journalism for supporting the final stages of research. I am also grateful to Matt Becker, editor of the University of Massachusetts Press, for his enthusiastic support, and Amanda Heller for her careful edits. Both improved this work.

I wish to extend a special thanks to Knight Kiplinger, longtime editor in chief of the *Kiplinger Letter* and grandson of Willard Kiplinger, who was generous with his time and open to my persistent and at times uncomfortable probing about his family's history. From my first contact in July 2019, Knight Kiplinger clearly understood the importance of what I was pursuing and opened many doors and many file cabinet drawers. He provided access to his family's personal and professional papers, unpublished manuscripts, and a detailed accounting of his grandfather's personal financial dealings and his family's real estate holdings. This book represents my own independent reporting and analysis of Willard Kiplinger's life and career, and I am grateful for Knight Kiplinger's willingness to let an outsider examine his family's past. Julie Shapiro, an archivist of the Kiplinger corporate files, provided immense help for this research, digging out dozens of key documents and offering her perspective on Willard Kiplinger's legacy.

THE
INSIDER

Introduction

WILLARD KIPLINGER SAT quietly in the corner of a spacious office in the State, War, and Navy Building, now known as the Eisenhower Executive Office Building, next to the White House. A veteran newspaper reporter, Kiplinger knew when to ask questions and when to shut up. At this point it was time to listen, since his host, Raymond Moley, was talking on the telephone with President Franklin D. Roosevelt.[1]

In 1933 this is what Kiplinger did most Friday afternoons: stop by Moley's office, trade information about what business leaders were saying about the New Deal, gossip about Capitol Hill politics, and discuss which cabinet members were causing problems. It was also an occasion for Moley to vent and to preview some of the most controversial aspects of the New Deal, policies that would forever change the relationship between government and business. "My instinct told me he could be trusted, and I told him all I knew," Moley wrote about Kiplinger. "Later he told me that he was alarmed at my frankness."[2]

Sometimes debates about the direction of the New Deal took place right in front of Kiplinger. Various officials might break in to interrupt their meeting and discuss sensitive matters with Moley. Kiplinger, a well-groomed man with a trim mustache and dark suit, blended in well, looking like the typical businessman he wrote for (see figure 1). Kiplinger might have concealed his face by raising a newspaper, pretending to read. Make no mistake about it, he was there to listen.

Moley's office was at the epicenter of the New Deal. By his account, this is where the National Industrial Recovery Act first began to take shape, a radical new system of industrial regulation and a risky bet to stabilize and transform US business conduct. Moley was a Columbia University law professor who headed Roosevelt's "Brains Trust," a group of elite professors, primarily from Columbia University, who helped conceive the New Deal during the 1932 presidential campaign.[3] Moley's power was so significant in early 1933 that one administration official described him as "for all practical purposes, a Cabinet in one person."[4] Moley was among a handful of men in the treasury secretary's office in March 1933 as the Roosevelt administration, in an attempt to stop bank runs from spreading nationwide, shut down the US banking system and created a weeklong national banking "holiday," which successfully averted the crisis. Moley spent hours with Roosevelt drafting the speeches and helping sort out the new path for regulating business. Moley, after all, said he came up with the term the "New Deal."[5]

The New Deal, by empowering organized labor, reining in Wall Street, and creating programs such as Social Security, forever changed the relationship between business and the federal government. So it is no wonder that in 1933, Washington was besieged by anxious chief executives of automobile factories, steel mills, and dress manufacturers seeking to learn how the New Deal would curtail their operations or provide new opportunities. Some worried that the new president was out to kill free markets and push the United States into socialism. Labor unions were celebrating and signing up new members at a rapid clip, emboldened by federal support for their organizing activities. During this time it seemed as if everyone wanted to see Moley. He was in such demand that a joke circulated around Washington: "Franklin, can you do me just one favor? Can you get me an appointment with Moley?"

Kiplinger had a standing meeting with Moley each week, a major journalistic coup. One reason was that Moley also found the visits beneficial, since Kiplinger possessed a deep knowledge of Washington, its history, and its unusual culture. Kiplinger had reported on four presidents since 1916 and was the rare journalist fluent in the languages of politics and finance. "He kept me informed about what was going on in Washington beyond my own constricted area of work. He saved me many a mistake," Moley wrote of Kiplinger. "He [Kiplinger] knew Washington after having lived there for 17 years. I knew what the new administration was thinking about and planning. And so every busy week that spring and summer, I set aside an hour

Introduction

on Friday afternoons for a talk with Kip."[6] Kiplinger was extremely valuable to Moley in another respect. The four-page *Kiplinger Washington Letter* was closely read by business executives and other journalists. As a business journalist broadly sympathetic to the New Deal, Kiplinger could help the administration advance its goals and potentially dampen business opposition.[7]

Reliable information about the New Deal was scarce in the early days of the Roosevelt administration. The daily newspapers offered a confusing tick-tock of coverage about the major changes passed by Congress but not the analysis of the impact. Even members of Congress were confused and struggled to gain insight into how the major employers were supposed to boost wages and hire more people and still somehow stay in business. Readers of the no-nonsense *Kiplinger Washington Letter* would find some startling information about debates happening inside the Oval Office, Roosevelt's living room in Hyde Park, and Moley's Washington office. As a result, circulation rose 458 percent between 1930 and 1933 to 18,535 subscribers as the newsletter's reporting became very popular with business executives trying

FIGURE 1. Willard Kiplinger at the typewriter, circa 1930. —Photo courtesy Knight Kiplinger.

to comprehend the government's response to the Depression.[8] "We do not hesitate to say that we consider this service as valuable to us as anything else we subscribe to," said W. E. Wietzel, president of First National Company in Trenton, New Jersey, in a 1935 letter to Kiplinger. The bank made beneficial securities trades based on Kiplinger's reporting. "In fact, it has more than paid for itself on several occasions."[9] *The Kiplinger Washington Letter* didn't quote Moley, or anyone else for that matter, because Kiplinger believed he would get better information if he allowed business leaders and government officials to speak to him without attribution. This was one of his insights from his days as a reporter for the Associated Press from 1913 to 1919, including a three-year stint in the Washington bureau, where he wound up specializing in business and economics. As Moley recalled, "I believed that he knew what to print and what should be kept on background."[10] These meetings with Moley were an example of the insight Kiplinger was able to gain into the New Deal, which in turn led to the expanded popularity of *The Kiplinger Washington Letter*. Business executives found that the letter could help them interpret Washington news and manage the information explosion of the day.

Situated on different perches, Moley in the White House orbit and Kiplinger interacting with the city's power elite, the two men in varying degrees influenced the country's response to the Great Depression, the economic disaster from 1929 through 1933, regarded as the most severe economic contraction in US history.[11] Output of goods and services declined by one-third, and nearly one-fourth of US workers had lost their jobs by May 1933.[12] The historian David Hamilton summarized the carnage: "Between 1929 and 1933, 5,000 American banks collapsed, one in four farms went into foreclosure, and an average of 100,000 jobs vanished each week."[13] Causes of the Great Depression were numerous and complex, but the economist Peter Temin traced the origins to a global economic shock from World War I, which altered international debt arrangements and created a boom and bust in demand for US exports of food and fiber. The fall in demand for farm produce was compounded by a postwar deflation, which served to accelerate farm debts. "There had been no downturn of its magnitude or duration before, and there has been none since. It stands as a unique failure of the industrial economy," Temin wrote.[14]

Moley was a central player in the Roosevelt administration's attempts to halt this economic crisis and rein in corporate excesses. In broad terms, the New Deal at first sought to stabilize the banking system and impose new controls on what businesses could produce and what they could charge, as well as workers' hours and wages. The idea involved limiting predatory price competition, curbing excessive supply, and raising worker pay to stimulate demand. These were the outlines of the National Industrial Recovery Act and the Agricultural Adjustment Act, the two major interventions in business that Congress passed hurriedly in the spring of 1933.

The New Deal created significant uncertainty in the business community, and many executives traveled to Washington that spring to speak firsthand to leaders in the new administration. The calamity in the economy had an ironic benefit for Kiplinger: the Great Depression and Roosevelt's New Deal created such a demand for information that it proved to be a boon for *The Kiplinger Washington Letter,* which had been founded in 1923 (see figure 2). By 1925 its circulation was 1,179, and it grew slowly until 1929, then jumped to 18,535 subscribers in 1933.[15] John Ryerson, a longtime *Kiplinger* editor, recalled that the demand for the newsletter was driven by businessmen who "began to see they needed to follow what was going on in Washington."[16]

Mission of This Book

The Insider shows how Kiplinger, a pioneer in specialized journalism, served as a crucial link between conservative business leaders and government regulators during the New Deal, how he bridged the worlds of Presidents Hoover and Roosevelt. Kiplinger's influence came at a momentous time in the nation's economic history, the depths of the Great Depression, when the very notion of free markets and the future of capitalism were being questioned. Kiplinger's journalism explained the New Deal to a business community that had lost political stature during this economic disaster. Rather than pander to his business audience, Kiplinger repeatedly told these senior corporate leaders that a new order was in place. Laissez-faire economics was dead, and regulation was necessary. Kiplinger helped advance democracy and the rise of modern capitalism by arguing that corporations needed new regulatory structures to curtail their power. "Private industry has demonstrated it cannot govern itself in the public interest without some kind of direction, regulation or supervision from above," he wrote. "Government, therefore, must supply the control." Kiplinger in the summer of 1933 was openly advocating for businesses to comply with the National Recovery Act, describing "the necessity of ALL OF US cooperating for the common good."[17]

He urged businesses to engage in the political system and become decent

THE KIPLINGER WASHINGTON LETTER
CIRCULATED PRIVATELY TO BUSINESS EXECUTIVES
THE KIPLINGER WASHINGTON AGENCY
NATIONAL PRESS BLDG., WASHINGTON, D. C.

Dear Sir: Washington, Saturday, June 24, 1933.

A critical stage of the Roosevelt recovery program will come within the next month or 6 weeks. Important decisions will be forced by events here and abroad. High officials say privately that low point of depression for U. S. is definitely past, but that world factors will still be a major threat during July.

Aim of Washington will be to check July business let-down. Officials think this can be done, but don't yet know just how. Objectives are clear: Raise prices, make jobs, prime private business. Methods are NOT clear. We find considerable floundering, conflict of counsel, and lack of concrete plans for following through.

Certainty of inflation, with uncertainty of "amount" of inflation are relied upon greatly.

Washington will not tell WHEN or WHERE it will stabilize or revalue dollar, partly because it doesn't know and partly because this is a trump in reserve to keep prices rising.

Plan is to pursue nationalistic policy, seemingly compelled by failure of international cooperation, and by domestic necessities. Our outside spokesmen say they want international trade, but our inside administrators are busy building a system of internal semi-self-sufficiency. General methods: TALK inflation, make credit easy, create spending power through public works expenditures, raise wages, spread work through shorter hours, make profits possible, relieve debtors, keep banks strong. Farm act, industrial act, and inflation act provide authority. "If we can insulate ourselves against disturbing foreign influences, we can accomplish 2/3 of a sound recovery in the next 6 or 8 months."

But foreign factors point to an early show-down. Our government refuses to stabilize currency, partly because our government wants a dancing dollar to keep prices rising; partly because dollar uncertainty is our best trading stock at London.

Can U.S. get away with this? Perhaps, but remember other governments have high cards they can play. England and France could force a currency crisis that would upset whole American scheme.

Will France go off gold? Nobody knows. We report a growing belief here that she will. If this happens, it will start a new wave of shocks, probably force England to return to gold, stabilize pound, further depress dollar.

London conference will drag out for months, probably recess and reconvene in fall.

Fall export movement, centering in October, normally should lift dollar in foreign exchange, and curb domestic price rise.

It looks, therefore, as if dollar must be stabilized by Oct. But this stabilization probably would be temporary, thus continuing uncertainty as to ultimate policy into next winter.

COPYRIGHT, 1933, K. W. L.

FIGURE 2. *The Kiplinger Washington Letter*, June 24, 1933. —Photo by Rob Wells

corporate citizens, thus furthering democratic goals. Kiplinger's reporting embodied "associationalism," which promoted business stability through self-regulation and voluntary cooperation by way of trade associations. The case study of Kiplinger's actions during this period serves to highlight the political and historical importance of trade publications in shaping policy debates. Kiplinger was part of a movement that envisioned business leaders in broader roles in the public sphere and sought to empower them to reform capitalism and make businesses more accountable.

The Insider, with its focus on Kiplinger's remarkable work during the New Deal, aims to shed additional light on the little-researched field of commercial newsletters, the trade press, and business journalism in general. This book is timely, given the widespread use of newsletters by major news organizations such as the *Wall Street Journal*, the *Boston Globe*, and many others. *The Kiplinger Washington Letter* was highly influential in the field of specialized journalism as it represented a new stylistic departure for business journalism, one that blended explanatory and analytical writing, both emergent trends in journalism at the time. Kiplinger took it a step further by offering forecasts. This new blend of reporting, analysis, and forecasting was a rejection of the rigid stenographic style of daily journalism in that era. The newsletter synthesized and forecast Washington business, economic, and political news for busy business executives in a novel compact writing style that emphasized brevity. He innovated with close reader engagement and performed a type of early crowdsourcing that anticipated the active audience interaction of digital journalism. These developments, along with his advances in direct marketing, influenced the multibillion-dollar industry of specialized information as well as mainstream publications from *Newsweek* and *U.S. News & World Report* to Bloomberg, Axios, and others.

Why This History Matters

This untold history of *The Kiplinger Washington Letter* and its influence during the New Deal is relevant as our society grapples with questions about the role of journalism in a democratic society. Kiplinger left the sidelines of traditional objective journalism (the "straight news" reporting in which the journalist is a passive observer) to explore more analytical forms of writing and reporting in order to tell the deeper truths about the intersection of government and business. Similar concerns about the limits of objective journalism have been debated in our era as journalists covered the Black Lives Matter movement and the endemic corruption of the Donald Trump administration. Straight news reporting addresses only the top layers of these complex matters. It is fascinating that Kiplinger, covering President Woodrow Wilson's administration, found traditional straight news reporting insufficient to inform society about the complexity of government activities. Kiplinger's approach is instructive for the "chattering class" of modern cable news commentators. He produced analysis, yet it arose from a highly rigorous reporting process, applying the skepticism and independence of a traditional journalist. He used those reporting skills to sift and process the onslaught of information in his day—news, spin, rumors, propaganda. He was not offering the empty cable news commentary of today. Kiplinger demonstrated his independence as a business journalist by resisting the party line of an emerging neoconservative movement, the American Liberty League, with its millionaire businessmen who bankrolled an extensive free-market propaganda campaign, much like, more recently, the Koch brothers.

Furthermore, *The Insider* offers an important perspective on the ongoing debate about whether capitalism and democracy are compatible. A concentration of corporate power, rising wealth inequality, and the debate over a living wage are among the issues prompting questions, yet again, about the fairness and equity of modern capitalism. Kiplinger stood out in his era by supporting capitalism but insisting that businesses consider their obligations as members of civil society. Businesses needed to participate in the democratic process and accept compromises, he wrote, such as working with organized labor. In that sense, this book offers another dimension to the ongoing debate about the nature of liberty that is severely dividing our society. Conservative business leaders' defense of the laissez-faire economic order, in which individual rights reign supreme over societal priorities, reflects the bitter debate during the COVID-19 pandemic when individuals refused to wear masks or take vaccines, claiming an infringement of their individual liberties. This same argument was playing out in the corporate sphere in the 1930s as Kiplinger and others sought to persuade recalcitrant corporations to accept government oversight for the common good. We learn from Kiplinger how a journalist can participate in the political space without being an explicit partisan. Kiplinger's agenda was functional in nature, meant to repair a society devastated by the Great Depression, describe a new world order for businesses, and help capitalism evolve into a more modern era.

Journalist as Political Actor

During the New Deal, Kiplinger emerged as a credible individual in both the business and political worlds thanks to his specialized knowledge of finance and business and his access to key actors. He was a confidant to Hoover and to several of Roosevelt's top advisers such as Moley, Secretary of State Cordell Hull, and Treasury Secretary Henry Morgenthau Jr. Kiplinger's career encompassed varied experiences: reporting for the *Ohio State Journal* in 1912, then the Associated Press in Columbus and Washington, followed by a career change in 1919, working for the National Bank of Commerce as a Washington representative. That led Kiplinger to launch his own private "business intelligence" bureau in 1920 focusing on business issues in the capital, which in turn spawned *The Kiplinger Washington Letter*. By the time Roosevelt took the oath of office in 1933, Kiplinger, age forty-two, had been immersed in the Washington political culture for some seventeen years.

This book contributes to a broader line of scholarship arguing that journalists like Kiplinger should be viewed as political actors.[18] Kiplinger was engaged in the political process, but his journalism wasn't slanted toward one party. He worked behind the scenes, mediating and advising, seeking to improve government operations, and allowing for the smooth functioning of the business-government relationship. Extensive correspondence with Moley, some 140 letters exchanged between 1932 and 1966, reveals that Kiplinger was trying to help the Roosevelt administration succeed by counseling administration officials, suggesting policy improvements, and at times even mediating disputes. In 1934, for example, Kiplinger advised Moley about the political benefits of having Roosevelt acknowledge business concerns with the New Deal and reverse business leaders' negative sentiment. Roosevelt should meet with a group of businessmen and seek their input on economic recovery policies, Kiplinger told him. Such a plan would "make a play to the business interests, to show them that he really wants their help." Such meetings could be highly publicized or private, Kiplinger continued, adding, "Perhaps it would be better to start it quietly," and not until after the 1934 midterm elections.[19] Kiplinger added that he planned to begin speaking about this idea with his business contacts and would write about it in *The Kiplinger Washington Letter*. "Discounting the ultra-conservatives with their lack of imagination and giving maximum weight to a lot of truly liberal businessmen who are or could easily be sympathetic with the New Deal, it seems to me that the business elements have a good right to kick" or complain about the New Deal's poor administration.[20] Moley turned out to be an important voice for the business viewpoint in the Roosevelt administration.

Kiplinger's roots were in the traditional journalism of the Associated Press, but he crossed over into a reporting style heavy with analysis and forecasting with *The Kiplinger Washington Letter*. Launching the newsletter was a major struggle, and to make ends meet during this period, Kiplinger would directly participate in the political process from time to time as a campaign consultant. Kiplinger also was on the payroll, $150 a month as an "anonymous assistant and adviser," for US Representative Cordell Hull, Democrat of Tennessee, during his time in Congress in the 1920s. He worked for a minor Democratic presidential candidate, Governor William Ellery Sweet of Colorado, in 1924.[21] Even in that era, when journalism ethics were being codified by the American Society of Newspaper Editors and the Society of Professional Journalists, political moonlighting arrangements by journalists would have been controversial and a conflict of interest; in many news organizations today, a reporter involved in such a consulting arrangement would be fired.

Over the sweep of his career, however, Kiplinger was not openly partisan, and he dropped the outside political consulting work once *The Kiplinger Washington Letter* took off during the Roosevelt administration. Instead, his political role was more subtle as his journalism helped shape discourse by normalizing the New Deal regulatory state, a foreign and threatening concept, for his business readers. In his reporting he also sought to shape New Deal policy by urging the Roosevelt administration to take business leaders' concerns seriously and maintain a consistent application of rules across various industries. Kiplinger's journalism clearly stood out from the competition in one respect: he strove to explain the New Deal and its controversial aspects to business leaders and initially minimized opposition. Early in the New Deal, during a period when business leaders were complaining about haphazard and conflicting signals from regulators, Kiplinger offered an excuse, saying the National Recovery Administration was "too big a job to do all within the space of a few weeks, or even a few months. It deserves sympathy."[22] He also advanced the New Deal by acting as a type of emissary between Roosevelt's advisers. In 1934 Kiplinger said he was discussing with some administration officials the taxation proposals backed by US Supreme Court Justice Lewis Brandeis. "I am doing what I can to bootleg his ideas to Morgenthau," Kiplinger wrote, referring to Treasury Secretary Henry Morgenthau Jr.[23] Generally speaking, Brandeis "preferred to solve

Introduction

the country's business problems by use of the federal taxing power" and not through the complex regulations established by the National Recovery Act.[24]

Kiplinger also tried to heal some rifts in the administration, such as the divide between Moley and Morgenthau. "In the occasional moments when I allow myself to cease being a reporter and to be a wisher-for-things," he told Moley, "I wish for good relations between you and Morgenthau, not particularly for his sake and not for your sake, but for the sake of the situation at large."[25] He discussed his willingness to offer political advice. "I am afraid Tom Corcoran over-estimates my ability to help Tugwell on tactical or steering advice," Kiplinger wrote to Moley,[26] referring to Rexford Guy Tugwell, the assistant secretary of agriculture, a controversial leftist, and Thomas Corcoran, a Public Works Administration attorney and an influential Roosevelt adviser. Primarily, Kiplinger provided Moley with a detailed critique of various Roosevelt administration officials, ranging from Tugwell to Commerce Secretary Daniel C. Roper to Agriculture Secretary Henry Wallace. Kiplinger even tried to suggest a constructive role for people he criticized, such as Tugwell, the leading voice for economic planning and more aggressive curtailment of US businesses.

There were also instances when Kiplinger deliberately withheld damaging news about the New Deal from his readers. In a letter to Moley in August 1934, Kiplinger wrote, "If I were to print for three weeks running the internal facts which I am able to check and confirm, I would wreck NRA,"[27] referring to the National Recovery Administration. Perhaps this was a boast, but the general point remained: Kiplinger did not print some material critical of the New Deal at a time when he was counseling businesses to remain patient. Kiplinger offered plenty of constructive criticism of the New Deal, however. Coverage in *The Kiplinger Washington Letter* from 1932 through 1936 repeatedly described a dysfunctional bureaucracy, mixed messages from senior officials, Roosevelt's political opportunism, and sudden changes of direction. Hugh Johnson, head of the National Recovery Administration, sought to censor Kiplinger following a string of reports critical of his agency, leading to a backlash from other journalists supporting Kiplinger.

Explaining the New Order

More significant than his efforts at mediation and messaging were Kiplinger's repeated warnings to his business readers that a new order was in place, one that curtailed their power. "Central idea is this: Government hereafter will supervise, regulate and control private industry and trade," he wrote in May 1933. "Ownership, management and initiative will be left to private interests, but government will have power of COMPULSION if private initiative does not respond to what the government regards as the PUBLIC INTEREST. It is a step toward the idea that ALL businesses are inherently public utilities."[28] In his reporting Kiplinger sought to form a new normative conduct for businesses and establish new political expectations in the New Deal: "The old order of laissez faire has broken down. Business, if let alone, would not bring itself out of depression for 5 or 10 years. Federal government now stands out as the strongest element in the picture. Federal government, therefore, must and will dictate to business, and business will follow political leadership or the Executive branch," he wrote in 1933.[29]

The clarity of his message was striking during a period of enormous societal and economic tumult. By 1932 the Great Depression had left many business leaders exhausted, and they complained about a lack of market discipline, unfair trade practices, and cutthroat competition. George W. Alger, a top New York garment industry executive, was among major business leaders who openly called for government intervention to save capitalism: "I am convinced today that decent industry needs help from law, which it never required before."[30] Even staunch free-market economists such as Frank Knight at the University of Chicago conceded this shift in power away from the corporate sector. This was a moment when many agreed that laissez-faire capitalism was dead but disagreed on the regulatory structure that would replace it.

The historian Ellis Hawley framed the ensuing debate as pitting Woodrow Wilson's New Freedom approach against Theodore Roosevelt's New Nationalism, a Progressive-influenced agenda that called for supervising companies, labor, and social welfare programs to more evenly distribute the fruits of modern industrialism. New Nationalism adherents believed that the "concentration of economic power was the inevitable result of mass production and an advancing technology" and called for social insurance for the elderly, disabled, and unemployed and labor reforms such as a minimum wage and an eight-hour workday, all programs by which government could help democratize big business.[31]

As president, Franklin Roosevelt attempted to navigate these two schools of thought when crafting the New Deal with political compromises that business leaders found contradictory and confusing. Roosevelt borrowed the associational idea for regulating business prices and production in the National Industrial Recovery Act and allowed businesses to form cartels to boost prices while taking more drastic measures in agriculture, fixing prices and setting production quotas. At the same time, he pushed for new rights enabling organized labor to expand, serving as a countervailing force to corporate power and pushing to boost worker wages and purchasing power in the economy. On the one hand, the Depression produced insistent demands for planning, rationalization, and the erection of market controls that could stem the forces of deflation and prevent economic ruin. On the other, it intensified antimonopoly sentiment, destroyed confidence in business leadership, and produced equally insistent demands that big business be punished. The dilemma of the New Deal reform movement lay in the political necessity of meeting both of these sets of demands, creating organizations and controls to halt deflationary forces and stabilize the economy while at the same time preserving democratic values.[32]

These changes were happening at a time when the future of capitalism was being questioned in some quarters. Radicalism was on the rise. In the Midwest, outbreaks of populist violence occurred in 1933, such as farmers' strikes, and general industrial strikes in the summer that put some 300,000 workers out of a job. Hugh S. Johnson, leader of the National Recovery Administration, feared that the country was on the brink of collapse and revolution: "We could have got a dictator a lot easier than Germany got Hitler." Tugwell, an influential member of the Brains Trust, offered similar sentiments, reflecting on the day of Roosevelt's inauguration, "I do not think it is too much to say that on March 4 [1933] we were confronted with a choice between an orderly revolution—a peaceful and rapid departure from past concepts—and a violent and disorderly overthrow of the whole capitalist structure."[33]

By contrast, Wilson's New Freedom was aimed at systemic reform by targeting corporate monopolies and breaking up concentrated economic power on Wall Street. Examples of the New Freedom regulatory approach include the formation of the Federal Reserve System in 1913, which created the nation's central bank and helped modernize the banking system, and passage of the Federal Trade Commission Act, which policed unfair trading practices, and the Clayton Antitrust Act in 1914. Louis Brandeis, a central Progressive intellectual and later a Supreme Court justice, was a key proponent. In addition, the concept of having businesses band together through trade associations for the public good emerged from the business planning efforts during World War I.

Kiplinger's journalism explained the New Deal to a business community that had lost political influence in the Great Depression and was seeing a broad repudiation of laissez-faire economics. Even staunch free-market economists such as Frank Knight at the University of Chicago conceded this shift in power from the corporate sector. Knight wrote to a colleague in the summer of 1933, "We cannot go back to laissez-faire in economics even in this country.... Now it seems to me inevitable that we must go over to a controlled system."[34] During this period of economic transformation, new possibilities were opening for democracy. Certainly the labor movement was gaining power and influence in public and business affairs during the New Deal. The historian Nancy Cohen, in her examination of American liberalism, asked if the social relations of capitalism and values of democracy were reconcilable.[35] Kiplinger's answer would have been yes. His journalism reflected an underlying idealism that business progress could coexist with democracy, that enlightened businesspeople could help perfect society. His reporting still embraced free-market ideals but endorsed the use of government power to align with private interests for public benefit.

In May 1933 Kiplinger described a radical change in the concept of liberalism in business:

> In the past, each business unit was largely a free individual, doing what it pleased in its own way, competing under a system which glorified individual initiative and individual competition, with a minimum of governmental restriction. In the future, the business unit will be NOT the individual enterprise, but the industry or trade as a whole. The individual enterprise will be restricted, controlled, curbed, compelled to march as a private soldier in the whole-industry regiment, with the government as commander of the regiment. This probably means YOU.[36]

This theory of modified capitalism was an essential feature of Roosevelt's First New Deal, encompassing 1933–34, which featured stabilizing the banking and financial markets while attempting to regulate business production, eliminate price deflation, and boost employment. Kiplinger described it as the "greatest experiment of our generation," one that was leading to "economic nationalism."[37]

Business Backlash

Such passages in Kiplinger's *Washington Letter* were not popular with some portion of his readership, many of whom were conservative business executives. "Roughly we would estimate that 80% of businessmen at the present time are antagonistic to Roosevelt and the New Deal—in varying degrees," Kiplinger wrote in 1935, citing results of a reader survey.[38] A business backlash against the New Deal began to form in the summer of 1933 over regulation of the Wall Street markets and new laws encouraging union organizing in the workplace. Kiplinger's reporting did not back business advocacy groups like the American Liberty League, a group of powerful industrialists who were actively organizing opposition to the New Deal. A more recent equivalent would be the Koch brothers, with their emphasis on corporate supremacy and free markets. Instead, Kiplinger offered his own criticism of the New Deal, focusing not on ideology but on administration. Kiplinger faulted the Roosevelt administration for inconsistency in industry price control agreements and poor management in the grinding bureaucracy of the National Recovery Administration. Confusion within the NRA about business regulations, Kiplinger wrote in August 1933, was "shamefully bad."[39] At the same time, he sought to explain the philosophy of key aspects of the New Deal, such as the importance of organized labor. He knew this topic was not welcome among his audience. "Business men should understand labor's point of view, whether they agree with it or not," he wrote.[40] Kiplinger was critical of organized labor, but he considered it an important force in the US economy and wrote in depth about the movement's broader ambitions and its divisions. At several junctures Kiplinger sought to normalize the mainstream labor movement, the American Federation of Labor, or AFL: "This AF of L is 'conservative' in the sense that it stands for the capitalistic system. It wants merely an increased share in the fruits of the system."[41] Such commentary showed how labor goals aligned with the New Deal and how a new system of labor-management relations was inevitable.

Another way Kiplinger sought to shape business behavior was by promoting the associational ideal, a concept favored by President Herbert Hoover, which sought to rein in business excesses from the laissez-faire era of capitalism and instill a sense of social obligation in business management. These are important steps toward expanding democracy. Roosevelt and his advisers adopted this core concept of industry self-regulation and organization in the First New Deal with enactment of the National Industrial Recovery Act. Kiplinger reported on business leaders' complaints about the New Deal but also insisted they remain accountable to society and use their power for the greater good. Kiplinger envisioned a broader role for business leaders in civil society. "Actually business men are our principal class of public servants, although it would shock them to be told so," he wrote in *Scribner's* magazine, a leading public affairs journal at the time. "The fact is that they in the aggregate control the destinies of most of us to a far greater extent than do government officials.... For this reason, the treatment of business men by the government demands attention in the *public interest* quite apart from the profits and private interest of any particular business man himself." Yet he faulted business owners for narrow thinking "in the sense that they are focused on their particular interests, and that they think of their business as the *end* rather than the *means* of getting things done for the community or the nation.... Many have no understanding of broad economic or social abstractions. Consequently they are apt to think that anything which interferes with their operations, their 'freedom,' their 'liberty,' is wrong."[42]

Some in the business community were receptive to this message, acknowledging that change was afoot and accepting some government oversight role of the business sector. The US Chamber of Commerce, for example, was willing to accede to some level of governmental control of business "to a degree that would have seemed incredible a year ago," *Business Week* stated. It noted the irony that the Chamber, "rugged individualism's sturdy champion . . . favors now cooperation under government control."[43] *The Kiplinger Washington Letter* played an important functionalist role by setting boundaries on business conduct during the New Deal while also showing businesses opportunities to engage and influence the regulatory process. "I spend my morning talking to business men callers at my office here in Washington, listening to their troubles, suggesting courses which are in line, or not too far out of line, with government policies," wrote Kiplinger.[44] He told his readers that his analysis was aimed to "help you read between the lines."[45]

Role of the Trade Press

From the very beginning of modern capitalism, business journalism played a central role of supplying market participants with information about business conditions, supplies, demand, labor dynamics, all essential details for basic transactions to take place. After all, public stock markets cannot exist without news. Consider the newsletters produced by Count Phillip Edward Fugger in Germany in the sixteenth and seventeenth centuries. These first newsletters distributed news about business and markets from trade centers in Europe, allowing for price discovery in these evolving markets for commodities and goods.[46]

Introduction   17

The Kiplinger Washington Letter differed from trade journalism in this era by providing a much broader and more ambitious scope. Kiplinger offered specialized industry advice, but there was more: he explained the forces that drove politics and policy. In this way his writing represented the business voice in a broader conversation about the direction of capitalism and liberalism.

The Insider also highlights the political and historical importance of trade publications in shaping policy debates. This volume extends my ongoing scholarship about business journalism, which includes my first book, *The Enforcers: How Little-Known Trade Reporters Exposed the Keating Five and Advanced Business Journalism* (2019). *The Enforcers* documented the historical importance of trade journalism and described a level of investigative reporting in this field of specialized journalism. *The Insider* extends this scholarship by examining the role of journalism in an evolving relationship between two of society's most powerful institutions, business and the government. This investigation of Kiplinger expands the historiography of business journalism that to this point has focused primarily on mass market publications, particularly *Fortune* and the *Wall Street Journal*. This book also examines how a top business journalist influenced the cultural and economic agenda of business leaders.[47]

Kiplinger's functionalist style of journalism made his newsletter different from the competition. In 1933, as Roosevelt's administration rammed through far-reaching business regulations, *Business Week* and the *New York Times* reported in detail on congressional committee hearings and the evolution of the proposals. By contrast, Kiplinger's style of forecasting blended reporting with analysis and some speculation—always clearly labeled as such. He described the main elements of news events but focused more on their impact, the global picture, and advised readers on what businesspeople could do to engage with the process. Kiplinger urged business leaders, when testifying about industry regulations before the National Recovery Administration, to "present your facts simply, clearly, and as briefly as practical. If you do this, you'll get a sympathetic reception. If you don't, you'll find the Administration very hardboiled."[48] He also warned readers against making a personal trip to Washington to obtain an explanation of the National Recovery Act. Such trips, he said, were "apt to be a waste of time," since the NRA was a "mad house."[49] Whether this was intended or not, Kiplinger's advice also served to reinforce his brand by sending the message to readers: save yourself some money and depend on us instead to look out for your best interests. This is the sort of attitude that is at the core of trade journalism, featured in publications such as *The Bond Buyer* or *American Lawyer* which offer specialized reporting for specific business audiences. Throughout history, trade publications have aspired to expand the corners of the business world where they specialize.

By the time Kiplinger launched his business newsletter, journalists and academics were trying to grasp the impact of large private businesses on society. Changes in technology, growing urbanization, and the emergence of new railroad and communications networks gave rise to major industrial companies and new forms of bureaucratic organization. "The coming of the large vertically integrated, centralized, functionally departmentalized industrial organization altered the internal and external situations in which and about which business decisions were made," the historian Alfred Chandler wrote.[50] These huge new organizations, which had no precedent in US history, needed information to navigate the economy and business issues, a need Kiplinger identified and fulfilled in his newsletter.

Kiplinger's *Letter* was in sync with the evolution of capitalism in the early twentieth century as it moved into a managerial phase, one that boosted demand for specialized news and information. Managerial capitalism involved a change in daily operations whereby firms were run by a new class of managers not connected to the owners.[51] This was a break from the older paradigm in which corporate titans, such as J. P. Morgan or John D. Rockefeller, owned companies outright and dictated operational details. The shift represented a decline of power for investment bankers and financiers in favor of managers. Kiplinger supplied the essential information for this growing corps of professional corporate managers and helped propel this movement forward.

Kiplinger's journalism, by playing such an explicit functionalist role, helped capitalism evolve. His journalism supported the moderate forces within the Roosevelt White House who were using the New Deal as a transition to a more stable economy and to head off more radical planned economy experiments, such as proposals by Tugwell, the assistant secretary of agriculture. Kiplinger sought to put the talk of radical socialistic reforms in broader context. "Is the Roosevelt program socialistic? Certainly YES, the trend is more and more in this direction. But the ultimate aim is not thorough-going socialism. . . . The purpose behind new socialistic policies is not to embrace socialism, but rather to save capitalism."[52]

Associationalism

With the First New Deal, Roosevelt's main goal for the business sector involved stabilizing the economy to spur job growth and eradicate ruthless competition which was causing a downward spiral in prices, a phenomenon known as deflation. The National Industrial Recovery Act, the heart of the First New Deal and its regulation of business, called on companies to work with trade associations in order to formulate wage and production controls that would stem plunging prices and stimulate demand. The main concept used to drive the business sector overhaul was "associationalism," which promoted business stability through voluntary cooperation with regulators.[53] Trade associations such as the US Chamber of Commerce and the American Petroleum Institute arose during this time to fill this role, part of the evolution of the modern lobbying industry. Associationalism anticipated modern neoliberalism in one important respect. Neoliberals, who revere individualism and a limited government role in public affairs, would endorse the industry self-regulation that is at the core of the associational ideal.

Kiplinger in February 1933 dismissed the notion that Roosevelt's policies represented a radical departure from Hoover.[54] Here was one of the ironies of the New Deal: Herbert Hoover was a champion of associationalism, and Roosevelt used the same concept to build a business regulatory framework for the National Industrial Recovery Act. Hoover, after all, had applied associationalism as commerce secretary from 1921 to 1928 to help tamp down predatory business practices and improve efficiency. In his reporting and engagement with both the Hoover and Roosevelt camps, Kiplinger repeatedly endorsed the associationalist ideal. Although these regulations represented a far-reaching change in the government-industry relationship, Kiplinger framed it as something the industry itself had been advocating:

> This is dictatorship nominally but not actually. Your trade or industry must get busy soon and create a government advisory committee. . . . Is this revolutionary? YES. But it is practically the thing you have been advocating for years. This is an over-turn of the antitrust laws. This is a mandatory compulsion of intra-industry cooperation which heretofore has been considered desirable but illegal. Individualized unit competition is thing of past. Laissez faire is thing of past. In future the thing is not you, or your company, but your trade or industry, in its relation to public welfare. If your trade association is good enough, it will become government instrumentality. But most trade associations aren't good enough.[55]

Explanatory Journalism

The Kiplinger Washington Letter represented a new stylistic departure for business journalism, one that blended explanatory and analytical writing, both emergent trends in journalism at the time. Kiplinger took it a step further by offering forecasts. This new combination of reporting, analysis, and forecasting was a rejection of the rigid stenographic style of daily journalism in that era. Kiplinger began to move toward this new style after a confrontation with his editor at the Associated Press in 1918 over an analytical article involving the Treasury Department. The AP's Washington bureau chief was livid after Kiplinger reported on the behind-the-scenes maneuverings in a public financing controversy. Kiplinger thought he was going to get fired. The message to the young journalist: stick to the Treasury Department's announcements and keep any interpretation or analysis to yourself.[56] Such encounters inspired Kiplinger to leave the AP and develop a more analytical form of business reporting. As his style evolved, Kiplinger made a point of not describing his reporting as news, even noting that his publication was not a "newsletter." It was a "letter": *The Kiplinger Washington Letter.*

He made it clear that his publication did not substitute for a newspaper. "We don't give you much NEWS," he wrote in a 1933 letter to readers.[57] At another point Kiplinger wrote, "Our job is to treat news as raw material, to fit the pieces together to make a consistent pattern of political policy, to contribute the elements of judgment, perspective, analysis, interpretation, balance," continuing, "It is a saying within our office that FACTS are always less significant than the MEANING of facts."[58]

Another central element in Kiplinger's analytical style involved the agency of the individual journalist, one that valued the reporter's opinions and analytical skills. "I proceeded on the assumption that a reporter is entitled to have judgment," Kiplinger wrote. "He knows who killed the victim, when maybe the jury doesn't. He knows whether the oleomargarine bill will or will not pass." In a 1966 interview Kiplinger said, "So with the Letter, I violated all of the rules of reporting, giving opinion as well as fact."[59] As with anyone using a crystal ball, there are some forecasts that proved to be embarrassments. Not long before the 1936 election, Kiplinger told readers that the Republican Party nominee, Kansas governor Alf Landon, had a shot to unseat President Roosevelt: "Landon CAN be elected."[60] In fact, the election wasn't even close: Roosevelt won by a landslide, capturing forty-six states. The more severe mishap was in 1948, when

Kiplinger forecast Thomas Dewey as the winner over Harry Truman in the presidential election. Kiplinger "took no solace in the fact that he had plenty of company in underestimating Truman and he promptly refunded the subscription fees of many irate subscribers," according to an internal company history.[61] Irate indeed: subscriptions to *The Kiplinger Washington Letter* fell by 23,496, or 13 percent, in the year after the 1948 election.[62]

This review of Kiplinger's journalism adds a new dimension to the historiography of explanatory journalism in the twentieth century. Kiplinger left the world of transcription journalism to produce interpretive reporting a decade before the watershed event in 1933 when the American Society of Newspaper Editors urged newspapers to include "attention and space to explanatory and interpretative news."[63] Existing research examined factors such as the emergence of radio broadcast news, the reaction to propaganda after World War I, and the growing complexity of government and society.[64] Kiplinger's move into interpretive journalism shows that he was filling a void in business and economic journalism that emerged as a result of the changing nature of the US economy and regulatory landscape.

Broader Influence

Across the political spectrum—conservative small-town Rotary Club businessmen, leaders of the Communist Party, current and former US presidents, and top corporate executives—all read Kiplinger's political and economic insights. His work appeared on multiple platforms, from his four-page newsletter to freelance articles for the *New York Times*, and from academic articles to speeches and even nationwide radio broadcasts featuring the Philadelphia Orchestra. Kiplinger produced significant journalism for the general public, helping expand public knowledge about the business and economic sphere. He became a popular brand in financial reporting with his freelance journalism in the *New York Times, Today,* and *Scribner's* and his best-selling books, the 1935 *Inflation Ahead* and the 1942 *Washington Is Like That*, which aimed to demystify the intersection of business and politics, a realm previously confined to elites. Other newspapers reported on Kiplinger's predictions, further expanding his broader public influence. Kiplinger's personal scrapbooks contain some twenty-nine newspaper articles in 1932 mentioning his work, rising to forty articles in 1935, and then averaging a dozen articles a year through 1945 (see figure 3). Publications including the *Tampa Tribune, Christian Science Monitor, San Diego Union,* and *Cleveland News* referred to his work. Kiplinger's

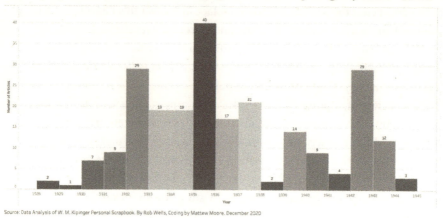

FIGURE 3. Newspaper articles mentioning Willard Kiplinger, 1929–1945. —Graphic by Rob Wells and Matthew Moore.

reporting was cited in the *Congressional Record* in 1930 and 1935. He was profiled in the *Saturday Evening Post*, the *Literary Digest*, and *Time* magazine.

In addition, Kiplinger wrote for academic journals such as *Journalism Quarterly* and the *Annals of the American Academy of Political and Social Science*.[65] He even wrote articles for *Cosmopolitan* magazine. From 1928 through 1937, Kiplinger was producing four to six significant magazine articles a year for outside publications. One longtime friend, Yates Cook, described Kiplinger as "a man of action. He didn't procrastinate."[66] The work dropped off after 1935, when *The Kiplinger Washington Letter* witnessed significant growth and he began to amass considerable personal wealth.

Kiplinger's prodigious output represented what Nancy Cohen would describe as a "tutoring of public opinion."[67] Through these activities, Kiplinger was part of a broader journalistic movement that included *Fortune* and *Business Week*, which opened a powerful business sector to public scrutiny and as a result opened up the possibility for some form of democratic pressure to control corporate behavior. To that end, Paul Starr has noted the unusual contributions of journalism entrepreneurs to enriching public discourse: "This entrepreneurial activity expands the scale and scope of the public sphere, extending its known frontiers. . . . [M]arkets, however much reviled, make vital contributions to a democratic public sphere that are unlikely to be made any other way."[68] One remarkable example of Kiplinger's journalism being used to advance democratic discourse involves his popularity in the radical labor press. The *Daily Worker,* the official newspaper of the Communist Party USA, and other radical papers quoted *The Kiplinger Washington Letter* in twenty-six separate issues from 1931 through 1940. In ten cases, the Kiplinger citation was on page one; in two cases, the *Daily Worker* and *Producers News* printed a replica of *The Kiplinger Washington Letter* on the first page. These radical journalists found Kiplinger's insights about corporate America to be essential reading. Earl Browder, general secretary of the Communist Party USA, quoted Kiplinger in his report to the party's Eighth National Convention in 1934: "Even the capitalists, in their confidential discussions, are adopting the view that the depression will be a prolonged one, that a quick recovery is impossible. Thus, the Kiplinger Agency, in its weekly letter of March 17, speaks on this point as follows: 'Washington feeling about the course of recovery: Most private discussions by the authorities here reflect a resignation to the idea of slow and irregular recovery, not rapid recovery.'"[69]

The New Deal era was a watershed for business and economic journalism, to the extent that Wayne Parsons described Washington, DC, as becoming the center of the journalistic universe: "Washington became an economic news centre that rivaled the pre-eminence of the financial district: from the 1930s onwards, governments were making economic news."[70]

The Kiplinger publishing enterprise was important in the history of business journalism in other respects. Kiplinger created the first personal finance magazine in 1947, *Kiplinger Magazine,* later renamed *Changing Times,* and then *Kiplinger's Personal Finance* magazine. He was also a co-founder of WETA-TV in Washington, DC, a leader in US public television. *The Kiplinger Washington Letter* and *Kiplinger's Personal Finance* magazine along with other periodicals claimed a paid circulation of 900,000 in 2019, while Kiplinger.com counted 30 million page views per month. The Kiplinger company and its various publishing interests had $33 million in revenue in 2018, down from $50 million in 1986.[71] In 2019 the Kiplinger family sold the business to Dennis Publishing in London, ending three generations of family ownership. The legacy of the family ownership continues, however. Beginning in 1983, the National Press Foundation has awarded a W. M. Kiplinger Distinguished Contributions to Journalism Award, which recognizes major figures in US journalism; at this writing the prize was $2,500. Award recipients have included Bob Woodward of the *Washington Post* and columnist George Will.

Newsletters

The Insider aims to shed additional light on the little-researched field of commercial newsletters, the trade press, and business journalism in general. We see Kiplinger's techniques of brevity, synthesis, analysis, and reader engagement influence the modern digital newsletter, a format used by the *Wall Street Journal,* the *Boston Globe,* the *Washington Post,* and many other major media companies. Cory Schouten, editor in chief of *Crain's New York Business,* wrote in 2020, "Our research shows newsletters are workhorses of reader engagement and subscriber growth and retention."[72] This genre of journalism is attracting plenty of interest and plenty of money. A newsletter aimed at millennial professional women, *theSkimm,* boasted more than 7 million subscribers in 2018 and had raised $29 million in capital after just six years of operation.[73] The political and business news website Axios is expanding newsletters into local markets, such as northwest Arkansas.

Kiplinger was a leader in specialized journalism, publications whose focus is people in a particular industry or business sector. These business-to-business publications generated nearly $12 billion in print and digital advertising revenue in 2017, according to Connectiv, an industry group.[74] By comparison, major cable and network television generated $7.9 billion in advertising revenue in 2017, a figure that includes Fox News, CNN, MSNBC, CNBC, Bloomberg TV, and the morning and evening network news shows, according to the Pew Center.[75] Kiplinger doesn't fit neatly in this category because the subscription base of *The Kiplinger Washington Letter* is so large, with print and online circulation of about 100,000, and also because the newsletter doesn't accept advertising.[76]

Despite their influence, there has been little academic research focusing on Kiplinger or his publishing enterprise. *The Kiplinger Washington Letter,* launched in 1923, claims to be the oldest continuously published newsletter in the United States. According to one industry analyst, Kiplinger "developed a crisp, staccato-style of journalism printed in typewriter type on letter-size paper that often has been emulated."[77] *The Kiplinger Washington Letter* once boasted of being "the most widely read business letter in the world."[78] A 1967 *Newsweek* obituary of Kiplinger noted: "There are at least 1,000 newsletters in the country today. Many of them borrow heavily from the Kiplinger techniques."[79] The *Saturday Evening Post* described Kiplinger in the 1940s

Introduction

as "the best-paid and most-influential reporter in the world: also the most independent." The magazine lauded Kiplinger for writing about Washington news in a breezy yet efficient style "that the folks back home understood."[80] Kiplinger's personal identity was wrapped up in his professional pursuits. He once offered a terse biographical note to his readers: "Personal. Some readers want to know who Kiplinger is. A journalist, trained as newspaperman, in Washington 17 years. Age 43. Native of Ohio. No hobbies. Personally the final writer of the Washington Letters."[81]

Brevity and conciseness were hallmarks of Kiplinger's journalism, presented in bare-bones fashion each week, four pages of typewritten text with no graphics or photos. Various phrases are underlined for emphasis, and some words are capitalized or are set in bold type. This book preserves the underlined phrases and bold text in quotations from *The Kiplinger Washington Letter* since these devices offer insight into how Kiplinger emphasized material for his readers. These quirky typographical conventions are elements of the "sweep line" writing style Kiplinger invented, designed to enable a busy business executive to skim a page and quickly grasp the most important points. As Kiplinger described it, the newsletter had an overarching goal: "Serve it up hot and brief."[82] *Newsweek* in its "Periscope" column and *McCall's* in "The Washington Newsletter" were among the dozens of publications that mimicked Kiplinger's stylistic inventions in the 1940s and 1950s. While few publications formally employ the sweep line style, the broad contours of Kiplinger's concept endure: a tightly edited, compact writing style aimed at helping the busy modern reader tame the information explosion. We could think of blogs, Substack, Twitter, and listicles as modern heirs to these ideas.

Another remarkable feature of the Kiplinger story was his generosity. He began a profit-sharing arrangement with his employees in 1923 and donated significant amounts of his company stock to the plan.[83] The Kiplinger Employees Profit Sharing Plan provided annual cash profit sharing, a bonus on top of regular salary that would equal 6 to 20 percent of an employee's pay. In addition, there was deferred profit sharing, equaling perhaps 15 percent of an employee's salary, paid into an investment account managed by the company. Workers also were eligible for a traditional "defined benefit" pension plan and, after that pension arrangement was phased out, a 401(k) savings plan, to which the company contributed 4 percent of a worker's salary. Kiplinger workers also had access to a company-owned Florida vacation lodge, called Bay Tree Lodge, on the St. Lucie River north of Palm Beach. A

1966 staff tribute to Kiplinger, a year before his death, thanked him for his generosity, the "oodles of fringe benefits . . . making us all creeping socialists. . . . The truth is, you're a damned good boss . . . as bosses go."[84]

Kiplinger could also be a tough taskmaster who would have his reporters and editors rewrite their stories multiple times and convene Friday afternoon "hell sessions" where stories were critiqued, bluntly. "Kip had a way of looking over folks' shoulders," recalled George Bryant, a former Kiplinger chief of staff and former Washington bureau chief of the *Wall Street Journal*. People who didn't perform well were fired.[85]

Audience Engagement

One of Kiplinger's most important contributions was his acceleration of trends already present in trade journalism: close reader engagement and crowdsourcing of information. Kiplinger perfected audience engagement techniques that served as a precursor to the active audience interaction of digital journalism. Throughout the business chaos of the New Deal, Kiplinger asked his business readers to write in and describe conditions in their industry and problems with the Roosevelt administration's regulatory initiatives, all of which would form the basis of articles. He also provided a specialized research service for his subscribers, who could ask about any business topic in Washington. Kiplinger's journalists would search out the answers and report back to the subscriber, a strategy that helped cement reader loyalty.

Reader engagement blurred with marketing. Kiplinger was clever in his sourcing and marketing techniques, reaching out to powerful and influential leaders through personalized letters. In 1931 he sent a complimentary subscription to Franklin D. Roosevelt, who was then governor of New York. This episode illustrates Kiplinger's ability to blend source development with audience engagement and business promotion. At the same time, the newsletter kept its price moderate so as to expand its reach to middle America and small-to-medium-sized businesses. The newsletter "has never restricted itself to an elite audience. . . . [T]he small or medium-sized manager and businessman or retailer or farmer is really the best potential reader of the Kiplinger Letter," said Kiplinger's son Austin in an oral history of the company.[86] For example, one reader, J. Preston Wenn, owner of a North Carolina sawmill operation, wrote to say that the *Kiplinger Letter* "is truly an executive tool for better management. . . . You are doing a great service for the American executive."[87]

Kiplinger's influence can be seen in the broad news coverage of his death. In postmortem tribute, one commentator said that Kiplinger had created "a whole new style of journalism."[88] While that claim stretches the point, it does provide some feeling for Kiplinger's standing in the field of the trade press. Austin Kiplinger was more measured in his assessment of his father's legacy: "During his time, he saw the federal government grow from a modest referee into a central figure in economic decision making. . . . W. M. Kiplinger was one of the first widely read writers to discuss the effects of national government on the economy in terms that people could understand. He let his readers know what Washington would mean to them in down-to-earth ways."[89]

Outline of Chapters

The Insider examines Kiplinger's news coverage and his role in shaping the public conversation about business practices, influencing business discourse, and envisioning a new relationship between businesses and government. It describes Kiplinger's life and impact but focuses on Roosevelt's first term and the First New Deal, 1932–1936, a period when *The Kiplinger Washington Letter*'s circulation expanded rapidly and Kiplinger himself became a national newsmaker in his own right. The analysis addresses three case studies. The first involves how the *Kiplinger Letter* and other media covered the March 1933 bank holiday, an event that signaled the failure of capitalism and the need for explicit government intervention. Kiplinger's coverage, his private correspondence, and competing media coverage are examined in two more events, the business rebellion against the National Recovery Act, which began in mid-1933 and accelerated in 1935, and labor's fight with big business and its historic victory with passage of the National Labor Relations Act, known as the Wagner Act, in 1935. *The Kiplinger Washington Letter*'s coverage is compared to a selective reading of reporting in the *New York Times, Fortune,* and *Business Week*. These issues and Kiplinger's influence were in sharp relief in the 1932–1936 period, a time when Moley was still close to Roosevelt and for which there is a wealth of correspondence between Kiplinger and Moley. In these three case studies, we see Kiplinger operating as a political actor while also contributing to the growth of explanatory journalism.

Kiplinger's upbringing in Ohio, the trajectory of his journalism career, and an overview of his business form the core of chapter 1. The tremendous success of *The Kiplinger Washington Letter* made Kiplinger a millionaire, and he shared a good deal of his wealth with his employees through his generous profit-sharing plan and other significant benefits.

The concept of Kiplinger bridging Wall Street and Washington is further explored in chapter 2 with the journalist's relationship with Herbert Hoover. The two first met when Hoover was commerce secretary in the 1920s and formed a friendship once Hoover left the White House, with a warm exchange of letters and some gifts. Hoover played an important transitional role in the evolution of business regulation by advancing associationalism, the idea of industry self-government through trade associations, to address the damage of predatory pricing and unrestrained competition. The associational ideal sought to rein in business excesses from the laissez-faire era of capitalism and instill a sense of social obligation in business management. Kiplinger actively promoted this ideal, an important step toward expanding democracy. Roosevelt and his advisers adopted this core concept of industry self-regulation and organization in the First New Deal with enactment of the National Industrial Recovery Act.

The Moley–Kiplinger correspondence forms the centerpiece of chapter 3, which explores the dual roles Kiplinger served as journalist and informal New Deal adviser. Similarly, Moley was trying to grapple with his own dual roles as political adviser and journalist. Moley left the Roosevelt administration in 1933 to become editor of *Today* magazine while maintaining a significant role advising the president through 1936, at which time he broke with Roosevelt and became a potent political critic.

Kiplinger's style of business journalism played an important functionalist role, a theme examined in chapter 4. This chapter explores how Kiplinger acknowledged industry's frustrations with the new regulations but constantly advocated acceptance of major precepts of the First New Deal. One aim of Kiplinger's coverage was to try to perfect democracy by scolding and mentoring the business community to improve its conduct. This is classic trade journalism behavior, helping to advance businesses by surveilling the market and reporting on emerging risks and threats. The goal is to improve the efficiency and operations of an industry. Kiplinger's ambition was far greater: helping to advance the entire scope of US industry. This fits within the "Enforcers Thesis," a theoretical framework I developed in my first book, *The Enforcers*, that documents accountability journalism in the trade press and how it can advance socially beneficial goals.[90] This chapter also explores how Kiplinger served as part of the movement to expand explanatory journalism in the 1920s and 1930s.

The business community, shell-shocked by the Great Depression, was slow to rise in opposition to the New Deal. Chapter 5 examines the business backlash, which grew from opposition to the new Wall Street regulations, particularly the creation of the Securities and Exchange Commission, and the early attempts to promote labor organizing through Section 7(a) of the National Industrial Recovery Act. Kiplinger's functionalist approach urged the business community to accept the inevitability of a new regulatory order and the demise of laissez-faire capitalism. This chapter contains a short case study of how Kiplinger and two leading publications covered critical business events in Roosevelt's first term, the national banking holiday in March 1933, and the business backlash against the New Deal, which arose in the summer of 1933. One surprising finding is that Kiplinger's coverage does not reflect the rhetoric of two leading business groups of the era, the National Association of Manufacturers and the American Liberty League, a lobbying effort backed by wealthy industrialists such as Irénée du Pont. The American Liberty League was a formative group in the evolution of neoliberalism and an influence in our own time on the Tea Party and Donald Trump movements. Kiplinger generally disparaged the League as reactionary and did not promote its agenda, even though it was popular with some elements of his business readership.

The growing business anger over Roosevelt's regulation erupted in a battle over the Wagner Act. Chapter 6 examines this watershed moment in the history of the US labor movement that greatly expanded workers' rights to organize and shifted the balance of power in labor-management relations. The final case study of media coverage shows how Kiplinger covered legislation broadly opposed by US business interests, balancing criticism of the labor movement with a plea to the business community to engage with the unions as more of a coequal force. This chapter also examines Moley's break with Roosevelt as the president turned sharply leftward with the Second New Deal, which emphasized class rhetoric and condemned the business community.

Chapter 7 concludes the book with an examination of how Kiplinger advanced and expanded trade journalism's potential social impact and ability to influence business conduct behavior in line with the Enforcers Thesis. It examines parallels between the neoconservatism of the American Liberty League and its descendants, such as the Koch brothers. Kiplinger did not let the American Liberty League dictate his news agenda, an important lesson for the independence of trade journalism and journalism in general. It also describes Kiplinger's impact on the evolution of interpretive journalism and his independence as an owner of a major media concern. These factors generally help specialized journalists, like Kiplinger, play an important role in fencing in corporate power and, as a result, help advance democracy.

FIGURE 4. Willard Kiplinger's well-used Underwood typewriter. —Photo by Rob Wells.

CHAPTER 1

"Pound My Beat and My Typewriter"

THE UNDERWOOD MODEL 6 is a marvel of industrial age engineering—steel, rubber, and chrome, weighing some thirty pounds. The machine owned by Willard Kiplinger has seen some significant mileage. The gloss black paint is chipped by the space bar and around the edges. Letters on several of the keys are no longer visible, while others—the X, V, and M keys—are crooked. The space bar is bent. The physical condition of this Underwood Model 6 typewriter, stored at the family's farm outside Washington, DC, speaks to the intensity and volume of material produced on it (see figure 4). It was one of the mechanisms by which Kiplinger communicated with the world—his thousands of pieces of journalism for both his publications and freelance work for the *New York Times* and others, the thousands of letters to top business leaders and readers of all stripes.

In his memoirs, Kiplinger described the need to prove himself in journalism since he could not enlist in World War I because of "flat feet and other defects. The secret worry that I might be a slacker or shirker drove me to pound my beat and my typewriter 12 and 16 hours a day."[1] That fear of failure stemmed from Kiplinger's childhood, when his father's business, a carriage and wagon repair shop in Ohio, collapsed during the financial panic of 1893. This work paid well, he recalled, which "let our family live better than some others, for we had fried round steak, fat gravy and mashed potatoes several times a week." The failure of his father's business was devastating. "It was a disgrace to fail in business, and my family felt the shadow of it for many years."[2]

This chapter examines the formative lessons that propelled Kiplinger's intense drive throughout his life, lessons that shaped his journalism and shaped his publication. "He had a burning ambition to succeed," according to his son Austin.[3] Willard Kiplinger was born January 8, 1891, in Bellefontaine, Ohio, a railroad town about sixty miles north of the state capital. He was reared there and in Dayton. Kiplinger had two brothers, Herman Miller and Clarence Gale. Kiplinger's mother, Cora, led a family door-to-door sales team peddling aluminum cookware across the Midwest and South, displaying a business sense that instilled an entrepreneurial drive in her sons.[4] The time in Bellefontaine was central to Kiplinger's worldview and helped develop in him a keen sense of what might appeal to a national audience of business readers. "He was always from Ohio," Austin Kiplinger said of his father. "And that was not a put-on." Willard Kiplinger "would relate things directly to High Street or West Liberty or Columbus, Ohio."[5]

Kiplinger's Early Years

Willard Monroe Kiplinger did not like his first or middle names; his mother picked Willard and Monroe in honor of two female temperance leaders. Instead he was known as "Kip," and he used the initials "W. M." in his journalism. Kiplinger was five foot eleven, of slender build, with blue eyes and light brown hair.[6] One former employee recalled that Kiplinger had huge hands. "I figured they'd have been good on a prizefighter or a blacksmith," said George Bryant, a former Kiplinger chief of staff.[7] Knight Kiplinger recalled his grandfather as "personally a shy person, not a strong public speaker, but he was very intellectually assertive, very curious, and obviously very driven to achieve success in journalism and his publishing business."[8] Kiplinger worked on his high school's newspaper and attended Ohio State University, where he served as editor of *The Lantern*, the daily student newspaper. He was one of the first two graduates of Ohio State's newly established journalism program.[9] Following his graduation in 1912, Kiplinger reported for the *Ohio State Journal*, starting off at $18 a week.[10] He made his reputation covering the 1913 flood in Columbus, driving around town with a rented horse and buggy to obtain names of more than one hundred flood victims.[11]

By September 1913 Kiplinger was working for the Associated Press in Columbus, where he covered the capitol. Denied a transfer to the AP's Washington, DC, bureau, Kiplinger quit in 1916, traveled to Washington anyway, and talked his way into a night shift job with the AP's Washington bureau. One reporting assignment involved following President Woodrow Wilson around town during his evening walks, a journalistic witness in case of an assassination attempt.

Kiplinger asked to cover financial topics for the AP, primarily the US government's attempt to mobilize business for World War I. This assignment gave him detailed knowledge of government and business, a training that promised a more lucrative paycheck. He found a new opportunity outside of daily journalism in 1919, accepting a job with the National Bank of Commerce, a New York–based commercial bank. Kiplinger was the bank's Washington representative, using his reporting skills to inform bankers about political developments and trends in the capital. He expanded on this concept in 1920, when he and two partners created a private "business intelligence" bureau that took on other corporate clients, later called the Kiplinger Washington Agency. The topical updates from this consulting work helped form the concept of a weekly newsletter for business readers. In 1923 Kiplinger borrowed $1,000 from Riggs National Bank to start *The Kiplinger Washington Letter*.[12] What Kiplinger learned writing for bankers proved foundational for the unusual style of the *Letter*. "They didn't want the outward signs of what was going on in the Treasury and the Federal Reserve Board. . . . They wanted the inner workings," Kiplinger recalled. The first issue, a single eight-and-a-half-by-eleven page, went out on September 29, 1923, to some five hundred current and prospective clients.[13] The letter "included on the least occasion prophecy—sometimes based on information but more often on opinion and hunch," according to his obituary in the *New York Times*. "After five years, the venture paid its way."[14]

The newsletter had a small following at first. "It was an instant flop and it stayed that way for six years," Kiplinger joked in a 1966 speech.[15] He scrambled to make a living during the early years of the *Letter*, and he took on various freelance projects, writing dispatches for the US Chamber of Commerce magazine *Nation's Business*, a bulletin for the accounting firm Ernst & Ernst, and freelance journalism for the *New York Times* and other publications. He also provided business services and specialized legislative and administrative research for corporations, which included lobbying, although the firm dropped the lobbying by the 1930s (see figure 5).

The hard work of launching the newsletter began to pay off during the New Deal, as discussed more fully in subsequent chapters. *The Kiplinger Washington Letter* became an influential source of analysis for business and political leaders nationwide. By the 1940s, Kiplinger's influence was noted by the *Saturday Evening Post*, which declared: "Almost everybody who is anybody reads the *Kiplinger Washington Letter*. It is the standard dope sheet on government and the men who run it, just as the Racing Form is standard on races and the horses that run them."[16] As Kiplinger became a noted speaker and a household name, he maintained a fondness for Ohio, for his roots. An editorial in *The Lantern*, the Ohio State student newspaper, recalled how Kiplinger would visit the paper's newsroom and chat with the student journalists. A student journalist once wrote of these visits, "Why on Earth was he [Kiplinger] sitting by himself on the rim of the copy desk or passing the time of day with someone as lowly as a *Lantern* reporter?"[17] He often carried his reporter's method and approach into his personal life. Austin Kiplinger recalled: "He could delve into anything. And many people, later on, noted this in his personal conversation. He would ask blunt questions that sometimes shocked people. Like: 'How much do you get paid?' 'Were you poor?' 'Do you like your husband?' 'Why do you live there?' He was probing under the surface, and it usually brought out information that other people might take years to get around to, or would never deign to ask."[18]

As he rose in prominence, Kiplinger experienced turmoil in his personal life. He had four children from three marriages. In 1914 he married Irene Austin. The couple had a son and a daughter, Austin and Jane Ann, but they separated in 1922 and divorced in 1925 at a time when he was struggling to get *The Kiplinger Washington Letter* established. During the early 1920s, Kiplinger's parents moved to the Washington, DC, area and helped raise Austin; Irene moved back to Toledo with their daughter. Clarence Gale Kiplinger, the journalist's younger brother, recalled: "My mother practically brought up Austin. . . . [H]e's more like a brother to me because we were both raised by the same mother."[19] Willard Kiplinger married Leslie Jackson in 1926 after a six-month courtship; they divorced in 1931. They had one son, Peter.

In 1936 Kiplinger married LaVerne Colwell, his longtime office manager, who joined his staff in 1921. Margaret Rodgers, a veteran business division staff member, recalled the scene when LaVerne broke the news. "One day Verne came over and burst in our door and held out her hand and said, 'Look at my diamond' and said, 'I've just married the boss,'" Rodgers recalled. "And we remember so well what she said, 'And I'm going to be his last one.'"[20] The couple had a daughter, Bonnie. Although there were periods of significant tension, his third marriage lasted thirty-one years.[21]

Kiplinger's focus and drive were at the root of conflicts in his personal relations. Besides the two divorces, Kiplinger had several significant disputes

FIGURE 5. Willard Kiplinger, circa 1930s. —Photograph by Harris & Ewing, Prints & Photographs Division, Library of Congress, LC-H25- 104108-DH.

with an early business partner, Paul Babson, and even with his son Austin, who found working for his father at times unbearable. In 1948 Austin left the family business before returning in 1956. Willard Kiplinger "was strong-willed, setting high standards for himself and others," according to Knight Kiplinger. "I think his being a workaholic probably did in his first two marriages. His primary passion was his craft, his business."[22]

Kiplinger's intensity could make for unpleasant experiences at work, particularly for the senior editors. He kept the top staff in the office Friday afternoons for a biting critique of the newsletter and magazine, dubbed "hell sessions" by the editors, meetings that soured employee morale. At these public critiques "he would tell you what was the matter with [an article]; why it didn't go right; how he spruced it up," editor George Kennedy recalled. "A lot of people on the staff thought he was stuck on himself and that he just wanted to tell you how smart he was and all the wonderful things he could do and that you couldn't do. But I think if you kept your pores open, you learned something about writing.... He had a damned good reason for most of the things that he did."[23] Oeveste Granducci, a longtime Kiplinger reporter, recalled rewriting a story sixteen times and it still wasn't good enough. "I took it in to him and he thought deeply about it after reading it and said, 'Gran, I think another rewrite is in order.' Well, I nearly blew my stack."[24] Kennedy and others recalled Kiplinger constantly rewriting, refining, and polishing the work of his editors, many of whom were experienced journalists. "Those were some of the reasons he hesitated to take vacations; he couldn't trust anybody to do his job," said Kennedy.[25] Bryant, Kiplinger's chief of staff, put it succinctly: "I found Kip a right tough task master."[26]

Some employees, like longtime magazine writer Robert Marshall, recalled a blunt and unpleasant job interview with Kiplinger. "He looked at me skeptically and made a few small unflattering remarks about my personal appearance and that kind of thing and then he looked at my resume," Marshall recalled of the 1951 encounter. "He harrumphed over that and announced that he didn't see anything interesting there and then swiveled around to face me head on and said, 'What makes you think you know how to write?' I told him that the fact that I had been making my living at it for the last 15 years encouraged me in this conclusion. So he harrumphed again and told Herb [Brown, a senior editor] that hiring me was Herb's mistake." Some veterans may have regarded Kiplinger's behavior in the job interviews as a type of performance, a rite of passage for the applicant, but the experience established a clear power dynamic. "I had been briefed in advance that I shouldn't expect the customary welcome given to a supplicant applicant," Marshall said, adding that he thought Kiplinger's conduct "was in good spirit essentially."[27]

While he could be a demanding and critical boss, Kiplinger also wrote warm letters to friends, checking on their health and family situation. He was a generous man to his family and employees, sharing a significant portion of the company's profits with workers through a profit-sharing plan and financially supporting the children of his earlier marriages. His longtime employees generally offered fond recollections. His personal secretary for fifteen years, Sally Almquist, recalled, "In all of that time he never once bawled me out for anything, never said anything mean to me, never."[28] Like Bryant, the former chief of staff, Granducci described Kiplinger as fair to his employees. "My feeling toward him was almost one of reverence and he had engendered in me a loyalty that I have never felt for anyone before or since," Granducci said. "He returned that loyalty as I found out on several occasions."[29]

Kiplinger loved to pull pranks and practical jokes on his staff and colleagues, though some of the pranks would strike us today as insensitive. Kennedy, one of the few Catholics in the office at the time, avoided meat on Fridays for religious reasons. He recalled Kiplinger approaching him on a Friday in the company cafeteria with two hot dogs on a plate: "He said, 'Eat 'em, eat 'em.' Well, he kind of put me on the spot." Kiplinger cut off a piece of the hot dog and ate it. "Tastes like fish to me. Try it," he told Kennedy. The hot dogs were made of tuna.[30]

While Kiplinger seldom participated in public events, he was a force in the creation of the Washington, DC, public television station WETA, and he participated in the Federal City Council, a civic group focused on local issues, headed by *Washington Post* publisher Philip L. Graham. He urged this group "to reach farther into the community and enlist black leaders," and he also worked with the Urban League to bridge the gap between the white and Black communities, Austin Kiplinger noted.[31] Kiplinger supported the United Negro College Fund, which helped support the historically Black colleges and universities such as Howard University, and he served on the fund's "national corporations committee."[32]

According to several profiles, Kiplinger didn't appear on the Washington social circuit, unlike other journalists of the era such as Raymond Clapper. Kiplinger "had kind of an anti-society bias. . . . He did not mingle socially at all. He shunned it," Austin Kiplinger recalled.[33] By contrast, Austin Kiplinger was prominent on the Washington social scene. Presidents Jimmy Carter and Gerald Ford attended the sixty-fifth anniversary celebration of the newsletter at Austin's invitation.[34] A memorial service for Austin Kiplinger, who died in 2015, was held at the Kennedy Center in Washington, DC.

Willard Kiplinger may not have attended dinner and cocktail events, but his personal files contain abundant personal correspondence with powerful figures such as former secretary of state Cordell Hull and Joseph Kennedy, patriarch of the political dynasty. He "had no desire for social prestige or political position. He had a burning desire for recognition and appreciation by his professional peers," wrote Austin Kiplinger.[35] The *Washington Evening Star* society pages offer some insight about Kiplinger's personal life—a rare vacation with his wife to California via a cruise ship in 1936; his participation in an official delegation of the National Press Club at the funeral of a prominent journalist, Carl D. Ruth; his acceptance of an honorary doctorate of laws degree from Ohio State University in 1937; Kiplinger's move from Washington to a new home on River Road in Bethesda in 1938; and the involvement of his mother, Cora, in the local Women's Christian Temperance Union in 1939. By 1937 Kiplinger was famous enough that his birthday would be noted along with those of other prominent individuals in various newspapers.

Kiplinger wrote often about the importance of maintaining political neutrality and objectivity in his journalism. A close review of his reporting in the 1930s shows little evidence of partisan advocacy. Kiplinger offered a rare insight into his political philosophy in a 1960 personal letter to his daughter Bonnie, then a college student. He started by discussing the French Revolution, the inspiration it gave to American colonists, and the emergence of two political camps, the Federalists and the Democrats. On graduating from college, Kiplinger recalled, "I was a zealot for Woodrow Wilson, Democrat, and his reforms. I was hot for James Cox, governor of Ohio, and his reforms. I was a whooping and hollering Democrat, and remained so for about 25 years." He continued: "THEN CAME ROOSEVELT AND THE NEW DEAL, A POLITICAL EXPLOSION. The common people took control. Social legislation which had been considered radical went through Congress like greased lightning. . . . [T]he New Deal was the political highlight of this century, this century to date." Even in this intimate format of a letter to his daughter, Kiplinger was circumspect about his current views.

> And now we have 1960. What are the parties like? Which is better? How should one vote? These are the questions in your mind. In order not to keep you dangling, I'll tell you that I do not know the answers. I do not know how I am going to vote. I take my personal vote very seriously and I am pondering. Even if I had made up my own mind, I would not tell you how to vote, for politics are like religion . . . a matter of conviction one way or the other, subjective balance of all points on both sides. Basically there isn't much difference. They [the two parties] are both liberal. They are both conservative.[36]

Willard Kiplinger's health declined in the 1960s, and he developed emphysema from smoking cigarettes. He unofficially retired in 1963 but struggled to let go of his business. "He knew he had to give up and he knew he had to pass his job on to somebody, but it was a strain on him to do that," Austin Kiplinger recalled. "I guess it would be like a woman giving up her child for adoption."[37] Willard Kiplinger died of congestive heart failure at age seventy-six at his home in Bethesda, Maryland, on August 6, 1967. "He had not taken especially good care of his health," his grandson said. "He was overweight, smoked, drank. Didn't exercise, the normal things."[38] Knight Kiplinger said that his grandfather did not drink to excess, however. Willard Kiplinger was remembered mostly for his devotion to his work. "WMK's professional style was intense," Austin Kiplinger noted. "He once said to me: 'You could take anything away from me except my job.' This was his central pre-occupation. And I think this is what made his later years so difficult. He knew he had to pass his job along, but he couldn't really bring himself to part with it. It was almost more important to him than his family, or friends, or life itself."[39]

The Kiplinger Business Story

The 1923 letterhead of the Kiplinger Washington Agency listed the following services: "Business Representative, Government Practice, Sales Investigation, Unpublished Information, Legislation Reports, Foreign Business, Trade Press Clippings." The agency "gave their clients information and judgment on court decisions, governmental rulings, bills in Congress, legislative reports, interpretations of tax regulations and occasionally helped speedup the handling of various applications before government agencies."[40] Kiplinger summed up those days: "We were into everything and would undertake most anything." Later, when recounting his role in lobbying for a major bank reform bill, the McFadden Act, in the mid-1920s, Kiplinger tweaked the phrase slightly: "We would undertake most anything as long as it was honest."[41]

In essence, Kiplinger anticipated the multibillion-dollar business of corporate intelligence. The services listed on the 1923 letterhead are provided today by governmental lobbying organizations and consulting firms ranging from Ernst & Young to PricewaterhouseCoopers or law firms such as Sullivan & Cromwell. In addition, media companies such as Bloomberg Government, Politico, and *Congressional Quarterly* supply granular intelligence about Washington and its inner workings. The appetite for news, analysis, and data about the federal government's activities is enormous. The lobbying industry spent at least $3.5 billion in 2018 trying to influence Congress and government agencies, according to the Center for Responsive Politics.

Serving this need, Kiplinger began assembling a small staff of reporters, notably John Ryerson, who wrote a specialty letter on taxes starting in 1925, and Granducci, who wrote a specialty letter on agriculture starting in 1929. By the late 1920s, the Kiplinger Washington Agency had about eight people

Kiplinger Washington Letter Circulation, 1925-1985

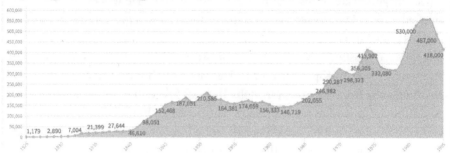

FIGURE 6. *Kiplinger Washington Letter* circulation, 1925-1985. —Graphic by Rob Wells.

on staff, including secretaries. Kiplinger created a variety of specialty newsletters in later years focusing on Florida (1956) and California (1965). Circulation of the main *Kiplinger Washington Letter* peaked at 560,000 by 1983 (see figure 6). In 1947 he founded *Kiplinger Magazine,* renamed in 1949 *Changing Times* magazine and renamed again in 1991 *Kiplinger's Personal Finance.* It is considered the first publication devoted to personal finance. A series of Kiplinger books included *Boom and Inflation Ahead* (1958) and *Kiplinger's Family Buying Guide* (1959). The publishing enterprise became known as Kiplinger Washington Editors, or KWE.

Direct mail solicitation became a hallmark of the Kiplinger business model. Kiplinger developed a significant direct marketing operation that handled "hundreds of millions of pieces of incoming and outgoing mail each year," a mailing operation so large that it had its own zip code in suburban Maryland.[42] By 1961 it was credited as the largest private user of mail in the Washington, DC, area, sending out some 56 million pieces that year.[43] At the time of his death in 1967, *The Kiplinger Washington Letter* had 200,000 subscribers and grossed about $4.8 million a year.[44] This growth made Kiplinger unusual in the newsletter business, where publications generally were limited to smaller audiences in a particular industry or field. Kiplinger still sought to provide the intimate engagement found in the trade press but at a much bigger scale. "Kiplinger differed in terms of the publishing model because their approach was very broad circulation at very low prices," said Joel Whitaker, publisher of *Newsletter on Newsletters.* The cost of a subscription to *The Kiplinger Washington Letter* has always been affordable. In 1923, a year's subscription was $10, or about $158 in 2021 dollars; now it's $199 a year.

Subscriptions to other specialized journalism publications, such as *Politico Pro*, can cost in the thousands of dollars.[45] One mark of success in trade journalism involved publishers who viewed their potential readers as a market rather than an audience. "The guys who pulled it off the best were the guys who were able to think and analyze as marketers," Whitaker said.[46]

The company experienced significant growth after World War II, requiring more office space. Kiplinger left the National Press Building, where the operation occupied an entire floor, and purchased a new building in downtown Washington, 1907 K Street, NW, in May 1946. Soon the company acquired property at 1729 H Street, near the White House, for a new building, which it occupied in 1950. "The Editors Building" featured a rooftop luncheon patio, a cafeteria, and two bowling alleys in the basement.[47] In 1960 the company expanded yet again. It kept its corporate and editorial offices in the Editors Building downtown but moved its printing, subscriber service, data processing, and mailing services operations to a new building called Editors Park in Hyattsville, Maryland, about seven miles from downtown Washington. Eventually, some seven hundred people would work at this facility, with another 150 people in the downtown facility. The company began to outsource these functions in the 1990s and eventually sold those divisions.

The company later distributed videos and tax software and created a book club on personal finance topics. Kiplinger published five books on economics and politics; a separate line of books on personal finance topics was produced by the staff beginning in the 1950s. The Kiplinger.com website started in the 1990s, a major personal finance website. All this activity led to a sizable publishing enterprise that was family controlled for three generations until its 2019 sale to London-based Dennis Publishing. The Kiplinger operation established such a brand and a reputation that it was approached "probably 25 or 30 times by organizations to ask if we were interested in being bought out," Austin Kiplinger recalled in 1977.[48] Potential suitors included McGraw-Hill, the *Los Angeles Times*, CBS, Dow Jones, and Prentice-Hall. The company enjoyed strong profits through the 1980s and 1990s and was able to return to profitability after the Great Recession. Shares in the Kiplinger Washington Editors, the parent of the newsletter and magazine publishing business, were not traded on public stock exchanges but were valued at $62 a share in 1979 and rose sevenfold (after splits) to $525 a share in 1990, hitting a peak of $2,230 a share in 2007. From the 1970s through the 1990s, annual operating earnings ranged from $3 million to $5 million per year.[49]

Kiplinger Conflicts

A careful review of Kiplinger's memoirs and other personal correspondence shows a long-standing concern with ethics in journalism. Yet there were some instances when Kiplinger crossed the line of journalistic independence and helped politicians, serving as a shadow political actor. In his unpublished 1960 memoir, Kiplinger admitted having been secretly on the payroll of a member of Congress, writing, "Also, and I should hush this up, I even got $150 a month as anonymous assistant and adviser to Cordell Hull, the publicly soft-spoken but privately terrible cussing Congressman from Tennessee who was then Chairman of the Democratic National Committee."[50] Although he did not elaborate about the duration of his employment with Hull, the context placed Kiplinger in the early 1920s as he was just launching the Kiplinger Washington Agency. Outside work for politicians was already a concern for journalists during that time. According to a study of press codes of conduct and ethics in the 1920s, "journalists were urged to avoid outside affiliations, particularly in business and politics, which might affect their judgment."[51]

Kiplinger devoted an entire chapter of his unpublished autobiography to the backroom dealings involved in his agency's lobbying on behalf of the McFadden Act of 1927, which let states regulate bank branching. This lobbying contract—Kiplinger stopped offering lobbying services sometime after this episode—"produced one of the biggest fees that the Kiplinger Washington Agency ever received.... Although I would not like to shout this from the house tops, we did some pretty powerful lobbying for the McFadden Banking bill, the famous measure that was introduced and fought over in each new session of Congress from 1924 to 1927."[52]

Kiplinger also recounted how Edward Filene, the New England department store legend, hired him to manage a campaign for a dark horse candidate for president in the 1924 Democratic primary, Governor William Ellery Sweet of Colorado. Kiplinger's account of his work on the Sweet campaign told a humorous tale of a campaign staff wildly out of sync with an independent-minded and idiosyncratic politician. Later that year, Kiplinger's "old friend William Gibbs MacAdoo [sic]," Woodrow Wilson's treasury secretary (and son-in-law), was seeking the Democratic presidential nomination. Kiplinger, while on assignment for the *New York Times,* "agreed to keep an ear to the ground and report anything I heard that would be of interest in his campaign."[53]

Kiplinger's letters reveal intimate contact with Roosevelt's advisers, to the point where Kiplinger would share advance drafts of his work and sometimes delete material deemed too controversial even though it was newsworthy. Kiplinger sent FDR confidant Thomas "The Cork" Corcoran an advance copy of the June 16, 1934, *Kiplinger Washington Letter*, which described the tensions in the Roosevelt cabinet between the "'Radicalism' of Tugwell vs. 'Liberalism' of Frankfurter group," which included Corcoran. "Tugwell group has doubts about capitalism's ultimate survival. Frankfurter group believes strongly in capitalism, with certain reforms. In practical APPLICATION of theories the Tugwell group is clumsy, indiscreet. The Frankfurter group has a better record of getting things done, and is much closer to the President than Tugwell."[54] Kiplinger told Moley on June 19 that he cut the paragraph "because Tom Corcoran was afraid it would disturb the waters or pour oil on the fire or something, in current efforts to make harmony between the Tugwell and Frankfurter schools."[55]

Austin Kiplinger

Kiplinger's workplace intensity led to an emotional split with his son Austin, who left the family business for eight years, from 1948 until 1956. "It was a terribly painful decision, I guess about as painful a decision as I ever really made in my life," Austin Kiplinger said in an unpublished 1977 interview for a company history. "We were deeply attached to each other." During this period, Austin, at age thirty, moved his family to Chicago, where he wrote a first-page column for the *Journal of Commerce* and later became a successful network television reporter and a local news anchor for ABC and NBC during the early days of broadcast journalism. He attributed his decision to leave the family business and relocate to Chicago to several factors. First there was his leadership role in a difficult and money-losing launch of the personal finance journal *Kiplinger Magazine* in 1947. Austin was placed in charge of all operations, yet his authority was being undercut by his father. "I felt it was simply an untenable position for anybody, and particularly for me because he took advantage of our personal relationship to some degree," he said, explaining: "WMK had the habit of passing responsibility without authority. . . . I was doing all the firing and the dirty work on the Magazine and he was having all the fun." He continued: "WMK was very jealous of what he called loyalty. And if anybody disagreed with him, he'd often accuse them of disloyalty. He used to accuse me of disloyalty if I had a different view of something."[56] Others observed that Willard Kiplinger was sharply critical of Austin's work on the magazine. "I think Kip used to get after Austin unmercifully," said George

Bryant.[57] John Hazard recalled Kiplinger's harsh confrontations with Austin: "WMK used to bawl him out in a way that he would never talk to me or I would have walked right out. I guess he thought he could get away with it."[58]

Another issue involved Austin's desire to shield his children, Todd and Knight, from the strain in Willard Kiplinger's marriage to LaVerne, as well as the stress between LaVerne and Austin's wife, Mary Louise "Gogo" Cobb. "WMK's relationship in his marriage was very, very poor then. . . . There was so much tension in the family that I didn't want my own sons to be brought up in that kind of a tension-related atmosphere," Austin Kiplinger recalled.[59] LaVerne, for example, "wanted her daughter [Bonnie] to be publisher of the Letter; nothing would satisfy her except that," said Lew Coit, Kiplinger's personal and corporate financial adviser from 1934 to 1967, a company director and once a vice president of the Kiplinger editorial division. "Of course, that didn't work out at all."[60]

Austin also felt a desire for professional growth and saw some time away from the family business as an opportunity for new experiences in journalism. According to Bryant, Austin's decision deeply shook his father. After Austin informed his father about the departure, "Kip got back over to the office and he couldn't talk. He went in and typed out just a little memo to the staff announcing Austin's decision and that was it. We didn't know what to say or to do."[61] Austin returned in 1956 and eventually took over the company as president and chairman.

The Great Depression

The growth and prosperity of the Kiplinger newsletter, ironically, had much to do with the Great Depression and the New Deal, which led to a general rise in demand for business and economic news from the nation's capital and a sharp increase in subscribers for *The Kiplinger Washington Letter*. "The need for clear, accurate information from Washington was never greater," wrote Austin Kiplinger.[62] Circulation of *The Kiplinger Washington Letter* boomed during this period. "There was a time when we couldn't keep up with all of the subscriptions that were coming in," said John Ryerson, a longtime Kiplinger editor.[63] Growth in any industry, let alone journalism, would seem counterintuitive during an economic disaster when people were queuing up in bread lines to survive. Yet, as the historian Frank Luther Mott observed, "one remarkable feature of newspaper history throughout the entire Depression era, however, was the maintenance of circulations. People had to have newspapers even though banks closed, their savings vanished and they were on relief."[64] Advertising in the newspaper industry fell significantly throughout the 1930s, yet *The Kiplinger Washington Letter* expanded during this period of great economic adversity.

During the Great Depression, a strong deflationary trend tore through the economy, slashing prices. Factories cut their production by nearly half between 1929 and 1932, according to a Federal Reserve Board measure of manufacturing production. Private construction collapsed from $7.5 billion to $1.5 billion during that time period.[65] These forces pushed millions out of work: unemployment soared from 1.8 million people in 1929 to 13.2 million in 1933, about one-quarter of the labor force.[66] Causes of this economic disaster were varied, but a significant factor involved restrictions on credit—making it more expensive for businesses to borrow money and expand—which caused a drop in business production and prices at the beginning of the Depression. The economist Peter Temin put the blame squarely on the Federal Reserve for turning a bad recession into the Great Depression.[67] The Federal Reserve raised interest rates beginning in 1929 to prevent the drain of gold from the United States and defend the value of the dollar, moves that further restricted credit availability in the economy. This credit and liquidity shortage intensified the number of bank failures. What started out as a somewhat "unexceptional downturn" in the US and global economy, Temin and fellow economist Barry Eichengreen argued, was magnified into economic chaos because of the actions of central banks and governments, which sought to defend the gold standard and did not expand credit.[68]

Economists across the political spectrum, ranging from Temin and Eichengreen to conservative icon Milton Friedman, have argued that the 1929 stock market crash didn't cause the Great Depression.[69] Yet the 1920s marked the rise of a shareholder and investor culture, one that quickly spun out of control and fetishized the market, encouraging people to engage in speculative excesses. "Coverage is still focused on the securities markets, however unconcerned most of the readership may be. The New York Stock Exchange is treated as the fountainhead of all news of the business," the historian Harold Caswell wrote in his early critique of business journalism.[70] Speculative fever and obsession with the market were a cultural phenomenon. Wealth inequality worsened in the 1920s and reached its most extreme point just at the start of the Great Depression. The economist John Kenneth Galbraith wrote: "By the summer of 1929, the market not only dominated the news. It also dominated the culture."[71] According to the *New York Times*, "November

1929 marked the final collapse of the maddest speculation in the history of the United States."[72]

The economic collapse led to violence in rural towns. In early January 1933, the *Times* reported, farmers in Plymouth County, Iowa, threatened to lynch insurance company officials who were seeking to foreclose on a farm. By January 31, the New York Life Insurance Company and other large companies had suspended foreclosures in Iowa, and the entire industry then banned foreclosures on owner-occupied farms throughout the United States and Canada.[73] *Fortune* examined farm strikes in the Midwest, protests by dairy and other farmers aimed at raising prices and reducing their debt loads, and found the uprisings were scattered in various counties and were not a uniform movement throughout the Farm Belt.[74]

Weak Business Journalism in the 1920s and Great Depression

Kiplinger's reporting came to prominence during a critical evolution in modern business journalism. There is ample literature and commentary describing the failure of business journalists to warn the public about the speculative excesses leading to the 1929 market crash. The historian John Quirt criticized the press, including *Fortune* magazine, for having "failed to anticipate that the slowdown which was underway foreshadowed a depression."[75] Several commentators have observed that there was little critical business journalism in this era. According to Kevin S. Reilly, "The prevailing business magazines were uncritical and often relied on ghost-written articles signed by famous names."[76] Most business journalists did not penetrate the veneer of business self-promotion. The historian James Aucoin wrote about the general decline in investigative reporting in the 1920s and 1930s, with major newspapers overall failing to expose the speculative frenzy that led to the 1929 stock market crash. He wrote, "The press acquired a shameful record of failing to expose the causes and effects of the stock market crash of 1929, the human cost of fascism's rise across Europe, and public corruption during these decades of crisis."[77] Herbert Hoover recalled that upon entering the White House in 1929 and witnessing a major boom in the stock market, he contacted newspaper editors to try to curb the speculation in the press and on Wall Street, fearing a dynamic like the disastrous South Sea Bubble: "To create a spirit of caution in the public, I sent individually for the editors and publishers of major newspapers and magazines and requested to warn the country against speculation and the unduly high price of stocks. Most of them responded with strong editorials. This had no appreciable effect, however." Hoover believed that the culture of speculation in the late 1920s was in part driven by the press: "The real trouble was that the bellboys, the waiters, and the host of unknowing people, as well as the financial community, had become so obsessed with the constant press reports of great winnings that the movement was uncontrollable."[78]

Yet there are some common misconceptions about the breadth of the public's participation in the markets in that decade. The US Senate hearings into the market crash determined that Wall Street firms in 1929 held the accounts of 1.55 million customers; this was a fraction of the US population of 120 million at the time. And of these 1.55 million accounts, about 600,000 were engaged in margin trading. Galbraith wrote: "The cliché that by 1929 everyone 'was in the market' is far from the literal truth. Then, as now, to the great majority of workers, farmers, white-collar workers, indeed the great majority of all Americans, the stock market was a remote and vaguely ominous thing."[79] *The Kiplinger Washington Letter* didn't tout stocks or provide a standard weekly market recap but instead would describe the stock market moves in the context of broader business and economic activity.

Many in the news media were complicit in the market's frenzy. In his review of news coverage, Galbraith reached a similar conclusion: "Most magazines and most newspapers in 1929 reported the upward sweep of the market with admiration and awe and without alarm."[80] John Quirt called the *Wall Street Journal* "one of the main cheerleaders" of the stock market leading up to the 1929 crash. Three days before the October 29, 1929, collapse, the *Journal* carried an article headlined "Hoover Asserts Business Sound." Quirt observed, "Such, then, was the sanguine view that prevailed in the *Journal* and elsewhere." The day after the crash, on October 30, 1929, a *Journal* headline read "Stocks Steady after Decline." The Hoover administration issued encouraging statements about the economy. "These canards," noted Quirt, "which would draw ridicule for years to come, were dutifully recorded and amplified in the press."[81]

Kiplinger's reporting on the Great Crash was mixed. As early as May 1927, *The Kiplinger Washington Letter* reported: "We note an undercurrent of feeling here that securities markets generally are too high . . . [b]ut that nobody in authoritative position seems to give any definite idea as to when they may break."[82] In November 1928, Kiplinger began warning about stock market speculation, writing, "All official and unofficial comment out of Washington touching upon the stock market is 'warning.'"[83] But by 1929, *The Kiplinger Washington Letter* began to back off from its market crash prediction, which Kiplinger later regretted: "When [we] should have been warning hardest, we kind of poohed out."[84] The company biographer described the situation in similar terms: "Unfortunately, after all its warnings, in the spring of 1929 the members of the Kiplinger Washington Agency softened this approach and became slightly infected with stock market-itis themselves."[85]

One bright spot in the 1920s business coverage was Alexander D. Noyes of the *New York Times*, who expressed concerns about the bull market. Noyes had covered the 1901 market bubble, an experience that informed his skepticism. "By far, the greatest force for sobriety was the *New York Times*. Under the guidance of veteran Alexander Dana Noyes, its financial page was all but immune to the blandishments of the New Era," Galbraith wrote. "A regular reader could not doubt that a day of reckoning was expected." Galbraith praised other elements of the business press, such as the financial news service Poor's and the Standard Statistics Company, which "never lost touch with reality."[86]

Business journalism struggled with a reputation for corruption and graft. Galbraith found that numerous journalists were no longer interested in "subtle blandishments and flattery," but "instead they demanded cold cash for news favorable to the market."[87] Within this context, Kiplinger's independent and analytical business journalism stood out by generally upholding consistent and ethical reporting standards. Internal correspondence shows how Kiplinger refused to reveal sources even under pressure from President Hoover or the treasury secretary. He wrote critically about powerful individuals central to his beat, such as Hugh Johnson, head of the National Recovery Administration during the New Deal, who sought to punish Kiplinger for his frank reporting. The standards Kiplinger observed were not upheld by other prominent journalists at the time.

There were several high-profile cases of corruption in business journalism in the 1920s and beyond and numerous examples of incompetence. As Quirt observed, "The practice of paying journalists to print tips and rumors was not unusual in the 1920s, as it had been in earlier decades."[88] A 1932 US Senate Banking Committee hearing into market manipulation detailed corruption among business journalists at the *New York Daily News* and the *Wall Street Journal*.[89] The hearings revealed that in 1929–30, *New York Daily News* markets columnist Raleigh T. Curtis received $19,000 in bribes from a stock promoter, an amount worth $294,307 in 2021 dollars. The author of the

Wall Street Journal's "Broad Street Gossip" column, William Gomber, and its "Abreast of the Market" column, Richard Edmondson, also were bribed by stock promoters.[90]

At the time, business journalism was still an evolving field that lacked consistent professional standards and a firm independent identity. According to Quirt:

> One reason so much of the reporting during that period lacked a measure of doubt was the curious view that business journalism had of itself. It saw itself not so much as a tough-minded chronicler of events as it did as an extension of the community it wrote about. Pliant editors and reporters ingratiated themselves with stock operators and adopted their upbeat perspective.... Tips and rumors were seldom investigated and press releases and other handouts frequently were printed without critical comment.[91]

Galbraith described many business reporters as drunks and incompetents: "The financial news or 'biz' section was a journalistic backwater."[92] Reporters were "two-hatters" who sold ads and wrote favorable stories about advertisers. The business section "was also a dumping ground for burned out city-side reporters and others looking for a place to camp until retirement," wrote Quirt.[93]

Many Washington journalists simply were incompetent in matters of business and economics, which gave Kiplinger a significant edge in the field. In a 1934 letter Moley told Kiplinger:

> The present set-up of newspaper men in Washington is not yet quite able to make the shift to economic and social terms. They are, as you point out, all political reporters; they are not trained in economics. The interest of the general public now is economic and not political. That is why, in addition to other reasons, Washington services such as your own, and special interest publications which you mention, in my judgment have become so essential to well informed people.[94]

Kiplinger's Influence

Kiplinger was unusual in the world of specialized journalism in that he became a noted figure nationwide for his business and political forecasts. By 1935, a public speech by Kiplinger about the economic outlook was considered a newsworthy event, earning coverage in newspapers ranging from the *Washington Evening Star* to the *Indianapolis Times*. His views were distributed to the American public through multiple channels. Besides his own publication, which had at least seven thousand subscribers in 1932 (see figure 7), readers would encounter Kiplinger's economic, business, and political insights in general circulation newspapers and magazines and in books such as *Inflation Ahead! What to Do about It* and the best-selling *Washington Is Like That*.[95] Kiplinger appeared on the occasional national radio broadcast, providing business commentary on a program called *The Business Forum of the Air*, which featured the Philadelphia Orchestra. A group of bankers in 1936 paid for this national broadcast to promote the virtues of capitalism. During the intermission in the music, Kiplinger would deliver a short commentary designed to "enlighten the public on the broad general aspects of business and depict the principles of the American industrial system and what they mean in the standard of living of the average family."[96] While mainstream capitalists valued Kiplinger's insights, so did radical labor organizers. The *Daily Worker*, the newspaper of the Communist Party USA, quoted Kiplinger in twenty-two separate issues from 1931 through 1935.[97] On the front page of its April 11, 1931, edition, the *Daily Worker* printed an image of an issue of *The Kiplinger Washington Letter* that focused on prospects for wage reductions. The caption read: "Here is a letter sent only to big business men who pay a staff of inside experts to summarize the movements and intentions of the big corporations and the federal government officials for them. The letter also serves as propaganda among business men for what they want. Now they want more wage cuts."[98] Across the political spectrum, from top bankers to

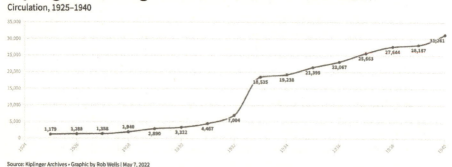

FIGURE 7. *Kiplinger Washington Letter* circulation, 1925–1940. —Graphic by Rob Wells.

"*Pound My Beat and My Typewriter*" 51

Communist Party leaders, Kiplinger served as an important source of information and analysis during the New Deal.

One of the few books about the newsletter industry described Kiplinger as foundational and "widely imitated," adding: "His newsletter is considered a 'classic,' occupying a niche of its own. Despite the success of Kiplinger, other publishers were slow to follow his lead."[99] Kiplinger's compact newsletter format was a formula that "often has been emulated."[100] The success of these commercial ventures spurred organizations of all types to create their own newsletters.[101] New entrants to the field copied the Kiplinger format and reporting techniques. The Kiplinger organization documented twenty-three publications they considered to be imitators, a list that runs from 1942 to 1967. It includes a newsletter by the Rodney Mason Agency, *Newsweek*'s "Periscope" column beginning in 1945, the "Washington Newsletter" in *McCall's* magazine, as well as unspecified columns in the *Wall Street Journal* in 1962 and the *Columbia Journalism Review* in 1963. *Newsweek*'s feature "The Periscope" clearly followed the Kiplinger format of underlined sentences and staccato wording with quick bites of information from Washington. *U.S. News & World Report* in 1957 published *Tomorrow*, a "Newsgram" straight "From the Nation's Capital," which used the telegraphic style of the *Kiplinger Letter*.[102]

Kiplinger's influence was felt in other ways. In 1948 he created a charitable foundation, funded in part by donations of his company stock, which helped launch the Washington Journalism Center in 1966. This program, now defunct, provided fellowships to journalism students to gain advanced training and reporting experience in the nation's capital.[103] Former ABC News reporter Ann Compton and Fox News anchor Brit Hume are among the notable recipients of fellowships early in their careers.[104] The Washington Journalism Center merged into the National Press Foundation in 1992. After Kiplinger's death, the Kiplinger Foundation endowed a chair and a mid-career program in journalism in his name at Ohio State University, his alma mater.[105]

Kiplinger's credibility stemmed in part from his close contacts with business leaders. For example, he was a featured panelist in a high-profile "Town Hall of Washington," the first event hosted in the one thousand–seat US Chamber of Commerce auditorium in December 1934 that featured Agriculture Secretary Henry Wallace and Education Secretary John Studebaker. A look at Kiplinger's personal scrapbooks, which contain more than three hundred separate items ranging from newspaper clippings to flyers announcing his speeches, demonstrates that impact. An analysis of the scrapbook shows some twenty-nine newspaper articles mentioning Kiplinger in 1932, rising to forty by 1935 and then dropping off.

Kiplinger did not join many groups, but he was a longtime member of the Federal City Council, a private civic organization in Washington with one hundred prominent leaders ranging from defense secretary Clark Clifford to *Washington Post* publisher Phil Graham. Yates Cook, the council's longtime executive director, considered Kiplinger "one of the most visionary leaders that we had on the council. . . . Mr. Kip was certainly the type of individual that never made any small plans." The council recommended regional economic development plans and was involved in some early advocacy for the Washington Metro subway system. Cook was struck by Kiplinger's interest in improving the plight of African Americans in the region, and he recalled that the journalist volunteered to help with the landscaping of an African American church, First Baptist Church of Kensington, Maryland. Kiplinger "was as visionary as any person I ever met on the question of race relations," Cook said.[106]

Hugh Johnson and "Censorship"

Another episode illustrating Kiplinger's influence involved a public dispute with Hugh Johnson, head of the National Recovery Administration, in which Johnson sought to ban Kiplinger from briefings and limit his access to staff. Johnson's move led to an uproar in the journalism community with several journalists offering defenses of Kiplinger, including Moley, further raising Kiplinger's profile as a leading journalist covering the New Deal.

Johnson was a large personality, a brigadier general during World War I known for his work with the War Industries Board, where he became a protégé of Bernard Baruch, a business leader and financier highly influential with Roosevelt. Moley recruited Johnson to help draft a system of price controls and production quotas that later formed the basis of the National Recovery Act, which made Johnson a household name. "Johnson for a time eclipsed the President in the headlines," Moley wrote.[107] Johnson crafted an iconic publicity campaign to boost support for the New Deal by having businesses display the NRA "Blue Eagle" symbol to show "We Do Our Part" in helping with the economic recovery. In September 1933 the Blue Eagle was promoted by a parade of 250,000 through New York City. While talented and energetic, Johnson was highly abrasive. Kiplinger described Johnson as a "bull in a China shop" who was bitten by the publicity bug.[108]

At first Kiplinger's coverage of Johnson was balanced, praising Johnson's energy and acknowledging the tremendous challenges he faced. But in August 1933 Kiplinger expressed concern about Johnson's ability to handle the strain of administering a centerpiece of the New Deal: "Johnson's health has become a matter of public importance. He works 20 hours a day, does personally the work of ten ordinary men, becomes a spectacular and heroic figure, but is nearing the breaking point. Most people regard him as the best available man for the job, and no one wants him to fall down at this critical time."[109] Kiplinger's portrayal of Johnson soon turned critical, warning that the government and Johnson would become "more dictatorial" in pursuing the aims of the National Recovery Act.[110] That fall he wrote that Johnson was a good person but that the NRA had gone too far, too fast. Johnson's NRA "is drunk with newspaper publicity, both nationally and locally."[111] The alcohol metaphor is striking, given that Johnson was struggling with a drinking problem.[112] A tipping point in the relationship came when Kiplinger reported that a deputy to Johnson had submitted his resignation.

Johnson began to fight back, condemning Kiplinger's reporting as excessively critical and inaccurate. He objected to Kiplinger's speculating about Johnson's retirement as well as his reports about confusion within the agency, uncertainty among businesses dealing with the NRA, and complaints about excessive promises unfulfilled, such as pledges to increase employment by 5 million people. By mid-October 1933, Johnson had sought to ban Kiplinger from speaking to his staff and ordered Kiplinger to submit any queries to him or his publicity director, Charles Michelson, who also served as publicity director for the Democratic National Committee. Johnson's ban extended as well to newsletter journalist James True, publisher of *Industrial Control Reports*.

Major national journals ranging from the *Washington Star*, the *New York Herald Tribune*, and the *Baltimore Sun* to *Time* magazine defended Kiplinger in articles and editorials. The coverage burnished the reputation of *The Kiplinger Washington Letter* and introduced it to more general readers beyond the core of Kiplinger's stable of business executives. The *Star* noted that Kiplinger "has been fair to the N.R.A." and that the main result of Johnson's action was "a lot of valuable publicity for the Business Letter Services, which hardly helped Johnson's purpose."[113] Moley, newly installed as editor of *Today* magazine in the fall of 1933, wrote an editorial defending Kiplinger, even though Johnson was a close Moley ally. "We regard any charge of unfairness applying to him [Kiplinger] as unwarranted," stated the unsigned editorial. "His letters do not contain anything but fair criticism. We may not have agreed with him but we have never felt that he exceeded the bounds of the kind of criticism that any administration ought to welcome.

"If every Washington correspondent were a Kiplinger, the public would be better served and the country would be better governed."[114]

Kiplinger's personal files contain a carefully worded statement intended as a press release that soft-pedals the dispute with Johnson, in particular an apparently contentious meeting between the two. It reads: "I see that I am involved in a controversy with General Johnson which is interpreted by some writers as indicating censorship of the press by Johnson. I think this is an exaggerated interpretation. I don't see any censorship in those angles of the situation in which I am involved." Kiplinger added that he didn't attend Johnson's press conferences but instead provided forecasts and analysis of the news. He offered a public account of his personal meeting with Johnson that contradicted his private writings on the matter. "The conference was amicable and I did not resent it," he said in the statement.[115] Yet in his unpublished memoir, Kiplinger recalled that Johnson and his staff yelled at him and the meeting became an interrogation. Kiplinger "was bawled out in the singeing and picturesque language for which the General was famous." NRA spokesman Michelson would then berate Kiplinger "when Johnson got out of breath." When those two took a pause, Johnson's secretary, Frances Robinson, "a hard-boiled young woman . . . got in her licks . . . The upshot of it was that I was forbidden to talk to anyone in NRA except Johnson or Michelson." Kiplinger was shaken by the experience. "When I arrived back at the office, my colleagues reported that I was white as a sheet," he wrote.[116] Other company documents offer a similar account of an intense showdown with Johnson resulting in restricted access.

What accounts for the conflicting private memoir of an interrogation and a public press statement downplaying the conflict? The press statement could have served two useful purposes. One, it would have portrayed Kiplinger as above the fray, not dependent on Johnson, and able to produce the same quality of journalism despite the controversy. A second purpose: the press statement would have served to calm emotions surrounding the episode and allowed Kiplinger to repair the relationship with a powerful cabinet official. At the time, Kiplinger told readers that Johnson and the NRA were limiting access to his journalists, requiring that all news for publication come through Johnson himself or Michelson. "This rule is not observed by many enterprising reporters, including ourselves," Kiplinger wrote. He then went on to rebut Johnson's complaints about Kiplinger's coverage point by point: "We have reported confusion of policies within NRA. Johnson says this is inaccurate." As for the restrictions on information from the NRA, Kiplinger pledged, "We will do our best," relying on other Washington sources to continue to report on the agency. Kiplinger then provided readers a "restatement of our editorial attitude":

> We believe in the fundamental purposes and aims of NRA. We have doubts about the success of the short-range emergency phase. We do not doubt the ultimate success of the industry codes, through which business will get what it has been yelping for all these years, relief from anti-trust laws, etc. We believe that the principles of government supervision of private industry, and some sort of cooperative economic planning, will be permanent. We believe that many NRA policies and methods have not been wise. Feel that this is inevitable in the process of accomplishing a social and economic revolution. But do NOT feel that this is any time to abandon the critical attitude, or that constructive criticism constitutes "almost treason."[117]

Johnson's attempt to shut Kiplinger out had little effect. In December 1933 Kiplinger offered a hard-hitting observation that Johnson was alienating people who had offered thoughtful criticism and the executive had entered the "epithet stage . . . He is more and more disposed to think that no one can be right except himself."[118] The next week, Kiplinger reported that Johnson would be replaced by the end of the year, although it would be another nine months before Roosevelt fired him, in September 1934.

Coverage of Johnson in other media was critical but not as biting as the Kiplinger reporting. *Business Week* in a May 1933 article initially misread Johnson, his ambitions, and his thirst for publicity: "Hugh S. Johnson, 'soldier, lawyer, manufacturer,' makes no speeches, wants no publicity, moves toward command of the business army out of a background of wide experience."[119] Yet *Business Week* reported on his missteps as well, such as with a July 7, 1934, photo of a picket line outside Johnson's offices protesting his firing of a labor leader within the National Recovery Administration.[120]

In his correspondence with Moley, Kiplinger offered stronger and more personal criticism of Johnson, particularly observations about his alcoholism. "Stories of his inebriety are now circulating nation-wide," Kiplinger wrote, adding that he had received "many letters" about Johnson's conduct on a recent vacation in San Francisco. "Not a day passes," Kiplinger noted, in which some visiting businessman did not ask him "to explain why the President keeps a man like Johnson."[121] Still, Kiplinger retained some degree of admiration for Johnson's talent and willingness to take a stand: "With all of his faults, he was a courageous and forthright man whose instincts generally were good."[122] He credited Johnson for being the first senior Roosevelt official to bluntly criticize Adolph Hitler after the rampage of Nazi firing squads through Berlin in June 1934 and told readers that Johnson was saying publicly what many officials were saying in private.

Kiplinger's Wealth

In 1947 Kiplinger's influence was noted by the *Saturday Evening Post*, which described him as "the best-paid and most-influential reporter in the world: also the most independent."[123] The description "best-paid" was a significant understatement as Kiplinger accumulated significant wealth during his career. Internal company records show that Kiplinger earned $87,537 in salary and stock dividends in 1935, worth $1.7 million in 2021 dollars, which rose to $101,000 in 1936, or $1.9 million in 2021 dollars, the largest amount he earned during the Depression. His 1946 tax return shows that Willard Kiplinger and his wife, LaVerne, still employed as a manager, reported household income of $360,091, an amount worth $5.3 million in 2021 dollars.[124] Their income that year was 132 times the median household income of $2,659, putting the Kiplingers in the top tier of US wealth.[125]

Kiplinger's eventual personal wealth was in the tens of millions of dollars. An exact figure is difficult to discern since he donated thousands of shares of his Kiplinger Washington Editors stock during his lifetime to a company profit-sharing plan and to the Kiplinger Foundation. To get a sense of the scale of Kiplinger's wealth, consider that the unified value of his estate at the time of his death in 1967 was reported to be $2.3 million, an amount worth $18.8 million in 2021 dollars. Yet that figure represents the product of careful tax planning to reduce the size of his estate tax bill, as should be expected for the publisher of a personal finance magazine. The estate of his wife, LaVerne, was valued at $10.2 million at her death in 1999, or $16.7 million in 2021 dollars.[126] The couple employed an integrated estate strategy, so some gifts and transfers during Willard Kiplinger's lifetime were reflected on LaVerne's estate tax return. The value of LaVerne Kiplinger's estate is difficult to gauge since she lived on for thirty-two years after her husband's death, and shares in the company appreciated significantly during that time.

One measure of the magnitude of the Kiplingers' stock donations is that the couple donated stock worth $1.9 million at the time of the journalist's death in 1967, primarily to the company profit-sharing plan and the Kiplinger Foundation. A subsequent rise in share values and a stock split in the 1990s and 2000s resulted in "a total benefit to employees and charities of almost $70 million," Knight Kiplinger reported. Another piece of context regarding the extent of Kiplinger's wealth: following his death, the Internal Revenue Service and the estate executors had a four-year fight over the proper valuation of the estate. The IRS argued that the privately held Kiplinger stock, priced at $300 for the controlling class A shares and $200 for the nonvoting class B shares, was appraised too low. The IRS wanted the stock valued at $700 for both classes of shares, three and a half times the value of nonvoting stock. The IRS and executors reached a settlement of $500 for the class A shares and $300 for class B shares, resulting in an additional federal and state tax payment of $300,000.[127]

The Kiplinger Foundation, created in 1948, supported journalism education, and colleges and civic organizations more generally, primarily in the Washington, DC, area.[128] The foundation made matching grants to schools, colleges, and educational organizations on behalf of its employees on a two-to-one basis up to $5,000 per year.[129] According to its last tax return in 2018, the foundation made contributions that year of $423,000. It underwent a major restructuring in 2018 and transformed into a donor-advised fund, called the Kiplinger Family Foundation, managed by Fidelity Investments; the foundation held assets of about $10.5 million in 2021.

In addition to acquiring real estate, Kiplinger enjoyed collecting historical art and acquired more than five thousand prints, paintings, maps, historical documents, and other items focused on the history of Washington, DC. There was a Washington history gallery in the Kiplinger Washington Editors' H Street offices, available for public viewing by appointment.[130] In 1956 Kiplinger commissioned Norman Rockwell, the famous illustrator and painter, to paint an oil portrait of the journalist. Rockwell accepted the commission and spent a weekend with his wife at Kiplinger's home in

Bethesda, where he made sketches for the portrait. "Well! At last I finished the Eisenhower and Stevenson portraits so real soon I'll be painting the greatest. You," Rockwell wrote to Kiplinger after the visit.[131] The Rockwell portrait later was displayed in the Kiplinger corporate offices. Kiplinger also commissioned the sculptor Max Kalish, a fellow Ohioan, to produce fifty bronze statuettes of prominent World War II–era leaders for a "Living Hall of Washington" project completed in 1945. President Roosevelt, House Speaker Sam Rayburn, financier Bernard Baruch, United Mine Workers president John L. Lewis, Labor Secretary Frances Perkins, comedian Bob Hope, and journalists Ernie Pyle and Raymond Clapper were among the subjects featured in the exhibit. "He wanted future generations to see what the men and women looked like, in realistic sculptures," recalled Knight Kiplinger.[132] Willard Kiplinger donated the statuettes to the Smithsonian Institution, where they were displayed in the Museum of American History and then, after 1988, in the Kiplinger headquarters in downtown Washington.

While there's little evidence that Kiplinger had an extravagant lifestyle, he enjoyed luxuries such as commissioning the Rockwell portrait, owning a Cadillac, sending his daughter Bonnie to private school or on overseas trips, and amassing a significant portfolio of real estate in Maryland and Florida. The Kiplinger Washington Editors company was not immune from the decline in the print publishing business, which led to a downsizing in the mid-2000s, as at many other news publishing operations. Kiplinger Washington Editors, Inc., the parent of the publishing enterprise, was sold in February 2019 after three generations of family management to a British company, Dennis Publishing, Ltd. The Kiplingers retained the extensive real estate portfolio, which was worth more than the publishing division.[133] "We were once an extremely wealthy family," said Knight Kiplinger in 2021. "And we are still well off."[134]

Real Estate Holdings

Willard Kiplinger loved buying real estate, and his investments in properties in Florida and Washington, DC, transformed the nature of his company, providing it with wealth to sustain the publishing enterprise and its numerous employee benefits, such as the generous profit-sharing plan. "Ironically for a man whose magazine pioneered personal finance journalism—he didn't take much personal interest in the stock market," Knight Kiplinger observed. He was fascinated by real estate and devoted significant time to residential and commercial real estate deals. "As the scion of German-American farmers in Ohio, and the grandson of a contractor who built commercial blocks in Lima, Ohio, in the late 19th century, Kiplinger seemed to feel that real property was the bedrock of financial security."[135] The Kiplinger corporate investments in real estate eventually appreciated faster than the company's publishing operations. The parent holding company, called Outlook, Inc., counted publishing as about 20 percent of its total assets, with real estate and financial assets making up the majority. Real estate investments supported the journalism.

Willard Kiplinger's entry into the real estate world began in the 1920s, when he started a small home-building business with his father in Arlington, Virginia, near Washington, DC. Kiplinger's parents had moved to Arlington to help him raise his son Austin after the divorce from his first wife, Irene. One significant personal real estate purchase came in 1937, when Kiplinger and his third wife, LaVerne, bought fifteen acres on River Road in Bethesda and built a white brick colonial-style home with spectacular azalea gardens. The property, reduced to about twelve acres, sold for approximately $5.5 million in the mid-1990s. In 1952 Kiplinger purchased a historic vacation lodge near Stuart, Florida, which launched a lifelong interest in the Florida real estate market. He tended to purchase raw land with company funds and held the properties for long terms, letting "inflation and population growth work their magic" and selling for a strong profit, which in turn enhanced the profit-sharing plan and shareholder dividends. Kiplinger's younger brother Clarence Gale Kiplinger retired to Florida after a career as a chemical engineer and hunted for real estate investment deals. Many purchases were made throughout Martin County, including land sold to be the site of the Hutchinson Island nuclear power plant south of Fort Pierce. Other purchases included a regional shopping mall in Jensen Beach and a 704-acre tract along the St. Lucie River that became a mobile home park, apartments, condominiums, and the 157-acre Kiplinger Nature Preserve.[136] Some of Kiplinger's smaller land purchases were donated to start a county library in Martin County and help fund the expansion of a local hospital. Land acquired in Potomac, Maryland, was donated to the National Symphony Orchestra, which sold it for home development.

Following Kiplinger's death, Austin and his sons began to engage in a wide variety of commercial and residential property development deals, the proceeds of which also benefited Kiplinger shareholders and employees.

Two notable developments involved new mixed commercial and residential projects in Urbana, Maryland; in suburban Frederick County, a fast-growing region northwest of Washington; and in Palm City, Florida, in Martin County. Editors Park, the company's former printing and marketing center in Hyattsville, Maryland, was developed as hundreds of apartments and townhouses in 2018. Austin's most notable personal purchase in 1954 was a four-hundred-acre farm in Seneca, Maryland. Across the Potomac River in Sterling, Virginia, is the Trump National Golf Club.

Profit Sharing

Kiplinger was an early and enthusiastic advocate of profit sharing with employees. "The profit-sharing was top-to-bottom, from the executives and writers to parking lot attendants, from the subscription clerks to the night cleaning crew and cafeteria workers—all of them Kiplinger employees who shared in every benefit equally, in proportion to their pay," noted Knight Kiplinger. "When *The Kiplinger Washington Letter* and *The Kiplinger Tax Letter* really took off in the in the nineteen thirties, the money was rolling in. And my grandfather just shoveled it out the door in year-end staff bonuses, which were sometimes a hundred percent of base annual salary."[137]

Kiplinger and co-founder Paul Babson created a profit-sharing plan that evolved into the Kiplinger Employees Profit Sharing Plan. The plan, formalized in 1952, had two main features. First, employees were eligible for annual cash profit sharing, which ranged from 6 percent to 20 percent of their annual base salary. "It is earned, it is not a gift," Kiplinger wrote to his staff after a bounty year in 1948. "It is earned by the organization as a whole through the effort of the individual members, including you."[138] Second, the plan offered deferred profit sharing, whereby about 15 percent of an employee's salary would be invested in an account for them that would be paid out on their departure or in retirement.[139] In some years it was a windfall: in 1966, deferred profit sharing was 28 percent.[140] Austin Kiplinger, in announcing a 15 percent cash profit-sharing bonus in 1968, told employees, "This high rate of profit distribution is never guaranteed, but with maximum effort, our chances will be better than even."[141]

A 1954 Christmas bonus letter to LaVerne Kiplinger, Willard Kiplinger's wife and still an employee, spelled out her annual salary and bonus, illustrating the details of the profit-sharing arrangement:

- Salary: $7,700
- Total Bonus: $1,155 (15% of base salary)
- Total Cash Income: $8,855
- Pension and/or life insurance payment, invested by the company: $2,581
- Deferred profit sharing: $881
- Total compensation: $12,317.
- Then add vacations, holidays, sick leave, continuity of job, absence of ups-&-downs, etc. What are these things worth? Set your own figure.[142]

Between 1952 and 1979, the company paid out $14.2 million to employees in year-end cash bonuses and withdrawals from the deferred compensation plan. In one instance, a worker who served as a messenger and loading dock clerk departed around 2010 with a lump sum of $540,417 from the profit-sharing plan and a separate pension.[143] The profit sharing and access to the company's Florida vacation resort were not extended to some 125 unionized printing and bindery workers in Hyattsville, Maryland, because of their separate union contract.[144]

Comparable figures for other companies are difficult to obtain, especially for that period. For some general context, one benchmark is an annual survey conducted by the Plan Sponsor Council of America. In 1990, contributions to profit-sharing plans averaged 9.1 percent of annual payroll versus 8.4 percent in 1989.[145] The Kiplinger profit-sharing distributions, which often were cash payments of 15 percent of salary, clearly were above the industry average.[146]

The Kiplinger Employees Profit Sharing Plan held various stocks, bonds, and nonvoting shares of the Kiplinger Washington Editors, Inc., the formal name of the publishing enterprise. At one point after Willard Kiplinger's death, the Kiplinger Employees Profit Sharing Plan owned about a third of Kiplinger's privately held stock, with the rest held by various family members. Beginning in 1952, the company would donate 25 percent of net profits greater than $350,000 to the plan and 50 percent of net profits greater than $500,000. In some years the Kiplinger organization would not turn a profit, on account of either business downturns or investment in the magazine, but management sometimes would supply funds for profit sharing anyway. Profit-sharing plan contributions were reduced after 1978 to allow the company to retain a greater share of the earnings and additional funds for growth and shareholder dividends.[147] Yet employee balances in the plan continued to rise along with the increased value of the Kiplinger stock. The Kiplinger Washington Editors discontinued the formal profit-sharing plan in 2008 during the Great Recession but continued to give year-end cash bonuses.

Willard Kiplinger donated significant amounts of his company shares to the plan beginning in 1953, and dividends from these shares were plowed back into the fund.[148] The fund swelled to $1.1 million in 1959, or $9.8 million in 2021 dollars, thanks to appreciation of its investments. By 1961, the value of Willard Kiplinger's personal stock contributions to the fund was $245,091, worth $2.2 million in 2021 dollars.[149]

In addition, workers were eligible for a traditional "defined benefit" pension plan sponsored by the employer which paid out a fixed sum in retirement. The Kiplinger Employees' Pension Plan reported assets of $39.6 million in 2017 and terminated in 2018 with payouts to the remaining vested employees.[150] In 1996 the Kiplinger Washington Editors had closed its the pension plan to new hires and offered them a 401(k) savings plan for tax-advantaged retirement savings. Many other employers were making similar changes. Kiplinger initially made a quarterly contribution of 6 percent of employees' salary without a worker matching requirement, an amount that later was reduced to 4.5 percent during the Great Recession. The Kiplinger 401(k) savings plan last reported assets of $25.2 million.[151]

What are the origins of this generosity? For one, from the beginning Kiplinger envisioned his Kiplinger Washington Agency as a type of partnership.[152] "It's more like a law firm than it is a commercial business," Austin Kiplinger observed.[153] Second, newsrooms had a paternalistic culture in this era. The apprenticeship model, steeped in paternalism, was an important foundation for the editor-reporter relationship in newsrooms. The communications scholar Clifford Christians wrote: "The older apprenticeship training was carried on by editors who had taught many reporters the finer points of writing and the methods of covering a story.... The relationship of reporter to editor was like that of apprentice to master or father to son, and frequently cherished as such."[154] Some of Kiplinger's employees, such as his longtime secretary Sally Almquist, spoke of a type of familial bond with him. "We loved him, and he loved all of us. He was genuinely interested in our personal lives, in our children, in our outside accomplishments or failures. Any trouble in the family of even the lowliest of us worried him, and help was offered (and many times given quietly)," Almquist wrote in the *Washington*

Post after Kiplinger's death.[155] Kiplinger established his company during an era when "welfare capitalism" was in vogue, when companies provided social benefits ranging from paid vacations to recreation facilities which created a sense of employee goodwill and enhanced productivity but also represented a form of social control.[156]

In a 1966 article for an employee newsletter, Kiplinger explained the origins of the profit-sharing concept. He began with a reflection on pay inequities at a job he held in his youth: "It irked me to see the owner of the business so affluent. He came to work in an 'electric' [streetcar], while I walked. He drank two ten-cent double Cokes at the soda foundation, while I was nursing my nickel one. I thought in a sort of vague way that he ought to share a little more with the rest of us." Kiplinger didn't "have any lofty or doctrinaire theory about profit sharing." Instead, he said: "It's just plain and simple, and in Ohio hick it's this: 'Them as does the work ought to git a share of the profits, if any.' . . . I'd like to say that it isn't charity and it isn't philanthropy. It's BUSINESS."[157] The company's reputation gained recognition, and the organization was named one of America's "Most Ethical Companies" by *Ethisphere* magazine in 2007.[158]

Bay Tree Resort

Other benefits for Kiplinger employees and retirees included access to a Florida vacation property, Bay Tree Lodge, on Sewall's Point on the St. Lucie River in Stuart, Florida, north of Palm Beach. Kiplinger purchased the lodge and some twenty acres in 1952 for $80,000 ($812,664 in 2021 dollars) on behalf of the Kiplinger Washington Editors, Inc. The property contained numerous residences with a total of twenty-two bedrooms.[159] For sixty-seven years, most Kiplinger employees and their guests could stay for free for up to two weeks at Bay Tree. "The house-rules for use are merely 'enjoy yourselves and leave everything as you found it.'"[160] The annual cost for the property upkeep was $600,000; three full-time staff maintained the resort. Until 1985 the employees' stays were free, but after an IRS ruling that year, the value of the lodging was added to their income as a taxable benefit. Guests later were assessed a modest cleaning fee. The Bay Tree Lodge benefit for Kiplinger employees ended after the company's 2019 sale to Dennis Publishing, Ltd.

Were the Bay Tree resort, the profit sharing, and other employee benefits part of some overarching plan for the Kiplinger corporate culture? Perhaps so, but there were episodes when Kiplinger's generosity was paired with unusual, perhaps impulsive behavior with money and company management.[161] In the summer of 1955, Kiplinger wanted to reward the supervisors in the magazine's subscription fulfillment department for their hard work. He saw that a new boat cruise was running from Washington to Bermuda and arranged for seven supervisors to take the cruise. Kiplinger spent considerable time planning the trip, even picking out the staterooms for his employees. "He had the best time planning for that trip ever," said Margaret Rodgers, a longtime Kiplinger office supervisor, who went on the cruise. Nevertheless, several employees questioned the wisdom of putting so many supervisors onto a cruise ship for a week on relatively short notice. "I just didn't know how we were going to run the business with all the supervisors gone," Rodgers said.[162]

Some former employees recalled that Kiplinger displayed a certain nonchalance about money in his everyday dealings. "I kept a supply of money in the desk for him because he never had any money in his pockets," said Kiplinger's secretary Sally Almquist. "Money meant nothing to him really. He didn't care if he had any in his pocket or not."[163] Kiplinger's brother Clarence made a similar observation:

> It's my impression that in the early days when Willard began to make relatively big money and had a surplus, he always felt that he shouldn't keep it, as though it didn't belong to him, it belonged to the rest of the gang. He had the fundamental idea, which is nice, that the people that helped put that thing together were the people who ought to get the money, not him. He didn't want the money. Money, I don't think, ever meant much to my brother except for the love of the chase ... the chase of getting it. But after you got it, what good was it?[164]

Lew Coit, the financial adviser who helped design the company profit-sharing plan and helped create the journalist's estate plan, thought that Kiplinger lacked basic sophistication about investments. "Kip didn't know much about economics or the money market, or investments, or securities, or what to do with your money," Coit said. In part that naïveté dated back to 1929, when Kiplinger suffered stock market losses through an investment fund. "I don't think he knew much about stocks," Coit said.[165] Kiplinger avoided stock investments until the mid-1940s, when he asked Coit for financial advice about managing the significant profits being generated by *The Kiplinger Washington Letter*. Coit's characterization of Kiplinger as financially unsophisticated is at odds with the journalist's extensive experience covering finance and economics up to that time, reporting on Treasury Department bond auctions, writing a popular book on inflation, and addressing federal budget and spending issues.

Almquist and others remembered Kiplinger's generosity, including his habit of sending his monthly Social Security checks to friends or charities, for example.[166] According to his brother Clarence, Kiplinger "made so much money he started giving it away."[167] For example, he "bought a whole city block down in Stuart [Florida] and gave it to the library and the women's club as a donation." Kiplinger, an early supporter of the public television station WETA, would write personal checks to make sure the station could meet its payroll in the early days, Knight Kiplinger said.[168]

Some employees also saw a certain rashness in Kiplinger's personnel decisions, such as the hiring of economist Ford Hinrichs as an in-house expert. "He'd collect people," said Irv Brooke, a business manager who began at the company in 1955. This decision proved unpopular since the Kiplinger journalists were already speaking to a wide range of economic experts and felt they were now obligated to follow Hinrichs's forecasts, which tended to be pessimistic. "That's the last thing the guys on the Letter needed," Brooke said.[169]

George Bryant, former Washington bureau chief of the *Wall Street Journal* and a senior Kiplinger editor, remarked that while Kiplinger had a gift for reading the masses, "I don't think Kip should have been allowed to hire anybody."[170] Hazard however, noted a common theme running through recollections of Kiplinger's behavior: "He used to spark ideas like mad."[171]

CHAPTER 2

A Bridge between Wall Street and Washington

IN LATE FEBRUARY 1933, less than a month before leaving office, Herbert Hoover sat in the White House, still desperate to help right the economic and social disaster unfolding throughout the country. Unemployment was at 25 percent and rising. The stock market was down 85 percent since September 1929, the month before the Black Friday crash.[1] Media coverage portrayed Hoover harshly as uncaring and cold. Homeless camps became known as "Hoovervilles"; a newspaper to keep the homeless warm was called a "Hoover blanket"; an empty pocket turned inside out was a "Hoover flag."[2] Hoover's own actions contributed to public outrage. In the spring of 1932, some 43,000 World War I veterans and supporters marched on the capital, many unemployed, seeking payment of deferred bonus pay for their service. Hoover ordered US Army troops to peacefully remove the protesters from camps in the city, yet General Douglas MacArthur exceeded the orders and launched an attack, leading to the death of two veterans.[3] Against this backdrop, Hoover reviewed his incoming mail on this winter morning and found something unexpected: a fan letter, one written by a prominent journalist.

Willard Kiplinger had dropped any semblance of journalistic objectivity and written Hoover a warm personal letter. "Every third or fourth morning I felt like turning in to the White House to thank the man who lives there for carrying on in his hard job which involves no compensations except, perhaps, that of self-satisfaction," Kiplinger wrote. "I have followed you closely for a good many years. I have avoided you personally, because my work requires that I be impersonal and constructively critical of public men and public policies. But I should now like to relax into the personal and tell you that I, as one private citizen, feel appreciative of your hard work. I have felt desire to tell you this to your face, but it might be awkward and embarrassing."[4] The tone was a bit curious since Kiplinger had interacted with Hoover on several occasions, including one time when he took his son Austin to visit Hoover when he was commerce secretary. Hoover wasted little time responding to Kiplinger. "I have, of course, read with interest your work during these four years," he wrote. "You have had a penetrating and wise view of most subjects. . . . I deeply appreciate your cooperation and am grateful for the friendship which your letter shows."[5]

Kiplinger had long admired Hoover. This letter marked one of a number of instances when Kiplinger broke with journalistic objectivity, a break probably made easier by the fact that Hoover's political career was all but finished in the winter of 1933. There's little evidence that Kiplinger's admiration of Hoover slanted his journalism, but he wasn't shy about expressing that admiration in the newsletter. "Dear Mr. Hoover," Kiplinger wrote a few days later in *The Kiplinger Washington Letter* as Franklin Roosevelt was being inaugurated. "Thanks for your hard work on a tough job."[6] Such warm feelings were not shared by many in the Washington press corps who were angered that Hoover had shunned a number of them and instead doled out exclusives to a few favorite journalists. Several journalists also were deeply disturbed by the militaristic response to the marching veterans.[7] Kiplinger's relationship with Hoover was different. The two shared a similar ideological outlook known as associationalism, the notion that private businesses could band together and work for the common good. Furthermore, Hoover's policies represented a subtle yet important step toward the regulatory state, a foundation that Roosevelt built upon in the National Industrial Recovery Act. Kiplinger was in the unusual position of being an insider who knew the Hoover White House and Roosevelt's New Deal, and was able to straddle them in his journalism.

In 1931 Kiplinger sought to be an emissary between these two men when he urged Roosevelt, then the governor of New York, to endorse an aspect of Hoover's economic recovery agenda. Roosevelt declined. "I cannot very well endorse the Hoover 'unity plan' without breaking the rule that I have very strictly adhered to of refusing to discuss purely national issues so long as I am Governor of this state," Roosevelt replied. Offering faint praise for Hoover's initiative, he continued: "I hope the President's plan will be successful but if it is, it will be purely from a psychological reason as the total sum to be raised is of course, pitifully inadequate to meet the situation. However, it is certainly an honest effort to do something and as such, I can heartily approve."[8]

This chapter describes how Kiplinger bridged the worlds of Wall Street and Washington, the worlds of Herbert Hoover and Franklin Delano Roosevelt. In doing so, the account places Kiplinger's journalism at a pivotal time in the evolution of US business history, a period when robber baron era capitalism was officially ending and a new, modern regulatory environment was about to arise from the New Deal. This changing regulatory environment led to an increased demand for information, one that Kiplinger fulfilled with his business journalism. Kiplinger acknowledged that reporting on the upheaval wrought by the New Deal "was no easy job, for it looked like a revolution (and was).... Our audience of businessmen were mystified, but essentially sympathetic at that time, and craved more and more explanation."[9]

Hoover's Regulatory Worldview

Hoover sought to achieve business stability and rationalize a steady expansion of government into daily commercial life through the ideal of associationalism, which envisioned "private firms coordinated for socially beneficial goals without direct government regulation."[10] Under such an ideal, vicious competition in the market would be policed by trade associations and other industry groups that would impose cooperation from within. Hoover arrived at these ideas from deeply held religious beliefs. Joan Hoff Wilson, in her 1975 biography *Herbert Hoover, Forgotten Progressive*, explained how Hoover's Quaker heritage shaped his regulatory worldview. Hoover was taught that people are to "act as socially responsible individualists.... This sense of the harmony and unity of voluntary community cooperation, what Hoover later called 'progressive individualism,' was probably the most important legacy of his Quaker upbringing."[11] In Hoover's view, American individualism needed a balance of freedom and regulation. According to this school of thought, Hoover was a transitional president between the era of pure laissez-faire capitalism and the creation of an active and engaged federal government.[12]

Hoover won considerable acclaim for directing relief efforts to aid Europe after World War I.[13] His ability to coordinate between the business and government sectors represented an important evolution in the relationship between the public and private sectors. As commerce secretary under President Warren Harding, Hoover in 1921 "saw himself as the protagonist of a new and superior synthesis between the old industrialism and the new, a way whereby America could benefit from scientific rationalization and social engineering without sacrificing the energy and creativity inherent in individual effort, 'grass- roots' involvement, and private enterprise," observed Ellis W. Hawley. Hoover began transforming the Commerce Department to serve business groups by supplying economic research and helping businesses coordinate and improve their operations without explicit regulatory mandates.[14] The fundamental values underlying this associational movement involved reliance on scientific expertise and an appeal to businesses to operate in accordance with community values and address the broader interests of society. With Hoover's encouragement, the number of trade associations grew from approximately seven hundred in 1919 to over two thousand by 1929. The government for the first time launched programs promoting standardization to help firms improve efficiency. Hoover's advocacy of associationalism in this era was important since organized labor was weakening in the 1920s and therefore was unable to emerge as a countervailing force to powerful corporations.[15] According to Laura Phillips Sawyer, Hoover "effectively promoted a new socioeconomic order by advocating a technocratic vision wherein federal administrators played a key role in gathering and disseminating useful business information for the purpose of better management of the competitive economy."[16]

The associationalist movement was endorsed by some business leaders, known as corporate liberals, who saw the need to rein in capitalist excesses out of fear that a socialist backlash would remove them from power. The associationalism concept dates to the beginnings of the American republic, when Alexis de Tocqueville observed the proliferation of civic and business associations to help communities achieve socially beneficial goals. "Among democratic nations, all citizens are independent and weak; they can achieve almost nothing by themselves and none of them could force his fellows to help him. Therefore, they all sink into a state of impotence, if they do not learn to help each other voluntarily," Tocqueville wrote.[17] The associationalist ideal also anticipated modern neoliberalism with its emphasis on self-regulation as a market-based solution to the excesses of capitalism. At the turn of the twentieth century, the business community decided to engage with the government on a more formalized basis through trade associations, particularly the US Chamber of Commerce, to fight "draconian and seemingly arbitrary rulings of the Supreme Court" involving antitrust issues. The historian Richard John wrote, "In so doing, the trade group helped transform into a working partnership a relationship between the courts and the business sector that had previously been highly adversarial."[18] Another influential group was the National Civic Federation, a group founded in 1900 by big businessmen, which was "the leading organization of politically conscious corporation leaders at least until the United States entered the First World War."[19] Other influential trade associations engaging with government at this time included the American Petroleum Institute and the National Association of Manufacturers.

Alan Dawley described associationalism as an evolution of American individualism and the struggle in liberalism to find a middle way between laissez-faire and statism. Associationalism was a "combination of modern larger scale organization and traditional free-market individualism, a synthesis of managerial and liberal thinking ... called 'the association idea.'" Put more succinctly, this concept made the state "into a kind of giant accounting firm for capitalism planning." According to Dawley, the associational idea served as an important transition point from laissez-faire to the modern regulatory state. "In that they [the associationalists] modified the liberal tradition of limited government to use the corporation as a chosen instrument of public policy, they represented a new kind of managerial liberalism," he wrote. "Herbert Hoover was their hero."[20]

The onset of the Great Depression exposed the failure of this self-regulatory approach as slowing sales made cooperation difficult among competing firms. "Associationalism, once widely accepted as a new and superior formulation of the 'American way,' became for many a mere facade behind which 'selfish monopolists' had abused their power and plunged the nation into depression," Ellis Hawley observed.[21]

As the Depression deepened, Hoover attempted to provide relief through more direct government aid, helping create the Reconstruction Finance Corporation in 1932 to assist businesses and local governments with loans. He also proposed additional foreclosure relief for farmers, loans to states to feed unemployed workers, and an expansion of public works projects. Yet Hoover remained unable to address the deep structural economic problems highlighted by the Great Depression. As Frank Freidel and Hugh Sidey noted, "At the same time he reiterated his view that while people must not suffer from hunger and cold, caring for them must be primarily a local and voluntary responsibility."[22]

Kiplinger and Associationalism

Kiplinger's endorsement of associationalism was repeated and explicit. For example, on May 20, 1933, Kiplinger advised business readers: "Make your own trade or industry plans in your own way. Take the initiative; don't wait for government initiative. See what you can do to (a) raise wages, (b) cut down working hours, (c) raise prices by agreement so as to produce a profit, (d) agree not to sell below your own individual cost, (e) but don't FIX prices too high or too crudely, for the antitrust laws still operate." His journalism advocating for associational cooperation helped serve the economic system by informing businesses about vital regulatory initiatives.[23] "It is desirable for business men to have an understanding of these underground political influences, because they affect POLICIES, because they explain many things which otherwise seem mysterious," he wrote in July 1933.[24] His reporting still embraced free-market ideals that were also essential components of the New Deal, such as the use of government power to align with private interests for public benefit, as he described in this insightful commentary in September 1933: "Many measures of industry control are 'uneconomic,' 'unsound' but they are SOCIALLY necessary. If you think in terms of sound economics, then you think with only one part of your mind. You must remember that governmental politics embrace both the long-range sound economic considerations, and the short-range social necessities. The Roosevelt government is a product of popular social dissatisfaction with the old order of long-range laissez-faire economic 'soundness.' The Roosevelt government MUST experiment with social controls,—real mandate."[25]

Such analysis drew admiration from colleagues. "I think Kip was one of the few men in Washington who really understood what the New Deal was trying to do," said George Bryant, a former Washington bureau chief of the *Wall Street Journal* and later Kiplinger's chief of staff.[26]

Re-envisioning the Corporate Executive

Kiplinger's zeal for business cooperation came as other media outlets were exploring new dimensions of business and its relationship with society. *Fortune* began reporting on business and economics in a much broader contextual format in which businesses were examined and celebrated as part of the cultural fabric. For example, *Fortune*'s spectacular photo essays by Margaret Bourke-White portrayed factories as works of art. The magazine published multidimensional portraits of corporations and their executives, such as the epic three-part series on the DuPont empire in 1934: "A family, a corporation, a social institution—i.e., a segment of capitalism."[27] Such reporting represents how the broader trend of interpretive journalism was influencing business reporting. As the historian Kevin Reilly wrote: "*Fortune* magazine had a prominent role in shaping the way professional business managers imagined themselves—and were imagined by others—as political and social beings.... During the 1930s, *Fortune* engaged in a cultural, as well as a political, dialogue with elite executives."[28]

We can view Kiplinger's advocacy of associationalism in a similar light. Kiplinger's newsletter helped businesses understand the inner workings of the federal government and provided the business community's feedback to Washington, activities that deepened businesses' understanding of their role in society. "Competitive economy was necessary in the days when production was difficult," Kiplinger wrote in June 1933. "Now competition is no longer necessary, because there is potential overproduction. The new problem is not economic development, but economic maintenance. Enterprises cannot act collectively for preservation. Enterprises need government intervention to compel cooperation, which is essential to preservation, to eliminate anarchy. Hence all these new laws under Roosevelt, a 'cooperationalist.'"[29] Like the *Fortune* profiles, Kiplinger was pushing business leaders into a new space, envisioning them as active agents in a broader trend to tame and reshape capitalism.

The Kiplinger–Hoover Relationship

Kiplinger and Herbert Hoover began interacting in the 1920s when Hoover was serving as commerce secretary. They were familiar enough that Willard Kiplinger brought his young son Austin to meet Hoover at one point. During this period Kiplinger once described Hoover as a friend, and he offered some positive portrayals of Hoover as commerce secretary and later as president.[30] In 1930 Kiplinger told his readers: "We consider Mr. Hoover a good President. . . . We believe he will be renominated in 1932. We believe the chances of his re-election are about 60–40 in his favor." Kiplinger's readers constantly asked about the roots of the public's dissatisfaction with Hoover. More than a year into the Great Depression, on November 22, 1930, Kiplinger provided this assessment of Hoover: "Assume first that Mr. Hoover is essentially honest, that he has the welfare of the greatest number sincerely at heart." One major failing involved Hoover's lack of a "public relations sense. . . . His publicity counsel has been VERY BAD on numerous occasions." Kiplinger also faulted Hoover's staff for poor personal style. "The White House secretariat has alienated many friends," he wrote. Hoover's cabinet members, while many were individually competent, "have not been organized into a fighting political team."

There is little evidence that Kiplinger interacted personally with Hoover much during the latter's time as president. "I never cultivated any President, because I discovered that you could get under obligation and it didn't do you any good," Kiplinger said in a 1966 interview. "I was a friend of Mr. Hoover and I dropped him when he went to the White House because I didn't want to impose friendship on news. I was afraid he would give me news and then sew me up, so I couldn't print it. I have always dropped personal friends when they get into high office."[31] Although; there are a few examples of Kiplinger corresponding directly with Roosevelt, he generally spoke to advisers and cabinet officials involved in the gritty details of policy rather than with the president.

Hoover Shipping Scandal

Kiplinger's insider influence was evident in a 1930 exchange of correspondence with Hoover in which Kiplinger displayed a willingness to criticize the administration for its shortcomings. The letters had to do with a brewing scandal over the United States Shipping Board, which oversaw the merchant marine industry at the time. In particular, the controversy involved instances of favoritism in mail contracts and the sale of trans-Atlantic shipping routes. The exchange with Hoover began after *The Kiplinger Washington Letter* reported on July 12, 1930, about the emerging problem: "In our opinion, the

Shipping Board situation offers the greatest potential opportunity for scandal of the whole Hoover administration, which is laying itself open to blame, not for initiating unethical practices, but for permitting continuance, with full knowledge." Kiplinger's criticism was blunt: "High administration officials assure us that <u>Mr. Hoover will work the thing out without open scandal and without political explosion</u>. We doubt it. . . . <u>Suggest you lay off shipping securities as a class until graft in the government has gone its course</u>."

Alarmed by the report, Hoover wrote to Kiplinger and said his article raised issues "of most serious character." Hoover asked if Kiplinger would speak to the attorney general.[32] The next day Kiplinger replied and agreed to do so confidentially, but he would not identify his sources: "I can retail to him a certain amount of common gossip within shipping circles with the understanding that this is smoke and might direct him toward places where there may be fire."[33]

The president's outreach did not dampen the critical reporting. The next issue of *The Kiplinger Washington Letter* led with the shipping scandal in even more blunt terms: "<u>Grave danger of impersonal policy scandal hangs over the Hoover administration</u>, and may have repercussions beyond the limited realm of shipping." It was "an open question," Kiplinger remarked, whether Hoover could navigate his way through the controversy without a full-fledged scandal. "<u>Has the Hoover administration forgotten Teapot Dome?</u> . . . <u>Our opinion:</u> The Hoover administration has no lack of essential integrity, but has been slow, stupid and blundering in its management of shipping matters. . . . Current administration of shipping matters does not deserve public confidence."[34]

Changes in Capitalism, Business Identity

Hoover was a leader in an important transformation of business culture. Prior to World War I, business and government agencies existed largely in separate spheres, with the market enjoying primacy in American political history. Kiplinger wrote about the "nightmare" President Wilson faced in mobilizing businesses for World War I: "The government was small and had few contacts among businessmen. Business itself was unorganized. There were very few trade associations. Every business was fearful of revealing figures or trade secrets to competitors. So cooperation was nil."[35] Hoover's work on organizing relief for Europe after World War I marked an important moment in the coordination of the private business community and the US government.

This was an era when the US business community was witnessing a transformation from a largely private economy, one in which business financed investments internally, to a mixed economy, in which the federal government emerged as a major force and even as an investor. The dominance of business in US society reflected the influence of liberalism, or the promotion of individual rights and free enterprise, represented in economics as sound money, fiscal orthodoxy, low taxes, and small government. In the nineteenth century, liberalism was equated with the laissez-faire approach to regulation, in which the government had a very small role intervening in corporate affairs, except to referee between competing interests. "Only in the United States had big business preceded big government," Richard John observed. During the nineteenth and early twentieth centuries, business dominated the political sphere, and elections "rarely had more than a marginal influence on the rules of the game."[36]

With the end of World War I, capitalism was evolving into a new managerial phase in which professional workers handled the daily operations, as opposed to businesses being directed by corporate owners like John D. Rockefeller or J. P. Morgan. The managerial phase also led to the rise of shareholder-owned firms, and the public's investing habits began to shift toward stocks following a successful war bond campaign during World War I.[37] Some companies responded and became more sensitive to shareholder and labor concerns, public relations, and dealings with the government, which opened the possibility for some democratic input in corporate governance, since individual shareholders could express their views through corporate elections.[38] "The managerial revolution had created in America a new form of economic democracy in which management acted as 'a referee between the three major elements in our economy—the customer, the worker and the capitalist,'" wrote Robert Griffith.[39] According to Gerald Davis, managerial capitalism was portrayed as a democratic movement, dethroning "land-owning aristocracy" as well as bankers and capitalists.[40]

A more prosperous social environment emerged in this period as companies offered initiatives such as social welfare benefit programs like pensions and health insurance, and company unions, all aimed at reducing employee turnover and preventing incursions from outside organized labor. Leaders of major corporations were involved in fashioning or influencing the new liberal social order in the early twentieth century to help stabilize society and lay the groundwork for future expansion.[41] The expansion of benefits was also intended in part to head off advances from organized labor. Known as "welfare capitalism," this trend gave employers "an ideology of control" over their workforce, masked by humanitarian pretenses.[42] As Davis put it, "Corporations had become the new guilds, creating lifetime attachments to members through devices that extended from health care to retirement pensions that rewarded those that spent a career with the company."[43]

Landmarks in Regulation

The New Deal programs evolved from the changes in business activities and the rising dysfunction in capitalism. There was ample precedent for the New Deal regime, building on government interventions in the marketplace over several decades, from regulation of the railroads in the 1870s to antitrust law in the 1890s to President Wilson's economic and business management during World War I. "The New Deal did not come out of a void," Bruce Ramsey observed.[44] The roots of a more active and powerful role for government in the economy traced back to the depression of the 1870s, with western and southern farmers seeking to impose some control on the economy including regulation of railroads, inflation of currency to help creditors, and elimination of monopolies. Out of this agrarian populist movement emerged the Interstate Commerce Act of 1887, a law inspired by the abuses of the railroad industry, and the first important federal legislation to regulate business behavior. The Sherman Antitrust Act in 1890 represented an important legal attack on corporate monopolies and power.[45]

Passage of these laws fed into a broader progressive and reform movement in the 1890s that called for government intervention to address the destructive consequences of industrialization and rapid urbanization. As Louis Galambos and Joseph Pratt observed, "The political economy of the United States was beginning to change in the Progressive Era in ways that gave business leaders pause, if not reason to fear for their future."[46] Large industrial corporations such as Standard Oil gained unprecedented political and economic power, fueling demands that government halt the ravages of industrialization and rapid urbanization. President Theodore Roosevelt called for controls of mergers "in the interest of public welfare." This was the climate that led to the landmark 1911 Supreme Court case that broke up

Standard Oil, a case followed by another victory for the antimonopoly forces, a successful 1912 antitrust lawsuit against E. I. du Pont de Nemours & Co. and its investment in General Motors.[47] In the 1912 presidential election, all parties called for some form of restraint on big business activity.[48] Scholar James Weinstein summed up the idea succinctly: "Liberalism became the movement for state intervention to supervise corporate activity."[49] Shortly after these victories, Congress passed the Federal Reserve Act in 1913, the first step towards exerting government control over the US banking system, and a year later the Clayton Act, aimed at preventing the emergence of monopolies, and the Federal Trade Commission Act.

A major force in passage of the regulations was businesses themselves, which sought to address extreme dysfunctions in the competitive marketplace. As Alfred Chandler, the iconic business historian, observed, "The growth of big business appeared to threaten the well-being of other businessmen."[50] Businesses sought federal regulation to control competitors and supply a form of economic protection.[51] For example, a 1934 *Fortune* survey found nearly two-thirds of big businesses wanted to keep the National Recovery Act, and fully 90 percent wanted to keep the minimum wage and hour provisions, since they helped guard against competition from smaller firms that competed on labor price.[52] The historian Colin Gordon viewed the regulatory trend as a response to "a chronic crisis of competition. The vast internal market that had encouraged the rapid growth of American industry also proved its undoing as disparate regional growth and federated political responsibility exacerbated market competition."[53] Thomas McCraw, an influential business historian, observed that federal economic regulation was essentially self-serving and wasn't designed with public protection as a priority.[54]

This concept of regulation taming the excesses of laissez-faire capitalism was a foundational theme as the regulatory state emerged from the 1870s to the 1930s. *Fortune* offered an insightful summary of the evolving role of business in society:

> The large corporation has come to exert a powerful influence upon the American tradition. As the corporation grew it emerged from an aggregation of individuals into a vital force upon the life and times. With its growth came new responsibilities beyond the sterile legality of responsibility to the stockholder. Here and there enlightened industrialists began to acknowledge their obligation to the social state of which the corporation was a part. Now has appeared

the New Deal, with a determination to legalize the broader conceptions of corporate responsibility; to protect, by law, not only the stockholder but labor and the public as well. To the businessman of the nineteen-twenties such a program sounds revolutionary.[55]

Some important journalism played a role in the regulatory evolution. At the turn of the century, journalists were writing about the ravages of uncontrolled capitalism. Investigative reporting about abuses in the meatpacking industry preceded the 1906 passage of the Pure Food and Drug Act.[56] Ida Tarbell's 1904 investigative reporting on John D. Rockefeller's Standard Oil was followed by a landmark antitrust lawsuit against Rockefeller that led to the breakup of Standard Oil in 1911.

Business's Response to Emerging Government Role

Top company executives, under attack by populist forces during the Progressive Era, began to mobilize public relations and propaganda techniques to enhance their image and retain power. As early as 1887, General Electric and Westinghouse hired publicity agents to promote their businesses.[57] Early roots of corporate lobbying can be seen in the late nineteenth century with debates over tariffs. Because of such business interest, "Congress had conceded industry's right to send its spokesmen into every committee hearing and to stand at every Congressman's door."[58] J. P. Morgan employed a significant public relations campaign to defend his business activities ahead of the 1912 Pujo congressional hearings on financial abuses in the market.[59] As Michael Schudson observed of this trend: "Public relations developed in the early part of the twentieth century as a profession which responded to, and helped shape, the public, newly defined as irrational, not reasoning, spectatorial, not participant; consuming, not productive. This had a far-reaching impact on the ideology and daily social relations of American journalism."[60] Corporate public relations came into focus during this period, with the American Electric Railway Association adopting a code of corporate public relations principles in 1914.[61] The rise of public relations led to a demand for information, including specialized news, and publications such as *The Kiplinger Washington Letter* sprang up to fill that need.[62]

New Deal Goals

With the New Deal, the Roosevelt administration had three basic goals: increase employment, increase purchasing power, and lighten the debt load, especially on farmers. Other objectives included solving chronic overproduction in agriculture and industry and establishing a framework to plan the national economy. From 1932 forward, an enormous portion of the current US regulatory apparatus was constructed, including the Federal Housing Administration, National Labor Relations Board, Federal Deposit Insurance Corporation, Federal Communications Commission, and Social Security Administration. What made the business community especially nervous was Roosevelt's vision of a new relationship between government and business. As Roosevelt declared in a 1932 campaign speech, "The task of Government in its relation to business is to assist the development of an economic declaration of rights, an economic constitutional order."[63] With this speech, Roosevelt left little doubt that the old economic order would be transformed.[64]

Kiplinger described the implications of the Roosevelt New Deal before the inauguration. On January 28, 1933, he wrote that Roosevelt's policies represented a "tremendous growth of state capitalism" with public investments replacing private investments.[65] In April, Kiplinger provided an outline of the radical regulation of industry, including production and price controls, telling his readers to expect "a new program for trade practice conferences" to standardize wages and working conditions.[66] "Are we headed toward a national planned economy? Yes," Kiplinger wrote later that month. "We shall be amazed that we did not recognize the revolution while it was occurring. It is now occurring."[67] Some Washington policy makers were concerned that the business community wasn't prepared for the speed and intensity of the New Deal. Kiplinger, in a preview of Roosevelt's May 1933 "fireside chat" radio address outlining the New Deal recovery program, spelled out the magnitude of the changes for the business community:

> Industry control is not temporary. It is permanent revolution. It is the beginning of a new economic era in which trade and industry will be encouraged or even forced to integrate, organize, regiment themselves, regulate themselves, under growing measure of government supervision and direction. It is the greatest experiment of our generation. It will take 10 to 20 years to perfect the operations of the new system. If it succeeds, we shall have a true socialization of industry,—private ownership and operation, but public control and planning. If it fails, the next step is communism, for there isn't the slightest chance that

we shall ever go back to the system of heretofore. This is a sober and practical view: it is not sentimental or emotional.[68]

The New Deal, Kiplinger observed in April 1933, was going to end up in court: "The Constitution is being stretched, of course. But it will take years to get court tests, and by then the emergency will be over."[69]

Another legacy of the New Deal was the energizing of the labor movement. The New Deal was possible only because workers felt empowered to strike and assert rights as never before. The new right to choose an outside labor union, included in Section 7(a) of the National Industrial Recovery Act of 1933, and enforcement of labor rights in the 1935 National Labor Relations Act empowered organized labor and made it a countervailing force to corporate power. These laws helped stabilize the availability and cost of labor, especially for large steel, coal, and other industrial concerns, and raised wages, thereby expanding consumer purchasing power, all of which would help grow the broader economy. The New Deal's dramatic impact on the organized labor movement and the news media's portrayal of this trend are addressed in chapter 6.

Fortune contrasted the Roosevelt administration to the "classical administrative set-up of the Age of Pure Capitalism" under President William McKinley in 1901, when there were eight administrative departments. By January 1932, Hoover had ten departments and eighty-seven independent officials and agencies. "Mr. Roosevelt did not invent governmental interference in business," *Fortune* observed. "What Mr. Roosevelt did was mightily to expedite a process already long apparent."[70]

One flashpoint in industry regulation, and one of the New Deal's enduring legacies, involved the creation of the Securities and Exchange Commission. The 1933 Securities Act and 1934 Securities Exchange Act empowered this new federal agency to police the public stock markets through regulation of stock sales and supervision of the New York Stock Exchange and other stock exchanges. Businesses objected to the SEC as a highly intrusive regulation of the free market that was curtailing their ability to raise money through stock offerings. By depriving them of the ability to gain financing and expand, businesses argued, the regulations inhibited them from hiring new workers, thereby defeating the New Deal goal of boosting employment. "The Securities Act of 1933 is so restrictive as to make practically impossible much financing that is necessary for economic recovery," argued the US Chamber of Commerce.[71] "Intended to protect investors with the least possible interference to business, the application of the act appears to have fallen far short of that objective in many respects."[72]

James Landis, a Harvard professor and the genius behind the Securities and Exchange Commission, designed it to be a relatively small regulatory agency that would emphasize free-market mechanisms to root out and punish market wrongdoing. The 1933 act forced companies to publicly disclose important changes in their operations. In theory, this information would in turn allow investors to make informed choices about which stocks to buy and sell. One pillar of this public disclosure regime was the news media. Articles about a company's new forecast of profits or losses or other significant corporate events would help the market police bad actors. Landis marketed the agency as a partnership with the stock exchanges and accountants and enlisted them to help achieve these public-minded ends. As McCraw observed, "Unlike so many other draftsmen of regulatory legislation, he [Landis] had recognized the importance of matching the sanctions to the problems and of imposing the sanctions at the fulcrums of the industry."[73]

The New Deal and the End of Laissez-Faire

While the Securities and Exchange Commission was a new intrusion into the markets, other New Deal regulatory proposals expanded initiatives started by Hoover. To boost struggling farmers, Hoover led the creation of the Federal Farm Board to help control production by supporting farm cooperatives through federal loans and the Reconstruction Finance Corporation to provide credit to ailing banks, railroads, and farm organizations. He urged state and local governments to expand spending on public works projects by endorsing the Emergency Relief Construction Act, which approved $2 billion in new public works spending and $300 million in relief programs run by the states. He urged business executives not to cut jobs. Pointing to the overlaps between these Hoover initiatives and the New Deal, Kiplinger in February 1933 claimed that the incoming administration didn't represent a radical departure from Hoover.

In his first term, Roosevelt reached out to business leaders in several ways and continued some of Hoover's reforms, such as the Federal Home Loan Banks to expand housing credit and public works projects such as the Hoover Dam. Like Hoover, Roosevelt was working within capitalism to save the US economy, relying on trade associations to organize businesses to boost employment and alter production to halt deflation. Some journalists observed the essential conservatism of the New Deal. Noting that American individualism was one of Roosevelt's core values, *Fortune* declared that the president's vision of a democratized industry "would be a self-governing industry."[74] Top industry executives joined a new Business Advisory Council to advise the president about commerce. According to Kim Phillips-Fein: "The New Deal did not mark a break with capitalism; on the contrary, Roosevelt always believed that he was acting to save private property. He was at times quite surprised by how much anger his policies aroused."[75]

Leaders of the New Deal, such as Federal Reserve Board governor Marriner Eccles, claimed that capitalism needed a fundamental change but worked within the existing structure to achieve these goals. Eccles observed that "laissez-faire in banking and the attainment of business stability are incompatible."[76] He was instrumental in shaping New Deal economic policy, proposing to raise aggregate spending on the economy by boosting consumer purchasing power through higher wages and employment to stimulate demand for goods and services in the economy. Eccles's ideas anticipated John Maynard Keynes's *General Theory of Employment, Interest and Money*, which established the dominant economic paradigm for much of the twentieth century, calling for governments to finance deficit spending during economic slumps and repay their debts during periods of surplus.[77] Eccles's ideas were well outside the mainstream of conventional economic thought, especially for someone of his pedigree: a Republican banker from Utah, a millionaire by his early twenties, and a former Mormon missionary. He complained about wealth inequality and promoted the need to boost consumer purchasing power. "As mass production has to be accompanied by mass consumption, mass consumption, in turn, implies a distribution of wealth—not of existing wealth but of wealth as it is currently produced—to provide men with buying power equal to the amount of goods and services offered by the nation's economic machinery," Eccles wrote. "Instead of achieving that kind of distribution, a giant suction pump had by 1929–30 drawn into a few hands an increasing portion of currently produced wealth.... The other fellows could stay in the game only by borrowing. When their credit ran out, the game stopped."[78]

Treasury Secretary Henry Morgenthau embraced Eccles's ideas, and this young western banker and reformer was named chairman of the Federal Reserve Board in November 1934. Eccles put the Federal Reserve in a subordinate position to the Treasury Department by setting monetary policies of lowering interest rates to help reduce government borrowing costs and thereby assist federal spending programs.[79] This was a significant break from previous Fed policy, which favored capital by fighting inflation and reducing debts and not necessarily putting employment and consumer spending first as economic priorities.

The Roosevelt administration faced a significant question: How far should they take the new regulatory order? Moderates like Moley wanted to work within the existing capitalist structure, while reformers like Tugwell, the influential assistant secretary of agriculture, looked at introducing new economic planning concepts. In Kiplinger's view, Tugwell "believed political power should be made ascendant over what he called business power."[80] Tugwell saw anarchy in the business sector in the early 1930s which demanded government intervention, "a system of democratic coordination." Tugwell's philosophy in *Industrial Discipline and the Governmental Arts* anticipated the associational organization of industries that was the centerpiece of the National Industrial Recovery Act. His ideas represented neo-socialism, which called for increased government control over industry while preserving private ownership and the profit motive.[81] Felix Frankfurter, the legal scholar and later a Supreme Court justice appointed by Roosevelt, also was an important influential force. As Kiplinger described it, the Frankfurter regulatory concept was "to take capitalism as it was and build on it with a series of policy regulations, leaving a sphere in which individual initiative would have free play."[82]

The Roosevelt administration sought to change practices in the old economic order that left workers with few rights and led to child labor and other forms of exploitation.[83] George Meany, then president of the New York State Federation of Labor, faulted the liberal ideal for resulting in systemic worker abuse. "Rugged individualism has brought about a condition under which labor was being purchased in a market where the only standards set were those dictated by the inherent human fear of privation and want," Meany said.[84] The onset of the new regulatory state with Roosevelt represented a major repudiation to business leaders. Kim Phillips-Fein wrote:

> For men like the du Ponts, the leaders of the American business class, the Great Depression was a political disaster as much as it was an economic one. Just a few years earlier, businessmen had been the heroes of American politics. They had been celebrated as the leaders of the nation. The old hostility to big business had finally been defeated, as the revolutionaries and anarchists of earlier generations were deported and driven underground in the wave of repression that followed World War I.[85]

Even staunch free-market economists such as Frank Knight at the University of Chicago conceded this shift in power from the corporate sector. Knight wrote to a colleague in the summer of 1933: "We cannot go back to laissez-faire in economics even in this country.... Now it seems to me inevitable that we must go over to a controlled system."[86]

Kiplinger bluntly explained to his business readers the consequences of the New Deal and its regulatory control over their companies: "Government control of industry will be permanent," he wrote on August 19, 1933, a prediction that certainly proved true. "Our present course is midway between fascism and communism. If the experiment flops, we shall swing—most likely towards fascism."[87] Kiplinger acknowledged that big business dysfunction was leading to social disruption: "It is socially too dangerous to allow concentration of economic power in the hands of a few. It is socially safer to have the business structure rest on many small pegs, rather than on a few big piles."[88]

Kiplinger reminded business leaders that they themselves had sought some of these far-reaching regulations and a closer relationship between government and industry:

> This is dictatorship nominally but not actually. Your trade or industry must get busy soon and create a government advisory committee.... Is this revolutionary? YES. But it is practically the thing you have been advocating for years. This is an over-turn of the antitrust laws. This is a mandatory compulsion of intra-industry cooperation which heretofore has been considered desirable but illegal. Individualized unit competition is thing of past. Laissez faire is thing of past. In future the thing is not you, or your company, but your trade or industry, in its relation to public welfare. If your trade association is good enough, it will become government instrumentality. But most trade associations aren't good enough.[89]

Kiplinger's analysis of the end of laissez-faire capitalism was in line with other major news organizations'. *Business Week* observed: "[The] passage of the Industrial Recovery Bill marks a definite break in the economic history of the country. The comfortable theory of free competitive enterprise—that each individual, seeking his own welfare thus will promote the general welfare—has broken down." It warned that if business leaders continued to fight and complain about Roosevelt's proposals rather than trying to engage and shape the outcome, business "will get something extreme and maybe dangerous."[90] By the end of 1933 it was clear a new order was in place, *Fortune* opined: "Mr. Roosevelt does not propose to restore the world of 1929 and would not restore it if he could. Proofs of that are numberless. The phrase 'The New Deal' is one." *Fortune* cited the 1932 speech to the Commonwealth Club in which Roosevelt observed that "equality of opportunity as we have known it no longer exists" and that the task facing the country was no longer settling untamed lands and exploiting natural resources but instead "the soberer, less dramatic business of administering resources and plants already in hand ... of distributing wealth and products more equitably, of adapting existing economic organizations to the service of the people."[91]

Capitalism on Trial: Wall Street Hearings

One vivid example of the diminished status of capitalist titans involved the 1933 US Senate Banking Committee hearings into the financial market abuses that led to the 1929 stock market collapse. These hearings documented financial incompetence, manipulation, fraud, and self-dealing by financiers and financial institutions. Charles Mitchell of National City Bank resigned as a result of revelations at the hearings. Richard Whitney, president of the New York Stock Exchange, was imprisoned on embezzlement charges and sent to the infamous Sing Sing correctional facility. Andrew Mellon, the former treasury secretary, was indicted but not convicted on tax evasion charges. The investigation, wrote George David Smith and Richard Eugene Sylla, "uncovered little in the way of substantively illegal transactions, but the effect of the hearings on public opinion was enormous."[92] In essence, the hearings put laissez-faire capitalism on trial.

The cover of *Business Week* featured a photo of J. P. Morgan, who once personally rescued Wall Street from collapse, brought before the Senate inquisitors in May 1933. The hearings, initially launched in 1932 after Hoover sought capital market reforms, drew considerable press coverage from *Business Week*, the *New York Times*, and others for the unusual sight of wealthy high-profile business leaders facing hostile questioning. Kiplinger addressed the practical significance of the Morgan hearings in his May 1933 *Letter*, stating that they would provide momentum for bank regulation and securities bills and lead to enactment of higher income taxes, closing of tax loopholes, "and devising of ways to soak the rich."[93] Besides focusing on the personalities involved, *Business Week* also addressed the policy implications of the hearings, such as momentum for increased wealth taxes.[94]

Kiplinger predicted in May 1933 that the hearings would damage a key

Roosevelt adviser: Treasury Secretary William H. Woodin, closely aligned with Wall Street. Kiplinger correctly thought that Woodin would be further weakened by the hearings and would be retiring at some point soon. This criticism is particularly notable since Woodin was just coming off a career-defining achievement. Only two months earlier, he had helped lead the historic rescue of the US banking system by devising the national bank holiday plan. Overall, the main contrast between Kiplinger and *Business Week* was clear: *Business Week* provided good analytical reporting on the day's news, whereas Kiplinger focused on analysis and forecasts about broader trends in government and the economy.

Economic liberalism suffered major setbacks as Roosevelt abandoned the gold standard, enacted new tariffs, and created a social safety net. He was able to push through such major reforms because business power had ebbed so significantly. "Many of these programs were measures that America's business class had resisted for a generation, and the government enacted them at a moment when the power and prestige of business was at its nadir. The employer's paradise had been lost," wrote Phillips-Fein.[95] Kiplinger described how these regulatory changes were causing a sea change in politics: "A new party is being born out of the Great Experiment." The Democratic Party was unrecognizable, with its departure on tariffs, states' rights, and taxation. Writing in the *Saturday Evening Post*, Garet Garrett framed the New Deal and its pursuit of a planned economy as a classic debate over the nature of liberty:

> The conflict is between two ideas of government so deep and so antagonistic that never have they ever been quite reconciled. One is the idea of a powerful, unlimited central government, acting directly upon the people in a providential manner, minding everything they do, and originally imperious only to do good to them. The other is the idea of representative, constitutional government, possessing only such powers as have been jealously surrendered to it by a free people—therefore, a limited government. And this conflict has its source in the first problem of political science—how to reconcile government with liberty. Government tends to devour liberty; and yet government is so necessary that people must surrender some liberty for it. How much? That is the arguable question.[96]

Throughout all these setbacks, businesses still flexed considerable political muscle. In late September 1933 the New York Stock Exchange won a showdown with the City of New York over a proposal for taxes on stock transaction and brokers' revenues. The stock exchange threatened to move from Wall Street across the river to Mulberry Street in Newark, New Jersey. That threat led to the collapse of the tax proposal.[97] Amid these attacks in June 1934, Roosevelt defended his policies, saying they were aimed at supporting legitimate business activities: "We have not imposed undue restrictions upon business. We have not opposed the incentive of reasonable and legitimate private profit. We have sought rather to enable certain aspects of business to regain the confidence of the public."[98] *Business Week* predicted that the president's message would help advance relations with business leaders.

The media industry was not immune from these seismic changes in government regulation. The newspaper industry lost an important labor case in 1934 when the National Labor Relations Board, or NLRB, reinstated a reporter fired by the *Call-Bulletin*, a San Francisco paper owned by William Randolph Hearst, a major critic of the New Deal. Hearst and the newspaper industry protested to Roosevelt, saying that the NLRB had exceeded its authority and that the labor regulations interfered with newspaper operations and threatened First Amendment free speech protections.[99] Roosevelt responded by telling the NLRB to stay out of labor cases, which were covered by separate industry codes. This was a major setback for organized labor and enforcement of the New Deal labor protections.

CHAPTER 3

A Two-Way Street

"WHEN I FEEL like boasting, which is every once in a while, I boast that I have done two or three good jobs in my lifetime, and the best was in the reporting of the New Deal," Kiplinger wrote in a personal letter to Raymond Moley in 1966. "And if so, I always add, it was due mainly to Ray Moley, who gave me the opportunity for insight."[1]

If we think of Kiplinger's journalism as a bridge between Roosevelt and Hoover, between the New Deal and business leaders, Moley was a foundational pillar. Kiplinger's reporting on the New Deal was a highlight of his career, and Moley was central to his success. This chapter explores the depth and the multiple dimensions of that relationship through more than 140 letters the two men exchanged between 1932 and 1966 that reveal secrets, tips, advice, and predictions. Together the letters demonstrate Kiplinger's influence on a pivotal architect of the New Deal and reveal an intimate dialog about the backroom fights within Roosevelt's cabinet. For example, Moley harshly criticized Secretary of State Cordell Hull and his free-market tariff strategies in a July 21, 1934, letter, comparing him to a "dentist who has pronounced sadistic tendencies. . . . He is a determined man, and where his prejudices are concerned he will ride hard and shoot ruthlessly." Moley concluded the three-page critique of Hull and his tariff policy by reminding Kiplinger, "I have written very frankly and in the strictest confidence."[2] In another instance, Moley, who was seeking to block US Representative Joseph "Jo" Byrns from becoming Speaker of the House, complimented Kiplinger for focusing on the Byrns controversy. "A good deal of public opinion can be whipped up on the outside and I am glad you are helping to do so," Moley wrote.[3] For his part, Kiplinger supplied a detailed and blunt assessment of

Washington's inner workings to Moley. Writing about Assistant Secretary of Agriculture Rexford Tugwell, a leading leftist, Kiplinger said, "The business element hates him, fears him, thinks he is at heart a communist." About James Farley, the postmaster general and Roosevelt's campaign manager, Kiplinger wrote: "A lot of new hasty rumors concerning his underground business connections are circulating again. Some people claim to KNOW the damaging facts. Of course these things are confidential. I tell you things which I don't tell anyone outside my office, and which I don't put into print."[4]

The Moley–Kiplinger relationship was a two-way street. Moley provided Kiplinger with intelligence about the administration. Then when Moley moved into journalism as editor of *Today* magazine, Kiplinger tutored him about the field, everything from discussing writing to suggesting stories and even recommending potential staff members. In 1966 Moley thanked Kiplinger, expressing his "appreciation for all you did for me on those days of 1933–1936."[5] The letters also reveal how these two men were managing their dual positions as journalists and political actors. Kiplinger sought to help Moley navigate his complex roles as a magazine editor and presidential confidant. "Because of your closeness to the President and because of your accessibility and interest in people's schemes, it's inevitable that people sell-you-down-the-river, perhaps not for money but for influence," Kiplinger wrote to Moley in 1935. "It is one of the difficulties in being simultaneously an editor and a statesman, or an adviser to statesmen, or whatever it is you are." For his part, Kiplinger described his attempt to balance his own conflicting roles as journalist and political adviser: "I tell you these things as a reporter, not as an adviser on policy, I have my ideas on what policy OUGHT to be, but when I shoot off my mouth on them, I am apt to get mixed up as a reporter."[6]

Moley's Political Education

Kiplinger and Moley shared a strong common bond on many levels, beginning with their birthplace: Ohio. Moley was born in 1886 in Berea, on the outskirts of Cleveland, making him five years older than Kiplinger, who was born in Bellefontaine, about 150 miles away near the center of the state, in 1891. Moley learned politics at the local level before pursuing an academic career. After graduating from Baldwin Wallace College in Berea in 1906, Moley briefly dabbled in local politics and was elected mayor of Olmsted Falls, Ohio, in his mid-twenties. He went on to earn his doctorate in political science at Columbia University in

New York in 1918 and began to specialize in criminal justice issues.[7] He helped campaign for Franklin Roosevelt in his successful 1928 bid for New York governor, and Roosevelt appointed him research director of a state commission on the administration of justice. The "Brains Trust" was born when Moley was asked in 1932 to gather some university professors to supply insight and advice to Roosevelt in that year's presidential campaign. He recruited Tugwell, an economist and later a major New Deal figure, and Adolph Berle Jr., a law professor and influential scholar on the corporate economy and business regulation. Roosevelt began relying closely on Moley for his advice, and Moley soon emerged as the leader of this unusual group of university scholars helping to craft a path out of the Great Depression. Moley was a prolific writer and authored some nineteen books over his lifetime, including *Fundamental Facts for New Citizens*, a 1922 guide for newly naturalized Americans published by the Ohio State Department of Education.[8] Moley also became a key speechwriter for Roosevelt in the 1932 campaign and claimed credit for developing the term the "New Deal" to describe Roosevelt's economic and social agenda.[9]

Moley was an essential adviser to Roosevelt during the interregnum between the November 1932 election and Roosevelt's inauguration as president in March 1933. For example, Roosevelt brought Moley along as his sole adviser to a tense and consequential meeting with President Hoover and Treasury Secretary Ogden Mills in the Oval Office in November to discuss foreign debts and World War I reparations.[10] Moley later was a central figure in the negotiations between Mills and incoming treasury secretary William Woodin that led to the banking holiday in March 1933, which closed all banks nationwide for a week to stem the tide of bank runs. Moley helped jump-start the legislative drafting of the National Recovery Act by recruiting General Hugh Johnson to help devise a plan of industrial regulation. One day in April 1933, Moley grabbed a stack of proposals for business regulation, put them on a spare table in his office, and told Johnson to figure out what might work. Johnson took off his jacket, sat down, and started reading, and thus began his first assignment in what would become the job of director of the National Recovery Administration. Johnson's proposal later would be modified in congressional negotiations, but that April day in Moley's office was the beginning of a job that made him one of the most famous and powerful people in the United States.

Amid all the activity in the new administration, Moley kept his appointment as a professor of law at Columbia University and intended to resume teaching in New York. Roosevelt, seeking to keep him in Washington, appointed Moley assistant secretary of state, a position without any statutory or administrative duties, so Moley could serve as adviser to the president.[11] Moley clashed with Secretary of State Hull, who was far more conservative and an ardent advocate of free trade and low tariffs. Tensions between the two escalated after their participation in an international economic conference in London that was widely viewed as a failure for the United States.

A Political Moderate

Moley was significant in another realm: he represented the conservative wing of the Roosevelt cabinet, one that included Treasury Secretary Woodin, a former Wall Street executive, and Hugh Johnson, head of the National Recovery Administration.[12] Moley's willingness to listen to and work with the business community contrasted with the radicalism of the far-reaching economic planning proposals advocated by Tugwell in the Agriculture Department and by Jerome Frank, a top attorney also at Agriculture and later chairman of the Securities and Exchange Commission. Moley's work on the March 1933 banking crisis was evidence of his desire to work within the existing capitalistic system. When Roosevelt imposed the weeklong national banking holiday, Moley was a central player in negotiating this plan, which held together the existing banking system instead of radically transforming it. "It cannot be emphasized too strongly," he wrote, "that the policies which vanquished the bank crisis were thoroughly conservative policies."[13] By contrast, the leftist faction in the administration called for major structural changes to the banking system. Moley believed that pursuing changes in basic banking laws during this time of bank runs would have sown more chaos and confusion and possibly damaged the economy:

> Had Roosevelt turned, in those fateful days, to the type of adviser that ultimately came into prominence in his administration, it is more than likely that questions of reform would have taken precedence over considerations of safety, with a resultant confusion and delay that would have wreaked damage upon our whole economic order. If ever there was a moment when things hung in the balance, it was on March 5, 1933—when unorthodoxy would have drained the last remaining strength of the capitalistic system.[14]

Perhaps the most prominent conservative in the Roosevelt cabinet was another key source for Kiplinger, Secretary of State Cordell Hull. Even a moderate like Moley possessed a strong distaste for Hull's free-market idealism. "Mr. Hull, who had never made any secret of his burning faith that the salvation of the world depended upon the revival of international laissez-faire capitalism, naturally looked upon his appointment as Roosevelt's endorsement of that faith. So did all its other adherents," Moley wrote. "And yet, with every day that passed, it became clearer that Roosevelt's domestic program was moving away from laissez-faire."[15]

Moley resigned from his government job in September 1933 to become editor of the new public affairs magazine *Today*, but he remained an active confidential adviser to Roosevelt through 1936. During that period, Moley recalled, "I spent 132 days in Washington assisting Roosevelt," and "there was scarcely a message or major speech by Roosevelt in the preparation of which I did not participate."[16]

Cultivating Moley

In 1932 Kiplinger began to cultivate Moley as a source, and soon a close bond formed as a result of their moderate political leanings and mutually beneficial exchanges of information. "Wish I had your bird's eye view of politics," Kiplinger later wrote to Moley. "I'm up in a watch tower, but you are higher and can see further. Wish a lot of people could take 'courses' under you in politics."[17]

The first exchange of letters began with Kiplinger somewhat boldly suggesting what Moley should be doing in the White House. In December 1932, about a month after Roosevelt's victory in the presidential election, Kiplinger urged Moley to undertake a fundamental reform of governmental organization. Kiplinger sent Moley a copy of the December 3 *Kiplinger Washington Letter*, which included an overview and analysis of the expected Roosevelt cabinet selections, including a positive review of Moley's role. "One of Moley's jobs ought to be to organize and coordinate the technical thinkers in government service," Kiplinger had written. "Government's right hand does not know its left hand, and business men are victims of governmental inconsistencies."[18] Moley replied three days later welcoming Kiplinger's proposal. "The suggestion you make on the last page is very good. It opens up a new and very important possibility that, frankly, I have not considered.... I hope I can have a chance to talk with you about it some time," Moley wrote. "I hope you will drop a letter into the mail whenever you think I would be interested."[19]

Kiplinger replied two days later with a two-page letter proposing a "Secretary of the Cabinet," whose office would coordinate policies in the executive branch, much like the role of the Office of Management and Budget in the present-day White House. Kiplinger suggested this new group of government technicians could assess worthy economic proposals. He endorsed the work

A Two-Way Street 93

of Malcolm Rorty, an American Telephone and Telegraph Company executive, a conservative, and a leader in the Econometric Society and National Bureau of Economic Research. "He [Rorty] has a 'plan' which appears to be more than the usual panaceas or economic rackets," Kiplinger wrote.[20] Moley later referenced Rorty's research when examining frameworks for the National Industrial Recovery Act, the centerpiece of the First New Deal.[21] Kiplinger also informed Moley about business self-regulatory proposals, highlighting the work of the economist Nelson B. Gaskill and the international business consultant Constantine McGuire. Such self-regulatory proposals aligned with the thinking of Louis Brandeis, the US Supreme Court justice and an influential force in the shaping of the New Deal.[22] Such ideas about government technical expertise regarding business and self-regulation were important aspects of associationalism, the concept of voluntary business cooperation with the government that shaped the basic dealings between government and business in 1933–1935.

FIGURE 8. President-elect Franklin D. Roosevelt and Professor Raymond Moley, his economic advisor, confer on matters of state at the Roosevelt home in Hyde Park, NY, February 27, 1933, as he made last-minute preparations to leave for the White House. —The Associated Press.

At the time, Moley had not yet moved to Washington, since Roosevelt's inauguration would not be until March 1933. Still, he promised to raise Kiplinger's suggestion with Roosevelt. "I am very much interested in the McGuire suggestion, so much so, that I am going to talk over the matter with the Governor," Moley wrote, and encouraged Kiplinger to keep sending ideas.[23] Kiplinger followed up the next month with a four-page internal memo from a Census Bureau official about creating a "bureau of business research." In one sense, Kiplinger's correspondence with Moley reveals a line of thinking favored by business-friendly economists, who would have felt at home with Hoover's approach to regulation.[24] Kiplinger sought to arrange a meeting between Moley and Hoover in 1936 after both men had left government.[25] Kiplinger also urged Roosevelt, in a 1931 letter, to endorse Hoover's "unity plan" to spur economic recovery, a suggestion Roosevelt rejected.[26]

Moley and Capitalism

Moley believed "there was nothing revolutionary" about the basic outlines of the First New Deal, designed to help the private economy with government credit, stem the slide in farm prices, better regulate the securities markets, and encourage self-government in industry to curtail cutthroat competition. "The maintenance of the capitalist system, with individual enterprise as its base, we took for granted," Moley wrote later.[27] To Moley, the New Deal architects believed that big business was not going away and must be brought to the table to curb abuses. He wrote:

> In several of his campaign speeches F.D.R. had touched upon the idea of substituting, for the futile attempt to control the abuses of anarchic private economic power by smashing it to bits, a policy of cooperative business-government planning to combat the instability of economic operations and the insecurity of livelihood. The beliefs that economic bigness was here to stay; that the problem of government was to enable the whole people to enjoy the benefits of mass production and distribution (economy and security); and that it was the duty of government to devise, with business, the means of social and individual adjustment to the facts of the industrial age—these were the heart and soul of the New Deal. Its fundamental purpose was an effort to modify the characteristics of a chaotic competitive system that could and did produce sweatshops, child labor, rackets, ruinous price cutting, a devastated agriculture, and a score of other blights even in the peak year of 1928.[28]

As the March 1933 bank rescue episode illustrates, Roosevelt adopted a series of political compromises designed to save capitalism from itself. Roosevelt spelled out the broad contours of his business regulatory philosophy, and the role of corporations in society, in a 1932 campaign speech to the Commonwealth Club in San Francisco, a speech once described as "his personal Magna Carta."[29]

> The issue of government has always been whether individual men and women will have to serve some system of government or economics or whether a system of government and economics exists to serve individual men and woman. . . . As I see it, the task of government in its relation to business is to assist the development of an economic declaration of rights, an economic constitutional order. . . . We know now that these economic units cannot exist unless prosperity is uniform—that is, unless purchasing power is well distributed throughout every group in the nation.[30]

Yet Roosevelt clearly broke with laissez-faire capitalism by imposing controls on prices and production through the National Recovery Act and the Agricultural Adjustment Act. The Commonwealth Club speech reflected his clear concern with the concentration of financial power: "This history of the last half century is accordingly in large measure a history of a group of financial Titans, whose methods were not scrutinized with too much care and who were honored in proportion as they produced the results, irrespective of the means they used," said Roosevelt. "Put plainly, we are steering a steady course toward economic oligarchy, if we are not there already. Clearly, all this calls for a re-appraisal of values."[31]

Moley recalled an April 1933 conversation with Roosevelt over the economic philosophy of the National Industrial Recovery Act. "You realize, then, that you're taking an enormous step away from the philosophy of equalitarianism and laissez-faire?" Moley asked the president. "F.D.R. looked graver than he had been at any moment since the night before his inauguration. And then, when he had been silent a few minutes, he said, 'If that philosophy hadn't proved to be bankrupt, Herbert Hoover would be sitting here right now. I never felt surer of anything in my life than I do of the soundness of this passage.'"[32]

Tariff Debate

The Moley letters reveal highly detailed intelligence about the administration's inner workings and policy debates. A three-page letter to Kiplinger on July 21, 1934, labeled "Personal and Confidential," provided Moley's analysis of the ongoing debate about tariffs, a central tool to control the flow of US trade with the world and a lever in international diplomacy. Congress had just passed the Reciprocal Trade Agreement of 1934, which gave the president power to negotiate bilateral trade agreements without seeking approval from Congress, a significant ceding of power to the executive branch. The concept was that the president could quickly cut deals with trading partners to open overseas markets for US agricultural goods and jump-start the economy. The agreement represented a major victory for Hull, the conservative secretary of state and ardent free-trade advocate who had campaigned for years to lower tariffs. Critics felt that this ideologically driven free-trade policy amounted to a "unilateral economic disarmament on the part of the United States" that removed negotiating power to halt discrimination against US goods overseas.[33] Moley, who feuded with Hull personally and professionally, feared that mishandling of the tariff would galvanize Republicans and could politically damage the Democratic Party.

Moley urged Kiplinger to pursue the topic for *The Kiplinger Washington Letter* and described ongoing confidential deliberations in the administration. Moley offered a highly unflattering view of Hull, describing him as a fanatic about reducing tariffs whenever possible. "Francis B. Sayre, the Assistant Secretary of State in charge of negotiations, was a mediocre man 'slow witted and gullible,'" Moley wrote. The fanatic and the slow-witted advisers oversaw "handling a vast economic and political question." He predicted that the administration would later develop a reciprocal trading agreement with Cuba during upcoming closed-door meetings and that Roosevelt would sign the agreement into law. "I have a genuine fear of the situation, not only for the disturbing effect that such proceedings will have on legitimate business, but for the danger of getting into a tariff campaign which will be disastrous for the Democrats if Hull's will prevails in the policy of this administration," Moley wrote to Kiplinger. "I am not trying to injure Hull; I am trying to help this administration."[34]

Following up four days later, Kiplinger thanked Moley for his letter, adding, "I have read it, re-read it, shown it to no one, and torn it up."[35] Kiplinger said that he was persuaded by Moley's argument about the tariff. He also told Moley about his friendship with Hull but noted that they disagreed on trade policy and public sentiment on tariffs. Some two weeks later Kiplinger wrote again, providing detailed suggestions and insights about the administration's emerging tariff policy. "Many manufacturers are badly scared over tariff bargaining" and feared that ongoing secret negotiations would hurt their business, Kiplinger warned. Business leaders were visiting Washington to learn what was happening, but getting no information from the State Department, they would leave town angry. Kiplinger told Moley that he was urging Henry F. Grady, chief of the tariff section at the State Department, "to set up some sort of public relations front to this tariff bargaining thing." Kiplinger then offered his own suggestions about the politics of the tariff issue: "If I were a politician, I wouldn't have the guts to tackle this tariff bargaining just at this time. I'd wiggle along on it until perhaps next year, until business were less harassed by NRA, by the unknown elements in inflation, etc."[36]

Insider's Advice

On November 12, 1934, Moley sought to enlist Kiplinger in writing articles to oppose the election of Congressman Joseph Byrns, a Tennessee Democrat, as House Speaker and instead advocate for Sam Rayburn, the Texas Democrat.[37] Kiplinger had at first offered a fairly neutral report about Byrns a couple of days earlier in the November 10 issue, noting a major intraparty fight between Byrns and Rayburn and how the Texan was favored by some in the Roosevelt administration. "Business interests probably prefer Rayburn, but will have little influence on the decision," he wrote. Kiplinger's tone in his reporting about Byrns sharpened after the Moley letter. The November 17 *Kiplinger Washington Letter* observed that the Roosevelt administration harbored "covert opposition to Byrns for speaker" amid concerns that he wouldn't be able to control an unruly House and contain spending proposals. Kiplinger alluded to a "sub rosa movement within the administration" to push for Rayburn. Moley's campaign was unsuccessful, as "Jo" Byrns was elected Speaker in January 1935, serving less than a year and a half until his death from a heart attack in June 1936. Rayburn would become Speaker in 1940.

The Moley letters reveal how Kiplinger was trying to help the Roosevelt administration by proposing policy improvements and at times even attempting to mediate disputes. Kiplinger provided the administration a range of suggestions on communication and political strategy primarily aimed at better selling the New Deal to business interests. "Seems as if the President or someone else with a loud voice ought to begin to prepare a sweep-up of the accomplishments of the administration during the past year," Kiplinger urged Moley.[38] He included a preliminary draft of this assessment, which would be published in the next *Kiplinger Washington Letter*.

Kiplinger also told Moley that Roosevelt should answer questions about whether he was aiming to continue the capital and profits system: "What is the administration's labor policy? (At present there is no way of telling.) ... From the business angle, the longer a statement of ultimate aims and intentions is put off, the longer business will continue to coast along without healthy revival."[39] In a June 1934 letter, he told Moley that Hugh Johnson and Donald Richberg, general counsel for the National Recovery Administration, should "keep their mouths shut" and not respond to criticism from lawyer Clarence Darrow about the New Deal. "If you have any influence with them, why don't you suggest that in any retort to the next Darrow blast that they be very cool and very moderate. This would create more public sympathy for the NRA cause than if Johnson and Richberg go on shooting acid at Darrow."[40] In July 1934 Kiplinger told Moley that he was "shocked at Joe Kennedy's appointment" as chairman of the Securities and Exchange Commission but was "giving great weight to your assurance that Kennedy personally and individually is on the level." Kennedy's wealth and his background as a stock market speculator made him a controversial pick as the nation's markets regulator, with some Roosevelt advisers concerned that Kennedy's Wall Street ties would compromise his ability to enforce new reform laws. In the same letter Kiplinger criticized Postmaster General James Farley, Roosevelt's campaign chairman, whom Kiplinger blamed for patronage appointments of unqualified people in the federal service, warning Moley that there was "so much dirty work arising out of men appointed by Farley."[41] He later praised Richberg for delivering a strong speech to the National Press Club, and he offered a positive appraisal of Harry Hopkins, head of the Federal Emergency Relief Administration and later commerce secretary.[42]

By the summer of 1934, Moley was still advising Roosevelt but was spending much of his time in New York. In his absence, Kiplinger was among the people supplying him with a steady stream of gossip and intelligence about the administration's inner workings. In effect, Kiplinger was serving as Moley's eyes and ears in the nation's capital, primarily reporting about the warring factions within the Roosevelt cabinet. He provided regular updates with insiders' assessments of Moley's influence in the administration: "I guess it would be accurate to say that you are 'highly regarded' by officialdom. That's SOMETHING, for there's more petty jealousy in this administration than I saw in any other."[43] Major themes in the letters involved Kiplinger providing communications advice to help sell the New Deal to business leaders and supplying critique, often constructive, of influential Roosevelt administration figures.

Criticism of Commerce Secretary Roper

In a March 1935 issue of *The Kiplinger Washington Letter*, Kiplinger offered a scathing report on the ineffectual tenure of Commerce Secretary Daniel C. Roper. In that issue, Kiplinger reported that business leaders believed "Roper is proving to be a disappointment.... A reaction against him is setting in, due to discovery after two years that his support of business is mainly vocal. Several influential business groups are secretly discussing plans for asking President to remove him. President will NOT do it, for Roper has powerful political backing." Kiplinger continued with a personal analysis of the commerce secretary: "Safe, sane, conservative, personally clean, honest.... Hates controversy, hates to fight, hates to take a stand on anything. Dodges responsibility systematically by appointing all sorts of advisory committees to 'confer.'... Meanwhile nothing gets done." Kiplinger added that Roper had been complicit in Farley's patronage system, that some of his closest advisers thought solely in political terms, and that some were "utterly incompetent." Roper's administrative style had "permitted political sabotage in every bureau, every function, of the Department of Commerce.... In the administrative sense there is no Secretary of Commerce, for he doesn't direct. The Department is ineffectual. It wastes millions of dollars through incompetence.... One reason why business men have so little influence in Washington lies in the Secretary of Commerce. Truth isn't pleasant," he told his readers. "but you ought to know it."[44]

In a letter to Moley two weeks later, Kiplinger described the impact of the Roper story. "It is highly personal and confidential and you'd better destroy this letter after reading it," he began. The report "shocked the old man and hurt him, but it also prodded him into activity and everyone within the Department reports that he is doing better. He consulted a number of his close friends about the truth of my comments and they were unanimous in telling him that in their opinion the situation was approximately as I outlined it." Morale had also improved in the Bureau of Foreign and Domestic Commerce, and a search was underway for a new assistant secretary of commerce. But in the end, Roper had to go, he wrote: "I continue to be firmly convinced of the desirability of getting a new Secretary of Commerce within the next six months. Roper just can't handle the job, no matter how hard he tries."[45] Kiplinger's wish was not fulfilled immediately, as Roper remained commerce secretary through December 23, 1938.

Portraying Tugwell

One recurring theme in both *The Kiplinger Washington Letter* and the Moley correspondence was Kiplinger's criticism of Rexford Tugwell, a leading leftist in the administration. Kiplinger repeatedly observed that Tugwell, while highly intelligent and talented, was too outspoken and had poor political instincts. In his private correspondence with Moley, Kiplinger predicted Tugwell would have trouble with Congress, even suggesting he would not win Senate confirmation: "It's hard for me to understand how anyone can be as stupid on political tactics as these men [like Tugwell] are."[46] Tugwell had started more reform proposals than he could handle, Kiplinger thought; these proposals would "create powerful enemies," and opposition in Congress would be widespread: "When they begin to open up on him in Congress within the next couple of months, he will find himself in a corner with too many fights to carry, even with the presidential backing, which I know he has, and he is quite likely to be forced out of his present job."[47] Kiplinger's prediction was off the mark: Tugwell was confirmed in June 1934.

While clearly not a fan of Tugwell, Kiplinger repeatedly offered Moley advice to make Tugwell a more effective fit within the administration. For example, he suggested that Tugwell should be a general presidential adviser and not assistant secretary of agriculture. "I just feel this way about Tugwell: He's bright and he's honest and he's energetic and he's thinking in the right general direction. He's too valuable an influence in governmental affairs, which are usually dictated by mediocre and stupid men, to be dispensed with prematurely. As Tugwell is going now, he is trying to start more lines of reform than he can handle when the pinch comes," Kiplinger wrote in January 1934. Although he had no relationship with Tugwell, Kiplinger told Moley he would be willing to meet with Tugwell personally to discuss these matters.[48]

In a letter the following summer, Kiplinger continued his criticism, this time of Tugwell's political speeches, suggesting that "he ought to be kept in the shadow."[49] He later noted that Tugwell would be out of the public eye during his September 1934 vacation, a development that would benefit Roosevelt: "Tugwell's sea trip is going to do the country and the party a lot of good."[50] He also kept Moley informed of business leaders' concerns about Tugwell, alluding in 1935 to a new rumor in business circles "all about how Tugwell secretly plans to have a government 'authority' over every major industry. Just now business is all hot and bothered about the 'radicals' plot against the automobile industry."[51]

Despite these concerns, Kiplinger at times would praise Tugwell in the newsletter. In September 1935 he observed that Tugwell "the reformer has reformed" as head of rural resettlement and emerged as a "cool and cautious administrator."[52] Two months later the tone reverted to one of sharp criticism. "Tugwell's Resettlement Administration is now No. 1 Washington mess," Kiplinger reported. "Part of the mess he inherited, part he made by neglecting his homework while he ran around the country making speeches, showing off."[53]

Today Magazine

Kiplinger had a lifelong interest in journalism education, and he could count Moley as his star student. "You have always had a bracing influence on me," Moley wrote to Kiplinger in December 1966. "Back there around 1935, you said in your usual succinct way, 'When are you going to be a journalist and quit being a politician?'"[54] Earlier he had written, "Your advice to me gave me a sense of responsibility to the public that I could not have otherwise had."[55]

The letters between the two men reveal Kiplinger's role as an important mentor after Moley left the Roosevelt administration in September 1933 for a new career in journalism as editor of *Today* magazine. Kiplinger assisted Moley by providing suggestions for story ideas and freelance writers on topics ranging from labor to farm policy. He would feed Moley insights from upcoming articles, which Moley would use to guide his editorials. For example, Kiplinger sent an advance copy of the July 7, 1934, *Letter* reporting on a survey of two thousand businessmen and their opinions of the New Deal. Moley arranged with Kiplinger to send *The Kiplinger Washington Letter* by overnight mail to his office for Sunday morning arrival so he could read it before writing his editorials for *Today*.[56] The exchange of letters involved discussions of news gathering, editorial voice, and other elements of journalistic practice. At one point Kiplinger held forth on the role of the media in society. "The editor MAKES public opinion. And the editor FOLLOWS public opinion in his community, or among his readers. Thus, by and large, the editorial opinion IS the mass opinion. It's both cause and effect."[57] Kiplinger even critiqued Moley's writing style: "Whenever I read an editorial of yours filling two pages, I always wish you wouldn't do it, or at least that you'd break the thing up so as to look like two or three or four editorials."[58] Mostly the letters were filled with Kiplinger's praise for Moley's work. Moley's articles on Hitler's rise in April 1934 were "shockingly impressive," Kiplinger wrote.[59] He suggested Moley advertise the magazine because not enough people read *Today*.

Editing *Today* magazine gave Moley a perch from which to advocate for his vision of the New Deal while still maintaining close ties to Roosevelt. The president, in accepting Moley's letter of resignation, clearly saw *Today* as an outlet for the New Deal agenda: "Your departure from an official position to undertake an editorship will give you opportunity to carry on the task of an equally wide field."[60] Although out of office, Moley was intimately involved with helping craft the Securities and Exchange Commission and pushing for passage of the Social Security Act.[61] Moley assured Kiplinger in 1934 that he was in regular weekly personal contact with Roosevelt, although, he added, "I am not letting newspapers know of my presence there when I am there." Because of this and his continued contacts, Moley felt he had been able to "hit it pretty accurately" with his columns predicting policy changes, particularly a December 2, 1933, column about monetary policy and other scoops about the German Jewish refugee policy, stock exchange regulation, and national employment insurance: "I think I am in a position to foresee fairly well what is happening."[62]

Kiplinger suggested how Moley might describe his relationship with Roosevelt and how his intimate access to the president could inform journalism in *Today*. For his part, Kiplinger said he would encourage readers to trust *Today* as an "unofficial spokesman for the administration, putting up trial balloons, representing what was in the President's mind, although not necessarily speaking directly and concretely for the administration. What do you think about this view? . . . I am thinking in terms of advising my own readers on what they ought to read and why."[63] Moley replied on February 14, 1934, saying he agreed with Kiplinger's viewpoint but didn't want a direct statement about *Today* as a venue for trial balloons. Yet Moley went on to describe several scoops he'd been able to publish on the basis of his access and insight into the White House. Kiplinger, in turn, helped Moley understand the business community's opposition to the New Deal. Business sentiment had "reached a new highly critical stage," Kiplinger warned in May. "The 'strike' of investors and business managers in general has deepened greatly during the past ten days."[64] Business leaders liked Moley's recent editorial on business confidence, he said, but some wanted a more definite statement from the president about his plans for the next two to three years.

Kiplinger also gently advised Moley to tread carefully as he became an increasingly vocal critic of Roosevelt in 1936: "Feel like reminding you again to be guarded in your critical comments on Roosevelt, especially in your conversation. Reasons: (a) People just naturally are suspicious of anyone who 'turns.' (b) 'Roosevelt made Moley' etc. (c) The name Astor, and what it implies."[65] Vincent Astor, heir to one of America's wealthiest families, was a founder and financier of *Today* magazine. As members of the US aristocracy, Astor and other millionaires were facing increasingly sharp political attacks during the 1936 presidential campaign as Roosevelt denounced the reactionary power of the wealthy class and the wide gap in wealth inequality in the country. Roosevelt privately grumbled that Moley, by working for Astor, had sold out to Wall Street interests. "Ray has joined the fat cats," Roosevelt told Tugwell in 1935.[66]

Today magazine also showcased Kiplinger's reporting, with his first contribution published in December 1933. One Kiplinger article was a featured cover story, a 1936 piece analyzing the federal budget; it was so popular that *Today* reprinted it in booklet form.[67] The information sharing between the two men reached the point where, in 1936, Moley began exploring some form of joint news gathering with *The Kiplinger Washington Letter*, asking if one of Kiplinger's reporters could cull material not published in the *Letter* for a *Today* column called "Forecasts and Reviews." Kiplinger rejected the proposal in September 1936 as impractical since his staff already was fully committed.

Kiplinger's Portrayal of Moley

Moley's name rarely appeared in the Kiplinger newsletter, in part because of the *Letter*'s policy of not identifying sources and using few direct quotations. An April 1933 edition of *The Kiplinger Washington Letter* described Moley as "practically the President's 'idea secretary'"[68] A few months later, in a passage about cabinet officials writing and broadcasting about the New Deal, Kiplinger observed, "Moley's writing is safe enough, neutral, dignified, not particularly illuminating."[69] But in the July 22, 1933, issue, in answering letters from readers Kiplinger opined: "Who is the ONE man most influential with the President? Hard to pick any ONE man. Perhaps Moley. He has NOT lost ground with the President on account of the London conference blow-up."[70] An August 1933 newsletter observed that Moley was being transferred to a new assignment on criminal justice but "is not being eased out of the administration."[71] Following Moley's official departure from the administration that September, Kiplinger noted Moley's reduced influence in a subtle manner, listing Roosevelt's trusted confidants as of November 1933 as Henry Morganthau Jr., soon to be treasury secretary; Agriculture Secretary Henry Wallace; Labor Secretary Frances Perkins; outgoing treasury secretary William Woodin; Postmaster General and campaign manager James Farley; and Harry Hopkins, head of the Federal Emergency Relief Administration and later commerce secretary.[72] Notably, Moley was absent from that list.

The warmth and professional respect between Kiplinger and Moley was evident in their letters, which multiplied after 1934, when Moley officially was out of government. The letters reflect Kiplinger's personal fondness for him: "I continue to miss you. There's no one here now who can point the direction as you did."[73] The two tried to arrange visits in Washington or New York and often sent follow-up letters expressing regret that they had missed the meetings because of their busy schedules.

Relations with Media

Certainly Kiplinger was not the only reporter talking to Moley. Ernest Lindley of the *New York Herald Tribune* and Roy Howard of Scripps-Howard Newspapers were among the other journalists with whom Moley maintained regular contact, although Moley's memoirs and private letters show that his exchange of ideas and advice with Kiplinger was not present in his correspondence with the other journalists. "Many of them were men trained in the old school of Washington reporting, where a breakfast omelet with Hoover was worth a working knowledge of Keynes or Kemmerer any day of the week and to know the provisions of the Federal Reserve Act was unmanly esotericism," Moley wrote.[74] Kiplinger possessed knowledge of finance and economics that was unusual in the Washington press corps at the time because he had covered the US Treasury Department since 1917, once worked for a bank, and had a broad network of business leaders and financial experts. Moley recalled his contact with journalists during the intense period of the spring of 1933:

> With economic reform bills pouring out of the White House, they needed background material desperately. I tried to help supply it, when I could, somewhat as I'd done on the campaign trips—not in press conferences, but informally. Four or five of the newspapermen would catch me as I went to lunch, or as I came into the hotel late at night, or stop by during "The Children's Hour."

There'd be questions, answers, and general rag-chewing. Some of the men came to be good personal friends—Ernest Lindley, John Boettiger, Francis Stephenson, Elliott Thurston, George R. Holmes, George Durno, Eddie Roddan, Paul Mallon, Kingsbury Smith, and, in a slightly different field, Willard Kiplinger. Others, like Ray Brandt, Ray Clapper, and Ray Tucker, I knew less well, but respected for their professional competence.[75]

The New Deal upset journalism in a fundamental way, making Washington, DC, a center of daily news and a fixture in the public consciousness. This was a major shift from the prior decade. The public in the 1920s was more interested in the exploits of baseball players and movie stars than politicians, and so the Washington bureaus of the nation's newspapers relied on press handouts and "went for days without getting a story on the front pages."[76] The sleepy news bureaus were jolted into action during the New Deal and began expanding to cover the dramatic events. Kiplinger's idea of launching a business news service focusing on Washington, therefore, was ahead of its time, leaving him well positioned to report on the unfolding events.

Moley's Break with Roosevelt

Moley's writing in *Today* demonstrated an increasing discomfort with Roosevelt's anti-business direction. He traced his split to June 1935, when Roosevelt, in the wake of the Supreme Court decision invalidating the National Industrial Recovery Administration, responded with tax legislation that targeted wealthy and profitable corporations. By September 1936, Moley's distance from the Roosevelt White House was apparent. No longer in the Roosevelt inner circle, Moley asked Kiplinger to "give us the lowdown on who is writing [FDR]'s speeches lately."[77] Moley wasn't completely out of the Washington loop, however, as he remained in contact with key figures ranging from campaign manager James Farley to Congressman Sam Rayburn, the Texas Democrat who would later become House Speaker.

In 1939 Moley published *After Seven Years*, an in-depth memoir that formalized his break with Roosevelt and was regarded as one of the most powerful critiques of the president and the New Deal. *After Seven Years* represented Moley's emergence as a national conservative voice. He later contributed to the conservative magazine *National Review* and was an adviser to President Richard Nixon.[78] In 1970 Nixon awarded a Presidential Medal of Freedom to Moley, whom he called "a very close personal friend and very valued counselor."[79]

Kiplinger's Relationship with Landon

Kiplinger's relationship with Alf Landon, the Kansas governor and Republican presidential challenger to Roosevelt, began with a fan letter, one that later caused him a bit of heartburn. Landon announced his presidential candidacy during a speech in January 1936, and Kiplinger fired off a congratulatory telegram, which wasn't that unusual for someone who networked endlessly. Landon recalled the incident in a 1971 letter to Austin Kiplinger:

> I am reminded of my first contact with your father—when he sent me a telegram of congratulations on my opening speech in the 1936 campaign in January on Kansas Day that year. The local press asked to see the telegrams I received and I handed them all over to them. They picked out your father's telegrams for one of the few they mentioned. He either wrote me or told me afterwards that it had caused some adverse comment among his Democrat news sources in the Roosevelt administration. He said he could live with that, but it taught him a lesson to be more careful about his communications. From then on, we became the best of friends.[80]

Writing privately to Moley in 1935, Kiplinger expressed admiration for Landon, who was rising in national politics. "The important current phase is the upswing in interest in Landon. I think Landon is a real 'liberal' or at least by the standards of four years ago," Kiplinger wrote.[81] In the May 2, 1936, *Kiplinger Washington Letter*, he wrote: "Landon, if nominated, will be a 'surprise.' . . . He is privately more liberal than most conservatives realize at present." Kiplinger's interest in Landon was flagging, however, as the campaign concluded. By September he admitted to Moley that he was underwhelmed by Landon as a candidate: "I am unable as yet to generate a whole lot of enthusiasm about Landon's public utterances and public appearances."[82]

The *Letter*'s campaign coverage in 1935 and 1936 didn't exhibit an obvious preference for Landon's candidacy, although Kiplinger covered the race closely. The November 9, 1935, issue described Landon as "a major figure in the field of Republican presidential possibilities" and portrayed him in a recent campaign speech as "folksy, plain, without prose, without striving to look like a President, smelling of earth and homely virtues." By April 1936 Kiplinger had perceived a problem for Landon's candidacy: "Wealthy business interests are whooping it up for him, and wealthy backing is considered a political liability this year."[83] He generally depicted Landon as an adequate but somewhat boring candidate. "Landon's acceptance speech seems neither very good nor very bad," Kiplinger wrote about Landon's appearance at the Republican National Convention.[84] "Roosevelt's political personality is vivid. Landon's is relatively drab."[85]

He offered readers a well-rounded assessment of Landon in June 1936:

> Genuinely shrewd politician, trained in the rough-&-tumble—qualities which Hoover always lacked. Wins friends, seldom antagonizes, woos especially his political enemies. Often slow in reaching conclusions, but stubborn when he reaches them. Mind of his own. Thinks of his office as a "job" never thinks of himself as a Great Man.... Not a good public speaker, but better than Hoover was in 1928 or 1932. Not a good poser; pictured homely traits are natural, not put on.... Not passionately partisan. Doesn't "hate Roosevelt," but believes his policies are wrong. Sincerity unquestioned. Ability yet to be appraised.[86]

Shortly before Roosevelt's reelection in November, Kiplinger expressed to Moley some profound and conflicting feelings about the president. He said that he expected Roosevelt to be reelected but worried about his thirst for power, even to the point of speculating that Roosevelt could turn into a dictator. "I'm having a lot of trouble with myself—again. I like SO many of the things Roosevelt has done," Kiplinger wrote.

> I'm sure he is going in the right direction by going some left. Etc. Etc.—You know what. And I DON'T like so many of the things the Republicans stand for."
>
> But—I'm afraid of Roosevelt. I can't convince myself that he will stay put on any issue. I feel he's so ambitious that he would do almost anything, just for the pleasure of exercising his own power. I could come closer to suspecting him of a fascist coup than I could Landon. I could imagine him a dictator, but I wouldn't imagine Landon.[87]

Kiplinger, reflecting on this era some years later, spared little criticism of Roosevelt's anti-business tone in his 1936 State of the Union address: "This was pretty much of a demagogic harangue, stirring class hatreds. Showed emotion, pique. More scolding of unspecified big villains. "[88]

Kiplinger gave several speeches in the fall of 1936 stating that the race would be close, which generated news coverage. Speaking to the Boston Chamber of Commerce in October, Kiplinger declared that Landon was the better choice because he would balance the budget and cut high taxes, both core items for an economic conservative.[89] Although Kiplinger predicted that Roosevelt would win the election, he foresaw a narrow margin of "6 to 5," even though Roosevelt won in a landslide.⁹⁰ The prediction wasn't far out of line with those of other news organizations, some of which showed Landon in the lead as late as September. A closely watched *Literary Digest* straw poll of voters in Maine, New Jersey, New York, and Pennsylvania had Landon leading Roosevelt by a two-to-one margin in early September.⁹¹ Kiplinger provided state-by-state projections about the Roosevelt–Landon race throughout 1936 that showed Landon in a competitive position. Yet on the eve of the election Kiplinger led his newsletter by predicting a Roosevelt victory by a 277–254 electoral college vote.⁹² In fact, Roosevelt won handily, with 523 electoral college votes, carrying forty-six states to Landon's two.⁹³ Landon didn't even win his home state of Kansas.

Landon and Kiplinger enjoyed a warm friendship in the years after the 1936 campaign. Landon gave Kiplinger two apple trees as a gift, and their letters invariably discussed the yield of the trees. "Both of your apple trees are bearing. Bushels from each this year. Too many for home consumption. I give 'em to friends, calling them 'Landons.' Even Democrats eat 'em," Kiplinger wrote in 1957.⁹⁴ Landon made regular visits to Kiplinger's home. "For many years, it was our custom to always arrange a breakfast on a Sunday morning whenever I was in Washington," Landon wrote years later. "My mouth still waters at the delicious hot biscuits that were always on the table. He would come to the hotel and pick me up. . . . At those breakfasts, we really discussed the great questions of interest confronting our country—and, really, personalities. I never breached his confidence, nor he mine."⁹⁵

Morgenthau Fight

Kiplinger's insider counsel to Hull and Moley and his coziness with Landon came back to haunt him and probably cost him an important relationship. Morgenthau suspected that Kiplinger was ghostwriting for Landon, a charge Kiplinger vehemently denied. The available evidence suggests that Kiplinger was not in fact a ghostwriter for Landon, although the two formed a friendship that lasted into the 1960s. There are no references in Landon's papers in the Kansas Historical Society to Kiplinger drafting speeches.⁹⁶ Kiplinger even wrote a letter to Moley denying the accusation.⁹⁷ Because of his close relationship with Moley, as well as his ongoing professional relationship as a contributor to *Today* magazine, it seems unlikely that Kiplinger would have lied to Moley about such a sensitive matter in private correspondence. In any event, the episode reveals the depths of Kiplinger's relationship with officials

A Two-Way Street

in the opposing political parties and provides insight about Kiplinger's increasingly conservative drift during this era, one that aligned with Moley's estrangement from the administration.

The Landon ghostwriting accusation also appears to have cost Kiplinger his friendship with Treasury Secretary Henry Morgenthau Jr. Kiplinger in early 1934 described his relationship with Morgenthau, who was becoming one of his major sources within the administration. "See a good deal of Morgenthau these days; my opinion of him already high, gets higher," Kiplinger wrote to Moley.[98] By November 1934 the relationship was such that Kiplinger was corresponding with the treasury secretary's wife, Elinor Morgenthau. Kiplinger sent a letter on November 14, 1934, praising her recent speech to a Jewish women's group. While on vacation at the Cloisters in Sea Island, Georgia, she replied in a warm two-page handwritten letter: "My dear Mr. Kiplinger, It was most thoughtful and kind of you to write about my talk at the Hadassah meeting, and I can assure you that I value your praise particularly because I have the greatest admiration for your opinions as expressed weekly in your letter.... We look forward with much pleasure to seeing you Sunday night—we feel vigorous and happy after a grand vacation."[99]

Kiplinger and Morgenthau were sufficiently close that the journalist devised an elaborate practical joke for the treasury secretary. It involved Roosevelt's controversial decision to devalue gold in 1933. The joke referenced how gold had been devalued in antiquity, by kings or rulers "clipping" pieces off gold coins to devalue them as currency. "So I had Ferruccio Pini, jeweler, design a medal with the gold dollar embodied in it and a caricature of the then Secretary of the Treasury, Henry Morgenthau, clipping it with shears," Kiplinger wrote to his son Austin some years later. "I showed the sketch to Morgenthau and he was displeased with something or other, probably the caricature. As I remember, the Secretary returned the whole thing to me with his card and I put off the project and eventually gave it up."[100]

Both the friendship and their professional relationship collapsed two years later when Morgenthau accused Kiplinger of biased reporting that favored Landon and of writing a speech for Landon. Kiplinger strongly denied the accusation in a blunt, tersely worded letter to Morgenthau in September 1936, in the heat of the presidential campaign. He had learned that Morgenthau had "'banished' us," he said, "some months ago when you saw that we were giving much attention in our Letters to Landon.

"You also dropped the remark that you wouldn't be surprised if we helped on the Landon speech. This must be sharply challenged," Kiplinger continued. "Fact is, there is only one man, in past administrations or in this administration, for whom I have ever done even slight favors along this line, and you know who he is and why," he wrote, a probable reference to his counsel to Moley or Hull. "I see now that I made a mistake and gave him the wrong impression." Kiplinger continued to defend his reporting on Landon and his attention to the candidate as legitimate: "Yes we have pipelines into Landon's camp. What good reporters wouldn't?

"I am writing you personally merely to say that I am sorry to lose you as a friend,—sorry for several different classes of reasons."[101]

In a subsequent letter to Moley, Kiplinger described the fight with Morgenthau: "P.S. and highly confidential: Morgenthau and I had a spat. He decided I was biased anti-Roosevelt and pro-Landon" and accused Kiplinger of an unspecified act of overt favoritism. "He was 100% wrong and I blew up, and blew hot steam all over him. So he cooled down and we are about to make up and be friends again. But I shall have to watch my step. He's a very suspicious person. I'm pretty sick of the thin-skinnedness within the New Deal. It's terrible. It's MUCH worse than under Hoover in 1932 campaign."[102]

Political Bias

As he sparred with Morgenthau and supplied a stream of political intelligence to Moley, Kiplinger also documented his thoughts on political bias in journalism. In the spring of 1936, amid the Roosevelt reelection campaign, Kiplinger drafted two memos to discuss reader complaints about bias. "The complaints on one side are usually about as numerous as complaints on the other side," he wrote.

> Spirit behind the Kiplinger Letters is non-partisan, unbiased. The Letters are devoted to no party and no special cause. Conclusions are honest, and are stated frankly without thought of the toes on which they may step. . . . 95% of our readers want these things: Critical writing, not a selection of ideas to fit their own ideas. Delicate subjects handled frankly. All shades of opinion, to check against their own opinions. Situations reported as they ARE, not as writers WISH THEY WERE. Letters are written for BUSINESS guidance, not for political guidance, not for election guidance."[103]

To his staff, however, Kiplinger was a straight-down-the-middle journalist who didn't take sides in political matters. "Kip's objectivity was fantastic and I believe that was one of the reasons for the success of his letters. It was impossible for the reader to tell whether something Kip reported on, or the Letters reported, was good or bad, right or wrong. It was just the facts, man, just the facts," said Oeveste Granducci, a reporter who joined Kiplinger in 1929.[104] Longtime editor George Kennedy recalled an incident in the late 1950s involving a highly critical article about the Eisenhower budget. Kiplinger had taken a rare absence from the newsroom, and the staff produced the *Letter* without his input, including a blistering assessment of the budget. "We said that Eisenhower's budget was a fake, that it was a trick deficit and that it wasn't true, deliberately faked for political reasons," Kennedy recalled. The White House was outraged by the item and banned a Kiplinger reporter from the Treasury Department. When Kiplinger returned, he told the staff he understood the administration's anger: "You can't call the President a liar and that's what you are doing. It's just a matter of handling the material right." Kiplinger reviewed the material and wrote the same story for the next week's issue, "but he didn't call anybody anything. They left out all the dirty words," Kennedy said. "But he got the same message over and that was a lesson I'll never forget. Never call a guy a dirty name especially if he's President."[105]

A review of Kiplinger's activities in the 1920s and 1930s reveals that his work as an inside political actor, providing counsel to various politicians, would cross ethical boundary lines in today's newsrooms. Kiplinger acknowledged as much in his memoir, writing "I should hush this up" about his outside work for Cordell Hull or his counsel to Moley.[106] He portrayed himself as a nonpartisan journalist and commentator to his readers and in speeches to journalism educators, his news interviews, and a few articles about the journalism profession. Much of the evidence shows that he upheld the goal of nonpartisan journalism. Yet the Hull, Moley, and Landon relationships show that he was willing to push—and sometimes cross—the line of partisan advocacy when he knew better. As Landon, the 1936 presidential candidate, recalled, news coverage of Kiplinger's congratulatory telegram led to some pushback among Roosevelt administration sources, and Kiplinger claimed the episode had taught him a lesson. Perhaps Kiplinger felt he could segregate this private counsel to politicians from his public journalism and that these activities didn't cross the line. One clear lesson involves the difficulty and messiness of maintaining that objective stance in journalism while trying to cultivate powerful individuals as news sources. It also reflects Kiplinger's hunger to be near power.

CHAPTER 4

Fetching Information and Guidance

THERE ARE COUNTLESS examples of Kiplinger's engagement with readers and his willingness to help business leaders navigate Washington, but few are as memorable as a tip he offered to Harold K. Wilder. In the fall of 1933 Wilder was secretary of the Laundry Board of Trade of Greater New York, and like hundreds of other business leaders, he was wandering around Washington trying to figure out how his industry would be regulated by the National Industrial Recovery Act. Confusion reigned. After he attended multiple conferences with federal officials, it became obvious he needed to speak firsthand with the head of the National Recovery Administration, General Hugh Johnson, and get him to sign off personally on the industry's plan for self-regulation. Without such a meeting, Wilder's industry was in danger of failing. He had tried in vain to get an appointment with Johnson, and he was stuck. No one would put him on Johnson's crammed schedule, and hundreds of other business leaders faced a similar predicament. Wilder reached out to Kiplinger, who passed along a surefire tip on how to meet Johnson: stake him out in the men's room.

Wilder recalled: "Mr. Kiplinger said something like this—'This may not help you but I happen to know that General Johnson gets to the office early in the morning, many times before 8 a.m., and his first stop is in the Men's Room here at the Department of Commerce (think it was on the fifth floor—at the end of the hall) and anybody that really wants to bump into the general might nail him on the way to his appointment there.'"[1] At the time, General Johnson had sought to ban Kiplinger from press conferences on the National Recovery Act because of his critical reporting, so passing along a tip about the general's personal habits could be seen as a form of payback. In any event, Wilder jumped on the tip. The first thing the next morning, Wilder staked out the men's room in the Commerce Department, on the fifth floor, at the end of the hall.

"I hung around the Men's Room and when the cleaning porter came in, I asked him if he had seen General Johnson," Wilder wrote in a letter to Kiplinger some years later. "And he said, 'No sir, but he is pretty regular. Comes in here every morning and goes right to that end stall. Yes, sir, he is a mighty regular man.'"

"Pretty soon, General Johnson strode in and went directly to his favorite stall," Wilder continued. "I waited a discreet time, and then went over and knocked on the door. A gruff 'what's the matter' came from inside." Wilder described his dilemma to Johnson and explained that he was "trying this method as an extreme means because the life or death of the laundry industry, particularly in the New York–New Jersey area," depended on Johnson's signing off on his industry regulatory proposal.

"There was a moment of silence, and he said, 'stick the code under the door' which I did," Wilder wrote. "A few moments passed, and the same gruff voice said, 'Here it is. I have initialed it. Good luck to you.'"

Wilder finally had the approval he needed. The laundry industry would not face ruin. The incident was "just an illustration of how a friendly tip from . . . Kiplinger resulted in at least one code being signed. . . . [I]t did indicate how a good reporter in Washington knew his way around."

Kiplinger learned many tricks and techniques for reporting beginning with his days at the Associated Press. Many were purely physical, such as standing outside a door where candidates were being interviewed for a top-level government position and asking them if they got the job. Other techniques involved spending time with the secretaries and support staff of an executive or government bureaucrat. He offered this sage advice: "I managed to keep my mouth shut and look wise—a valuable trick in the newspaper business."[2] Primarily, Kiplinger's most effective reporting strategy was his relentless networking, expanding his list of contacts and cultivating opinion leaders and key sources with a blizzard of personal letters, phone calls, and well-timed visits.

This chapter examines how Kiplinger's reporting aligned with the trend of interpretive journalism in the 1920s and 1930s. It explores some of his unusual reporting conventions, such as not naming sources in his newsletter reports.

It describes the stylistic features of the *Kiplinger Letter*, namely, a compressed writing style and the emphasis on forecast and analysis. This chapter shows how business newsletters engaged in a two-way communication with the audience, something not common in mainstream journalism at the time. Kiplinger leveraged his influential base of readers to better understand business, regulatory, and economic trends and to broaden the marketing of the Kiplinger brand. The combination of Kiplinger's interpretive form of journalism, his how-to advice for readers, and his public outreach through speaking events and freelance writing served to demystify economics, business, and finance for the broader public and helped democratize the financial markets.

One purpose of Kiplinger's coverage was to scold and mentor the business community into improving its conduct, ultimately improving democracy. This is classic trade journalism behavior: helping to improve the efficiency and operations of an industry and allowing businesses to see emerging risks and threats. Kiplinger's ambition was far greater than a typical trade journal's, however. His coverage was national and encompassed the entire scope of US industry. His reporting fits within the "Enforcers Thesis," a theoretical framework I developed about accountability journalism in the trade press and how it can advance socially beneficial goals.

Interpretive Journalism

Kiplinger's journalism, a blend of analysis and forecasts, marked a significant departure from his hard news roots with the Associated Press. His memoir reveals a frustration with his era's journalistic conventions, which emphasized a transcriptionist approach to covering government and discouraged interpretation. Kiplinger described two cases that brought calls to fire him on account of his interpretive reporting for the AP. While he was covering the Treasury Department in the Wilson administration, Kiplinger wrote, a senior Treasury official, Eugene Meyer, sought to get him fired for a scoop about a major bond issue from Treasury. The story proved correct and Kiplinger kept his job. In another instance, the editor of the *New York Post* asked the AP to fire Kiplinger for writing an interpretive story about European foreign policy; Kiplinger kept his job after the premise of his article was validated.[3]

This tension between strict "hard news" reporting, defined as summarizing the words and deeds of official sources, and the interpretive report, which provides analysis and context surrounding an issue, has been a long-standing issue in journalism. The debate can be traced to the professional journals as early as 1885. An early industry trade publication, *The Journalist,* "lamented the lack of explanation in news reports, noting that many reporters lacked the education and knowledge to explain important social phenomena clearly to their readers, in particular, financial crises and international conflicts," wrote the historian Kathy Roberts Forde.[4] She and Katherine Foss described reporting conventions in that era: "The idea that a news report should focus on the presentation of facts without interpretation or opinion in a neutral third-person voice emerged across the final decades of the nineteenth century and became the dominant idea of what a news report should be across the first decade of the twentieth century."[5] It wouldn't be until 1932 that the term "interpretative journalism" first surfaced in a 1932 college journalism textbook.[6] For business journalism, the interpretive style developed slowly. The roots of business journalism are in the sixteenth century with specialized newsletters and price sheets reporting on supply and prices of specific goods.[7] This bare-bones journalism provided essential information to help emerging capitalist markets evolve. As John McCusker wrote, such "business newspapers helped to perfect the market." Reporting on prices "cut a firm's transaction costs and [allowed] merchants to engage customers more closely, to challenge competitors more successfully," and to "generate more business for the city."[8] At a later point in history, Paul Julius Reuter, founder of the global financial news service that bears his name, elaborated on this idea: "News moves markets. . . . [N]ews is a market."[9]

From these origins, the interpretive style in business journalism emerged in *The Economist* in the 1840s, as the magazine's legendary editor, Walter Bagehot, provided context and analysis that "gave business a language and legitimacy which it had hitherto lacked," Wayne Parsons wrote. Bagehot's "weekly comments put capitalism into words and thereby provided a new forum of communication between business and the wider world."[10] The *Commercial and Financial Chronicle,* published by William Buck Dana, and *Fortune,* published by Henry Luce, are other examples of early interpretive business journalism—publications meeting a demand for more analytical information. Sidney Kobre and Marion Marzolf explained this interpretive trend as a function of the media seeking to better serve readers amid a growing complexity in society and broader shifts in economics and foreign affairs. "Newspaper readers now desire to learn especially the why of the news," Kobre wrote.[11] Journalists ranging from Raymond Clapper to Paul Mallon answered the call and offered interpretive reporting in their columns. Luce and Briton Hadden, who founded *Time* magazine in 1923, brought the interpretive style to a broader audience. The magazine's "pointed and vivid style, its contempt of 'stuffed shirts' and all kinds of stuffiness, and its occasional flippancy pleased the readers of a new post-war generation."[12] *Time* was notable for devoting more coverage to economics from 1933 forward. There were calls from outside journalism for a broader, more analytical view of public affairs to help citizens engage more effectively in democracy and comprehend the growing interdependence among nations. "Theologian Reinhold Niebuhr urged the press to provide 'more than isolated facts' about the world," Marzolf wrote.[13]

Kiplinger openly advocated for interpretive journalism. He lectured on the topic in college journalism classes and wrote an article in 1936 for an academic journal, *Journalism Quarterly*, titled "Interpret the News," in which he argued that interpretation was a natural and an essential evolution in journalism.

> News interpretation is an advanced form of news reporting. It takes a string of facts, or events, or situations, and pieces them together to show a trend. The interpretative reporter, starting with what the facts are, goes on to show what the facts mean. And the meaning of facts is much more important, illuminating and digestible than the facts themselves.... The reader should come first in the journalistic scheme of things. It is not enough to feed the reader raw news. He must have an understanding of the news. Brevity and interpretation are two things which will contribute to more understanding.[14]

The Kiplinger Washington Letter took the interpretive role so seriously that a reader would have had to be current with daily news events to make sense of Kiplinger's analysis. "We leave news to the newspapers," Kiplinger wrote in his unpublished memoir. "Our goal is to cover the reader and fetch him such information and guidance as he wants."[15] He expanded on this theme in a 1966 interview: "If there's a secret to the success of my newsletter, that is the secret. Mixing fact and opinion, judgment and appraisal, and not attributing the information we get."[16] A reader of *The Kiplinger Washington Letter*, for example, would not learn that Roosevelt uttered the words "The only thing we have to fear is fear itself" in his 1933 inaugural address, yet the reader would learn what to expect on banking policies from the new administration.

George Bryant, Kiplinger's former chief of staff, described the extremes Kiplinger would go to with the analytical approach. "He wanted some insight into a story that had already been written because he didn't have room in the Letter to write an exclusive," Bryant recalled. "This was terribly frustrating." In 1947, for example, Bryant obtained an exclusive copy of a White House

Council of Economic Advisers report, news that would be page one in the *New York Times* or the *Wall Street Journal*. But, Bryant recalled,

> Kip turned the whole thing down and said, "Let's wait until it gets in the papers, then we'll write something about it." He said then, "I know this [is] a blow to you and I think you're a good reporter. You got it and got it when you ought to have it. If you were still with the *Wall Street Journal* you would be on the front page with it, but it's too involved to tell in a short space and we can't tell about it really for the first time in a page. It's not worth devoting a whole letter to." And he was right about this.[17]

Kiplinger's vision of blending fact and forecast wasn't popular with some of his colleagues. A 1960 profile of Kiplinger in the *Washington Evening Star* noted that the practice of never quoting a source "looked pretty high-handed at the time to other newsmen, since it raised doubts he's talked to anybody."[18] Yet speaking to officials on a not-for-attribution basis was an essential part of Kiplinger's interpretive journalism, as he believed it provided him with more candid insights and analysis. According to Austin Kiplinger, his father "suffered a great deal from the sneers of some of his fellow journalists when they were writing standard political commentary. They considered his work inferior because it was about business and they were with the high rarified levels of national and international affairs, diplomacy and political policy."[19]

Interpretive journalism generally was not welcomed by Roosevelt, who "opposed reporter interpretation, believed it was a dangerous mix of fact and opinion."[20] In this respect Roosevelt's idealized view of the media harked back to Jeffersonian principles of supplying accurate and prompt information so citizens could make informed choices, the classic formulation of "objective journalism." While Roosevelt condemned interpretive reporting, the president's own media relations strategy, using off-the-record interviews and background briefings, encouraged Washington correspondents to write in an interpretive fashion.[21] Roosevelt held regular press conferences and socialized with journalists, but there was considerable tension between the president and his critics in the press. Negative media coverage of the New Deal began building in 1935. "The press as a whole is more anti–New Deal than pro," Kiplinger reported in April 1936.[22] Reporters resented the New Deal propaganda campaign, which involved the Democratic Party working with spokesmen of various government agencies to denounce critical journalists. Roosevelt made no secret about his disdain for columnists and analytical journalism and instead called for basic reporting of government activities without the analysis. Kiplinger firmly opposed that view. "'Straight news' consists largely of the things which officials do, say, or report. Straight news necessarily reflects largely the views of the administration in power," Kiplinger wrote. "Government pressures on the press are quietly increasing."[23]

Anonymous Sources and Reporting Techniques

How did Kiplinger's newsletter gain access to top officials? First, the reporters possessed deep knowledge in their fields. Second, the newsletter never quoted anyone, as Kiplinger believed that the public statements of business and government leaders were self-serving and deceptive. "When officials talk for publication they are apt to pose and parry and tell half truths," Kiplinger told his readers. "When they KNOW they will not be quoted they are apt to talk more freely and more truthfully. We never transmit to you anything which is truly confidential."[24] The sourcing policy also reflected Kiplinger's belief about the fundamental mendacity of Washington political culture: "Officials often do not mean what they say in published statements. They talk for the effect on the opposing side. They bluff. Their public statements must be discounted in light of private comments."[25] This anonymous sourcing policy emerged from his experience gathering information for the National Bank of Commerce. "While on that job for about three years, I found that much in the news is suppressed," he told an interviewer. "People don't like to talk to reporters. They regard reporters as the enemy, so they won't tell them the real lowdown." It was easier to get information working for a bank than being a reporter for the Associated Press. "I think it is not too much to say that there is a conspiracy to keep the real lowdown from reporters in Washington."[26]

The anonymous sourcing was not common during Kiplinger's era. Anonymous sourcing in news generally applied only to foreign reporting in the 1920s and 1930s, then to military reporting in the 1940s, and then spread outward to other beats in the 1950s. Anonymous sourcing was not mentioned in the American Society of News Editors' professional code of ethics in 1923, and journalism textbooks didn't mention it until 1955.[27] The practice remains controversial in contemporary journalism, particularly business reporting, which values transparency to establish credibility with participants in the financial markets.[28] After all, market participants can bet a lot of money on a stock or bond trade on the basis of a news story, so being told the exact source of the information is especially important. Bloomberg News, for example, strongly discourages using anonymous sources.[29]

Kiplinger asked readers to trust the organization to curate news and produce a fair analysis of events. He addressed the controversial sourcing policy in a 1929 letter to readers: "There is a certain danger in anonymous advices. The transmitting medium, ourselves, may be distorted, prejudiced, inaccurate in perspective. Part of our job is always to recognize the possibility, to minimize it, to preserve common judgment, to avoid the twisted ideas which accompany hobbies, to remember that we are paid by YOU, and that you will stick with us just so long as our batting average is high."[30] By explaining his editorial methods and standards, Kiplinger served to set himself apart from less ethical and more sensationalistic reporters of the era, such as columnist Drew Pearson, who faced a number of libel suits for his reporting.[31]

The second Kiplinger reporting technique involved regular contacts with some 150 "key men" in Washington each week, officials at various levels of the bureaucracy and government who Kiplinger believed knew what was happening.[32] In his unpublished autobiography, Kiplinger described his weekly reporting methods:

> If you were writing the Kiplinger letter, or your own, who would you go to for information? The great men, the famous politicians, members of the President's cabinet, the President himself? That sounds like a good idea but I'd advise against it. Actually, we, as reputable Washington reporters, can talk to most anyone we want to, the great and the near great. Sometimes we are earnestly invited. But mostly we politely turn such invitations down. This may sound foolish but the truth is, the great men at the top are not the ones who know the most about what's going on in Washington. Just a little below the top is a level of officials who formulate the plans that eventually become the policies on the top. They are the backbone of the administration. If you can get their confidence you can get the feel of what's going on.[33]

Some of the staff recalled Kiplinger's respect for his reporters, their news gathering, and their insights. "With Kip, reporting was paramount—good questions, good contacts, good sources of information," recalled George Kennedy, a longtime Kiplinger editor from the 1950s through the 1980s. "He let his staff people talk. He never interrupted unless they were getting verbose and wasting time. He wanted to hear what they had to say. He gave them the floor completely. This impressed me as a young reporter—the faith he had in me."[34]

Kiplinger didn't bother going to the Capitol to cover Congress or attend presidential events, according to a review of company correspondence and employee interviews. There is no evidence that Kiplinger attended Roosevelt's press conferences or had much contact with the president, who socialized with other journalists such as Ernest K. Lindley of the *New York Herald Tribune*, Raymond Clapper of Scripps-Howard Newspapers, and Frederick A. Storm of United Press. Some journalists found that Roosevelt used personal dinners and bridge-playing sessions as ways to manipulate news coverage. Others found that personal contact with Roosevelt was intoxicating. Arthur Krock, the *New York Times*' Washington bureau chief, seldom attended Roosevelt's press conferences in an attempt to maintain his independence. When the president asked about his absences, Krock told him: "I lose my objectivity when I'm close to you and watch you in action. You charm me so much that when I go back to write comment on the proceedings, I can't keep it in balance."[35]

Kiplinger's circle of contacts included top regulatory and business officials: Federal Reserve chairmen Eugene Black and later Marriner Eccles, assistant treasury secretary and later J. P. Morgan chairman Russell Leffingwell, and former treasury secretary and US senator William Gibbs McAdoo. Relationships with some of these men kept going many years after they left office. "I miss you boys in Washington," McAdoo wrote Kiplinger in 1919 after he had left the Wilson administration to practice law in New York. "One of the genuinely delightful features of my life there was the friendly and candid discussions we had at our weekly meetings about the questions of the day." McAdoo thanked Kiplinger for sending him a photograph, which was not identified: "I need not tell you how much I appreciate it because it is evidence of a very delightful friendship I formed with you at Washington and which I hope may continue as long as we both live."[36] This relationship proved very fruitful for Kiplinger, since McAdoo later was elected to the US Senate from California and would solicit Kiplinger's input about the state of current affairs. "What the hell is all the shootin' about?" McAdoo asked in November 1933, referring to the backlash against the New Deal and chaos on the gold policy. "I am a bonehead, no doubt, and perhaps that is why I am confused. Send me a line, in confidence, and tell me what you think of things."[37]

In 1931 Kiplinger reached out to Franklin Roosevelt, then New York governor, and sent him a complimentary subscription to the newsletter, a gesture that raised the journalist's visibility with a future president. "I should certainly be interested in receiving your Washington letters and appreciate very much your generosity in offering to put me on the complimentary list," Roosevelt wrote on July 8, 1931. He asked Kiplinger to mail the letter to his home on East Sixty-fifth Street, "which will insure their not being buried in the great mass of official mail which clutters my desk every day." Two weeks later Roosevelt wrote again to Kiplinger: "I like your survey of the situation—and I am glad to get the Washington letters."[38] The exchange of letters served an important purpose: a journalist now was on the radar screen of a major policy maker. On November 6, 1931, Roosevelt wrote to Kiplinger again: "I am glad you have found time to drop me a line in relation to national problems as I requested in a previous letter to you."

After gathering bits of news and gossip from these dozens of weekly meetings, Kiplinger and his reporters began the painstaking effort of analyzing and distilling the information into a four-page weekly letter. The editing process was legendary, with reporters working hours to produce a few insightful paragraphs on a major policy issue. Kiplinger was the best writer in the house and oversaw the final edit of the newsletter. Here's how the process worked when the Kiplinger organization was first starting: Kiplinger and his reporters would type up short memos or items, condensations of interviews after their meetings around town, and drop the pieces of paper into a basket in the office. "Then on Wednesday night after work we would spread these scraps of paper out on a big table, sort them and arrange them and have them typed up thus making our weekly letter," Kiplinger recalled.[39] In the 1930s, the letter generally was produced on a Friday night. Austin Kiplinger, then a teenager, recalled that his father worked much of the day, writing the letter. The younger Kiplinger would join his father at the office, do some homework, and then head over to the YMCA for a swim and a steam bath—the elder Kiplinger's favorite form of relaxation. They would eat dinner at a Chinese restaurant and then return to the office around 9 p.m., where the elder Kiplinger would finish the letter around 11:30 or midnight.[40]

Newsletter History

Kiplinger's use of direct marketing and his emphasis on concise analytical writing represented significant evolutions in the newsletter field. Newsletters were witnessing a boom in the 1920s and 1930s, but as the scholar Kathleen Endres observed, newsletters had been around for centuries. They are "both the oldest and the newest print news medium," which she traced to Rome in 59 BC and China during the T'ang dynasty, AD 618–907. "For centuries, these handwritten newsletters were the dominant print news medium.... Centuries before the newspaper made its appearance, handwritten newsletters spread the news of the day." According to Endres, newsletters were being reintroduced in the twentieth century, as they "seemed tailor-made for the specialized information needs of readers in developed countries."[41]

In the United States, newsletters responded to a demand for specialized business information that accelerated around 1840 to serve a growing industrial society and the information needs of an expanding capitalist economy. "The need and the opportunity for a business press grew out of the introduction of the factory system, and the dawning of the realization that the making and distribution of goods depended upon economic principles," wrote Jesse H. Neal, a leader of the trade group Association of Business Papers in New York in 1922.[42] Ferdinand Lundberg framed the demand this way: newsletters supplied information for "class conscious businessmen" who could afford to pay for the lowdown.[43]

The newsletter genre ranges from sophisticated commercial publishing to photocopied church bulletins. Newsletters are limited circulation periodicals, defined as "specialized information prepared for a specific audience," as opposed to a newspaper, which covers general news, from sports to crime to recipes, for a broader community.[44] Newsletters can be affiliated with trade or professional associations to keep their members informed or can be aimed at specific business sectors or industries.[45] The size and scope of this field is difficult to discern. The National Mail Order Association provides a listing of some fourteen thousand newsletters in the United States and Canada in 252 categories.[46] A 1994 study estimated that the newsletter industry reaped some $5 billion in revenues.[47]

Newsletters marked an evolution of these specialized media trends and were built on market intelligence supplied by banks themselves. According to Lundberg, "In format, but not in content, the news-letters resemble the periodic bank and brokerage house market reports which multiplied in the United States and Western Europe from 1850 onward."[48] *The Kiplinger Washington Letter,* in fact, evolved from Willard Kiplinger's work for the National Bank of Commerce and the Business Intelligence Bureau, where he wrote letters to bank clients on Washington events and policy from 1919 to 1923. Kiplinger's time working for the National Bank of Commerce was highly significant. It allowed him to understand the information needs of business executives, the audience that would later become readers of *The Kiplinger Washington Letter*. This understanding of the bankers' busy business life and his awareness of their desire for analytical and forward-looking information were formative ingredients in designing the newsletter.

Kiplinger was not the first to launch a newsletter aimed at business clients. Percival Huntington Whaley, a lawyer-journalist described as "the father of the modern news-letter," launched the *Whaley-Eaton Service Newsletter* in Washington, DC, in September 1918 with another lawyer-journalist, Henry M. Eaton. Within two years of their founding this newsletter, "there were scores of imitations started in Washington. All of them failed."[49] Kiplinger was the only really successful Washington rival. Kiplinger's journalism represented an advance for trade journalism since it envisioned a broad national audience of business and political figures, far beyond the targeted and narrow audiences of a typical trade journal. Kiplinger's reporting thus allowed a broader public to see the inner workings of Washington and the business community.

Veteran industry publisher Howard Penn Hudson wrote, "Willard Kiplinger set the style in 1923, using the newsletter as a jumping-off point for telling his readers the significance of the news."[50] The idea caught on quickly. By 1924, subscribers to the *Kiplinger Letter* included leading corporations of the era: Buick Motor Car Co.; Hibernia Bank and Trust Co.; Sears, Roebuck & Co.; Sun-Maid Raisin Growers; the National City Bank; H. J. Heinz Co.; William Filene's Sons Co.; and United Fruit Co., among others.[51] Kiplinger eclipsed the *Whaley-Eaton Newsletter* in the 1930s, and by the 1940s it boasted a circulation estimated at thirty to forty thousand, compared to the six to seven thousand circulation for Whaley-Eaton.[52] While significant, *The Kiplinger Washington Letter* still was a niche player in a media ecosystem that included competing daily newspapers, magazines, and books.

By 1940, Lundberg, writing in *Harper's*, described newsletters as "a revolution in journalism" that was upsetting the staid order in media publishing, an overstatement given that the true revolution would come in the next decade with television.[53] Kiplinger envisioned himself as an upstart and a disrupter and felt the scorn of some newspaper reporters. "Occasionally you may read in the daily press slighting comments about business letter services," Kiplinger told his readers in 1933. "Daily newspapers look with suspicion on any new medium. Old-established political writers, who treat politics as a sport, are the aristocrats of the profession. New style business writers, who treat politics as an integral part of economic forces, are frowned upon by the old school."[54]

Lundberg described how newsletters, as an innovative distribution channel with a low barrier to entry, posed a challenge to mainstream journalism in the early 1940s. His commentary is nearly identical to that in the 1990s, when the Internet was upending journalism:

> Today, anybody who has something to say or who has genuine news may with a typewriter, a mimeograph machine, and a mailing list reach an extensive audience. Great capital resources are not needed. Not only have the news-letters built up their own audiences on a financial shoestring but they have placed the press magnates in an awkward position. For if the press ignores vital material that the news-letters print then the newspapers are in danger of being regarded as unreliable by the informed public. And if the newspaper takes tips from the news-letters—as most of them do to avoid being outflanked—then they no longer have exclusive judgment on what shall enter the news-stream.

Lundberg even suggested that since they weren't funded by advertisers, newsletters, unlike newspapers, did not face a form of censorship that forced them to downplay negative economic news. "The news-letters escape whatever influence large advertisers bring," Lundberg wrote. Yet Kiplinger, along with the Whaley-Eaton and Research Institute letters, was also concerned about advancing business progress: "Editors Whaley, Kiplinger's, and Leo M. Cherne [of the Research Institute] admit that they do not publish everything that comes to hand, that they make an effort to be 'constructive' and pro-business."[55]

Marketing

By today's standards, the main tools Willard Kiplinger used for encouraging audience engagement were surprisingly direct: typewritten letters and the US mail. With hundreds of typewritten notes and mailings of sample issues, Kiplinger executed a marketing strategy that engaged elite influencers of his day, ranging from the British royal family to Fortune 100 CEOs, from cabinet secretaries and US political kingmakers to small-town Rotary Club officials. Kiplinger's blizzard of typewritten correspondence would be the modern equivalent of cultivating social media influencers on YouTube or Instagram to embrace a product, hoping it would spread virally through their networks. In modern journalism, reporters and editors are encouraged to develop a "brand," to carve out their identity as a subject matter expert or practitioner of a particular genre of journalism in order to build an audience. "He was always marketing his service, he was always looking for new subscribers, and he was always looking for new sources with whom he could correspond," Knight Kiplinger said of his grandfather. "I think it was important to him that his *Letter* be read by influential people. I think it was important to his self-esteem. Every journalist wants to be influential and read."[56] One example involved a January 1934 letter Kiplinger wrote to the head of the Federal Reserve Board, Eugene R. Black, an Atlanta native. The exchange of letters with Black, a central figure in US government and finance at the time, illustrates Kiplinger's deft source-building skills and his ability to cultivate relationships at the highest level of government. Kiplinger didn't address business but instead recalled an amusing adventure during his youth, selling aluminum cookware in Black's hometown of Atlanta. "Apropos of nothing whatsoever, I ought to tell you a story," Kiplinger wrote to Black.[57] The head of the US central bank replied: "I enjoyed your story immensely and it brought a smile and a bright spot in the week's record. Please believe that I am very grateful for the friendly thought which prompted your letter and especially the good story it contained."[58]

Kiplinger corresponded briefly with Black's successor at the Federal Reserve, Marriner S. Eccles, who sent a copy of a speech he delivered in Boston. "I have somewhat revised it with a view of making it available to some of my friends, as well as to a wider circle of bankers and business men who are interested in the matters discussed," Eccles wrote.[59] Kiplinger replied to the Federal Reserve chairman: "I thought your address before the New England Council was swell. It is interesting and down-to-earth. It is non-technical, and that's the sort of thing which is hard to do and which is seldom done. My congratulations on it."[60]

Kiplinger expanded his visibility by writing for numerous outside publications or speaking at public events, such as the 1936 radio broadcasts with the Philadelphia Orchestra. Kiplinger was prolific with his outside journalism, writing at least thirty-two freelance articles for the *New York Times, Nation's Business, Today,* and other publications between 1932 and 1940 (see figure 9). These were generally much longer articles in which Kiplinger wrote in a more fluid style than his staccato and clipped "sweep line" writing for *The Kiplinger Washington Letter*. Kiplinger's freelance writing served multiple purposes, also serving to raise his profile with sources and expanding the public's awareness of him as a business expert.

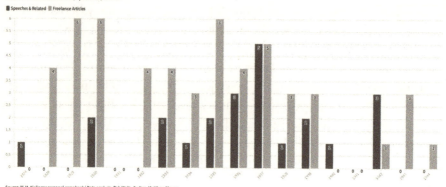

FIGURE 9. Frequency of Kiplinger's freelance articles, speeches, and related publicity, 1924–1944. Compiled from W. M. Kiplinger's personal scrapbook. —Graphic by Rob Wells and Matthew Moore.

Kiplinger began implementing a professional marketing strategy in 1925 when he brought on a new partner, Paul T. Babson, owner of a small business information service in Boston called United Business Service. Newsletters rarely are supported by advertising and instead rely on subscription revenues, so marketing to new readers was essential.[61] Babson designed a direct mail marketing campaign that sent out thousands of solicitation letters. He also persuaded Kiplinger to invest in addressing and tabulating machines. The new company paid information brokers for subscriber lists from publications such as *Literary Digest* or lists of people who had recently purchased automobiles. Kiplinger was an early user of mass direct mail, but other publications were using these techniques as well. Beginning in the mid-1940s, *Reader's Digest* became heavily involved in direct marketing.[62] The Kiplinger marketing techniques were successful and subscriptions grew significantly. By the end of World War II, Kiplinger was the nation's largest business newsletter, with a circulation of 187,000.[63]

Crowdsourcing

With direct marketing strategies, Kiplinger's newsletter began to gain visibility and currency with a general audience. Kiplinger also engaged in a type of crowdsourcing, urging his audience to report on business sentiment, further cementing their engagement with his publication. Kiplinger's broad base of subscribers—"there is hardly a small town in the country that has not a few

Kiplinger subscribers"—led to a daily flow of tips and questions.[64] In a 1949 interview Kiplinger remarked: "Fifty businessmen write me every day and I write them. They ask me questions and I ask them questions, and we swap news and views about how things are with them in their trades and localities. It is my business—to correspond with business men."[65] The profile of his readership by the late 1920s was summed up by Kiplinger as follows:

> Practically all of business men. Some are wealthy. Many are executive officers of large manufacturing and commercial operations. Perhaps 30 percent are bankers, mainly large bankers. We believe the group represents a fair cross section of the business community of the nation. It does not include any considerable element of wage earners, or labor, or professional men (exception for some lawyers and accountants), or farmers.... We have no knowledge of the politics of our clients; probably most are Republicans.[66]

Kiplinger's audience engagement techniques represented a new step in the evolution of journalistic practice at the time. The mass society and transmission theories of media communication were prevailing concepts in the 1920s and 1930s, holding that the media generally transmitted a message to an audience but got little direct feedback.[67] According to Elihu Katz and Paul Lazarsfeld, two pioneers in media effects theory, early mass audience research in the 1920s involved a classic transmission model that viewed the audience as "an atomistic mass of millions of readers, listeners and movie-goers prepared to receive the Message; and secondly, they pictured every Message as a direct and powerful stimulus to action which would elicit immediate response."[68] A prevailing view of media in the 1920s and even the 1930s involved focusing on the source and content, not on the audience's needs. It wasn't until much later that media scholars began to examine audience interplay, which was present in other forms in the pre–mass market era.[69] Early audience engagement and interactivity involved theater audiences singing songs or yelling instructions to performers.[70] The introduction of electronic broadcast technologies such as radio and television led media theorists to posit a "one to many" model of media transmission, an idea now outdated by the distribution reach and interactivity of social media.[71] Today, nearly anyone with the capacity to watch a YouTube video can also produce a video.

While Kiplinger's audience engagement was extensive, other publications were using audience surveys too. The Whaley-Eaton letter and the Research Institute of America *Business and Legislation Report* were actively engaging with their readers in the 1920s, soliciting story ideas and shaping some of their coverage on the basis of reader input and feedback. *Fortune* used a similar technique in June 1934 when it surveyed a cross-section of its readers to discern industry's opinion of the National Recovery Act, declaring, "*Fortune*'s subscribers can very properly speak for American industry because, in no narrow sense of the term, *Fortune*'s subscribers are American industry."[72] *Business Week* used this technique as well, printing answers to common reader questions in a periodic feature called "Recovery Catechism."

Kiplinger had an ongoing dialog with a broad range of readers, including middle America's business class, in which he asked them for their input and shared his forecasts, even when they were incomplete. Kiplinger endeared himself to readers by frankly admitting his shortcomings and the limits of his reporting. "Our letters absolutely dependable? No. Lots we don't know, lots we can't figure out," he wrote in April 1933. To underscore the point, Kiplinger offered a question-and-answer section where he didn't always provide answers. "Are we headed toward a MAJOR inflation? Probably yes. How far will inflation go? Don't know. How high will commodity price level go in next six months? Don't know."[73] In a swipe at some fellow prognosticators in the media, Kiplinger noted a week later: "Reason we are so fussy in explaining that the opinion lacks 'authority' is that too many published statements these days carry implication that they are 'inspired.' Our opinion is not inspired or motivated." This gives evidence of Kiplinger's conversational tone in the letter, despite the formal salutation "Dear Sir."[74]

Like other publications, *The Kiplinger Washington Letter* surveyed readers about local business conditions, in a way similar to the Federal Reserve's periodic "Beige Book" survey of the regional economy.[75] Today we would describe this as crowdsourcing information. One example was in the July 26, 1930, issue, where Kiplinger reported the results of a confidential survey of five hundred business leaders on Washington politics and business conditions. At the time, the US economy was in the first year of the Great Depression. Some three-fourths of the business leaders surveyed described Congress in "extremely derogatory terms," using phrases such as "disgraceful antics," "disturbing," "insincere," "hypocrisy," and "utter incompetence." On the economy, the business executives felt that August 1930 would be the bottom of the Depression; professional economists believed that the Depression would actually continue for another thirty months, until March 1933, although the economic misery for many would stretch out throughout the decade.[76] The business readers seemed resigned that the Depression was the result of an imbalance in economic forces and should be allowed to run its course: "An impressive thought running through hundreds of letters is that business depression is the inevitable result of a 'maladjustment of supply and demand in preceding boom years' and therefore is 'normal' therefore 'must be accepted as a matter of course.'"[77] In November 1933 Kiplinger gathered questions from business readers about the New Deal and had them answered by NRA officials. Kiplinger assured his readers that their views would shape the direction of his journalism. After one reader survey, Kiplinger said that the innumerable tips from readers would form the basis for future articles: "Business facts galore are given us and will prove useful for our guidance in future letters."[78]

Such surveys also enabled Kiplinger to gather data and insights about his readers, all of which he used to refine his marketing and journalism to further cement their loyalty. The gathering of audience data and sentiment is a hallmark of the modern newsletter practice of continuous research on an audience and their information needs. Another example of crowdsourcing was the November 18, 1933, edition, where business leaders wrote about their impressions of General Hugh Johnson's tour of the country. Many readers described him as bombastic.

Kiplinger formalized his ongoing dialog with the business community by creating a query service to allow readers to ask any question, whether or not the topic had been covered in the newsletter. This service was initially provided for a fee but later was free. This advice service was a hallmark of the Kiplinger publishing enterprise during its period of family ownership but was mostly discontinued by its new owner, Dennis Publishing. During its existence, the query service even applied to personal financial questions from subscribers to *Kiplinger's Personal Finance* magazine.

According to Knight Kiplinger, a reader could contact Kiplinger editors "and ask us for our judgment about something we haven't written about. He calls and says, 'I'm hearing from my trade association that there is this new policy taking shape at the Department of Energy. Do you think that's true? Do you think it's going to be enacted?'" After making some calls, a Kiplinger staffer would call the subscriber back and might say, "Yeah, your trade association is on to something here." Knight Kiplinger recalled the types of queries submitted by *Kiplinger Personal Finance* subscribers: "They're paying us just eighteen or twenty dollars a year, but we'll stay on the phone for an hour with a subscriber with questions about his mix of mutual funds, or the best way to make college tuition gifts to his grandchildren or something like that."[79] The magazine has offered much less of this kind of service under the new management.

Enforcers Thesis

The strategy of using audience engagement as a news-gathering tool is a standard practice for trade publications, which enjoy a shared language between journalists and the industry they cover. The term "trade press" refers to journalism that serves a specific industry audience, such as *Aviation Week and Space Technology* or *Women's Wear Daily*, providing a mix of oversight, community news, and continuing education for professionals in the field. "If you're working for a narrow audience, you have to be in touch with your audience," said Joel Whitaker, publisher of the *Newsletter on Newsletters*.[80]

We can also view the Kiplinger brand of journalism through a theoretical lens involving trade and specialized journalism. The Enforcers Thesis describes how accountability journalism in the trade press can advance socially beneficial goals. The thesis grew out of my case study of the *National Thrift News*, a gutsy financial industry trade newspaper that broke a major political scandal in the 1980s involving the real estate developer Charles Keating and his influence peddling in the US Senate.[81] The Enforcers Thesis argues that business journalists focus on normative ethical practices in an industry and tend to report on companies that violate those norms. In this process, business journalists who conduct this type of accountability reporting are enforcing a code of industry conduct and are identifying socially harmful business actors. This thesis offers a new perspective on trade publications, which have long been criticized for being captives of the industries they cover. The thesis, which applies to independently owned trade publications, is based on the concept of watchdog reporting and the ideal of journalism performing a surveillance function over the government and powerful institutions. Watchdog journalism is originally produced journalism that sheds light on an abuse in society. It can also involve rebroadcasting information generated by analysts, legal cases, regulators, or other entities that perform an oversight function. The *National Thrift News* episode, along with research into other instances of investigative reporting in trade journals, offers evidence that trade publications can play an influential role in shaping coverage of mainstream media and, in many cases, can raise important societal issues. The Enforcers Thesis urges scholars to think of the trade press more broadly. Paul Starr has written about the "diffusion of knowledge" and public education as a facet of the press in the early US republic.[82] Perhaps trade publications can extend a form of "industrial education" to the broader public by alerting consumers to threats and opportunities in the business community so they might avoid spillover problems in their financial lives.

The Enforcers Thesis examines structural and sociological factors that allow some business publications to report independently and candidly about powerful corporations. The thesis argues that there are three central factors that support accountability journalism at trade publications: journalist ownership of the media organization, a strong grounding in traditional journalistic values, and the willingness to assert journalistic autonomy from commercial influences. Kiplinger's profile fits the Enforcers Thesis: he owned and controlled the news organization, instilled rigorous reporting standards, and was willing to face down powerful actors, primarily in government. The case of *The Kiplinger Washington Letter* suggests an expanded boundary for the concept. Unlike traditional trade journals, the newsletter was not focusing on a single industry. Its domain involved the entire US economy, and by extension, the functioning of capitalistic society. Kiplinger's functionalist approach to reporting addressed the abuses of capitalism, and he offered solutions to make capitalism operate in a more socially beneficial manner. In essence, in his watchdog role over the business sector, Kiplinger had broader ambitions for the evolution of the US economy. Of course, one business newsletter alone could not bring about such a significant change, but as my research clearly demonstrates, Kiplinger's editorial voice was a significant influence in New Deal business discourse.

Functionalist Advice

In his reporting Kiplinger strove to provide practical advice for business leaders to respond to the changes in Washington so that they might operate more effectively in a democracy. His journalism reflected the concept of functionalism, which holds that the news media can maintain and advance social stability though transmission of norms and ideas such as cultural heritage, surveillance of powerful institutions, and correlation of information to help individuals make sense of current issues.[83] One way to think of functionalism is as "news you can use." In this case, it was news you could use to better comprehend and engage in the democratic process. Kiplinger also printed advice to business officials on best strategies for testifying at NRA hearings on industry regulations.[84] He even urged business leaders to settle their differences with organized labor. "Get together with labor, if possible, and work out disparities of understandings as to what should be included in codes. In many instances, this will be impossible, of course," Kiplinger advised in July 1933.[85]

The concept of functionalism grew out of sociology in the 1920s with the work of Émile Durkheim, Robert Merton, and Talcott Parsons.[86] Durkheim wrote about a common conscience, or a shared system of beliefs, which echoes an overarching goal of Kiplinger's reporting: to establish a new common code of business conduct in this fast-changing landscape.[87] Harold Lasswell's classic study "The Structure and Function of Communication in Society" in 1948 spelled out the transmission, correlation, and surveillance functions of the media. Lasswell explained how surveillance by the news media can disclose threats as well as uncover "opportunities affecting the value position of the community and of the component parts within it."[88] One criticism of functionalism is that the media tend to preserve the status quo. Ellis Hawley, for example, argued that big business wound up as a victor in the First New Deal through government sponsorship of cartels and the role of business in implementing regulations that limited competition from smaller rivals.[89] Yet Kiplinger pushed the status quo by describing the end of laissez-faire capitalism and declaring the formation of a new economic order. His functionalist approach to reporting not only served his business readers but also sought to bridge a rift between business and the Roosevelt regulators.

For example, in a February 1933 report, Kiplinger attempted to allay business fears by emphasizing the competence and forethought of the incoming administration. "There IS a Roosevelt program," he assured readers, outlining financial issues such as inflation, farm credit, banking policy, and restructuring of railroad and utility regulation. He also warned businesses of major changes ahead, a consistent theme in the coverage throughout the spring of 1933. "Taken as a whole it will sound good, although particular parts of it will be highly disturbing to many."[90] The changes were necessary, Kiplinger wrote, because inaction could lead to widespread social unrest: "The big idea is this: Administration is just on the point of concluding that business will not revive spontaneously and naturally to diminish unemployment with sufficient speed to eliminate danger or social disturbances in industrial centers. Conclusion is imminent, therefore, that government must apply direct force to business."[91]

One undercurrent in Kiplinger's writing, and in other commentary at the time, involved the potential for social unrest if the Roosevelt program failed to improve economic conditions for the working class. This concern inspired a sense of urgency in Kiplinger's writing. "How close is the nation to a violent 'break'?" he asked in the April 8, 1933, newsletter. The public needed to see some early improvement in unemployment by late May or early June, he declared. "Hence the social unrest crisis must be considered a POSSIBILITY throughout May." The memoirs of New Dealers Tugwell and Johnson both name social unrest or violent uprisings a significant possibility in the spring of 1933.

One prime example of Kiplinger's functionalist approach was the "Brown Letter," a special edition of the newsletter that reported just on the nuts and bolts of the National Recovery Act. He called it the "Industrial Control Postscript." Printed on brown paper to distinguish it from the regular *Kiplinger Washington Letter*, it served as a forum for addressing the flood of business news surrounding the New Deal. The announcement of its launch on June 1, 1933, carried patriotic overtones: "No charge is made for the special service. It is our contribution to meeting an emergency."[92] The Brown Letter had a specific functionalist mission: "What we can do for you: Receive your questions, try to get unofficial answers, report back in future letters."[93]

In the regular edition and the special Brown Letter, Kiplinger's mission was "to piece together the various fragments of Washington policy and make an understandable picture, and ship you the picture, so that you may fit your policies into it. We have no interest in influencing Washington policies. We don't have any CAUSE to promote, except the accurate understanding of political influences in their practical aspects. Perhaps this itself is a cause."[94] In another issue he elaborated on the theme: "We report government INTENTION, which is far more important than mere TEXT," he wrote in May 1933.[95] Kiplinger provided a practical step-by-step guide to dealing with the Recovery Act, advising readers," "Don't write General Johnson," head of the National Recovery Administration. "He can't tell you anything officially. What he has already told people unofficially is reflected herein." Instead, business leaders should read the law itself and certain publications to avoid falling prey to scam artists: "It may help to keep you out of the hands of the professional racketeers, who are busily engaged in selling advice which you can just as well get free from the governmental source."[96]

This functionalist approach was adopted by other publications such as *Business Week*, which included regular summaries of the progress of the New Deal. The *Business Week* coverage was not as explicit as Kiplinger's step-by-step advice on how to prepare for a National Recovery Act industry code hearing. Still, *Business Week* provided ample detail that would be useful for its audience, such as a May 1933 report giving specifics about a compromise on banking legislation between Treasury Secretary Woodin and Carter Glass, chair of the Senate Appropriations Committee. At other points, *Business Week* seemed to misread the significance of the New Deal political momentum. A May 10, 1933, article, for example, reported, "Whether Congress will at this session enact any measure aiming to increase federal regulation of industry appears at the moment somewhat in doubt."[97] Its coverage that May seems to suggest that *Business Week* lacked details about the Roosevelt regulation plan up to this point. "The picture puzzle of industrial control legislation," it reported, "is at last beginning to fall into place."[98] By contrast, Kiplinger was already providing extensive commentary about the aspirations and fine points of the New Deal regulatory project. There was little evidence of this pro-market functionalist coverage in *Fortune* or the *New York Times*.

Creating a Public Sphere

Kiplinger's audience engagement advanced a public sphere in the business world, especially among smaller businesses away from the East Coast political and financial centers. Kiplinger pushed business leaders to become more engaged in public affairs and to work within existing democratic structures by repeatedly urging them to adopt a cooperative and constructive approach during the chaos of the First New Deal. In essence, he was trying to broker a truce between a restive corporate sector and Roosevelt's forays into economic "dictatorship."[99] Smaller businesses were able to express their concerns and amplify their voices through Kiplinger's reporting, which offered them a forum in a publication closely read by political elites. As readers complained about the onerous regulations of the New Deal, Kiplinger urged them to organize and join trade associations, which would serve as vehicles to engage effectively with Washington and influence the regulatory process. He suggested that businesspeople write to the US Chamber of Commerce or the National Association of Manufacturers and examine their publications on how to curtail and modify industry regulation under the National Industrial Recovery Act.

This approach was highly influential and relevant for businesses. "He shrewdly foresaw that government and the decisions of government were to play a larger and larger part in our lives. There was a demand which he not only cultivated but richly supplied. This concept was perhaps his most brilliant expression of foresight and it spawned many imitators," wrote Moley in 1967.[100]

Kiplinger influenced organized labor as well, which found important insights in his reporting about the backroom dealings of major companies and government officials. "The 'Kiplinger Letter,' issued from Washington, is a special service for business men. It is not intended for mass consumption, and can therefore afford to be frank from time to time," observed *The Daily Worker*, the newspaper of the Communist Party USA.[101] The general secretary of the Communist Party cited Kiplinger when providing his members with important news about the economic outlook.[102] And the *Producers News*, a farm laborers' newspaper, told its readers that Kiplinger provided insight about "exactly what Big Business thinks of the NRA."[103]

By contrast, *Business Week* was framing politics and business as two separate spheres in its early coverage of the New Deal, opining on June 9, 1934, "Politics is a luxury that we business men cannot afford this year. Our interest in business recovery is greater than our stake in a bye-election," a reference to the upcoming 1934 congressional midterm elections. Yet *Business Week* followed this statement with a plea for business leaders to be more strategic in their opposition to the New Deal: "The irreconcilables who would destroy NRA, root and branch, are wasting their breath. There are serious defects in NRA and in the codes. But NRA has solid values as well—values which some of the most important industries in the country are not going to surrender. How much better, then, to join forces with those practical business men who accept NRA as something here to stay, and work toward its reform."[104]

Information Explosion

The Kiplinger Washington Letter performed another important functionalist role by helping the public manage information overload. By the mid-1920s, newspapers, magazines, books, and now radio were all competing for the public's attention. A growing urban population, the rise of new printing technologies, and cheaper newsprint contributed to a twelvefold increase in newspaper subscriptions between 1870 and 1920, from 2.6 million to 33 million. By 1910 there were more than 2,500 daily newspapers in the United States, and many medium-sized and large cities had more than one newspaper. A typical city dweller was buying more than one newspaper a day.[105] During this era, iconic magazines were founded: *Forbes* in 1917; *Reader's Digest*, 1922; *Time* magazine, 1923; *The New Yorker*, 1925; *Fortune* and *Business Week*, 1929. This growth in periodicals led to the emergence of major culture industries; the number of people working in the newspaper and periodical industries rose to 117,001 by 1925, a 9 percent increase from five years earlier.[106] Print journalism soon saw the emergence of a formidable competitor in radio with the first commercial radio station, KDKA in Pittsburgh, in 1920; by 1922, the United States had 576 radio stations.[107]

As the 1920s began, information overload was a significant topic. John Heidenry wrote in his study of *Reader's Digest*: "The idea of getting the most out of every minute was very much in the air in the twenties. . . . More Americans were buying their first automobile, joining the Rotary or other fashionable clubs, breaking out of the constrictive six-day workweek. Radio, motion pictures, and the Sunday drive in the family automobile now determined how Americans spent their leisure time, which reading and churchgoing had once monopolized."[108] Walter Lippmann, the influential political columnist, articulated the overwhelming challenge to comprehend the modern world. "The world that we have to deal with politically is out of reach, out of sight, out of mind. It has to be explored, reported, and imagined," Lippmann wrote in his 1922 classic *Public Opinion*. "Man is no Aristotelian god contemplating all existence at one glance. He is the creature of an evolution who can just about span a sufficient portion of reality to manage his survival, and snatch what on the scale of time are but a few moments of insight and happiness."[109]

By the mid-1920s, other media entrepreneurs such as Henry Luce and DeWitt Wallace launched publications specifically geared to help the overburdened reader manage the information overload. Luce, in his prospectus for *Time the Weekly News-Magazine* (later shortened to *Time*), spelled out the problem of summarizing news for an increasingly busy populace: "People are uninformed because no publication has adapted itself to the time which busy men are able to spend simply keeping informed."[110] *Reader's Digest* was a highly influential publication that emerged in this era, launching in 1922, one year before *The Kiplinger Washington Letter*. In it, DeWitt Wallace and his wife, Lila, produced a monthly condensation of important articles previously published elsewhere. The magazine, which initially carried no advertising, was popular, growing to 1 million circulation by 1935 and 3 million by 1940.[111]

The dilemma of information overload had long-standing roots. Author Ann Blair traced complaints about information overload back to antiquity. She found laments about the abundance of books in Ecclesiastes 12:12 and from the Roman writer Seneca in the first century CE.[112] The Dominican friar Vincent of Beauvais compiled one of the first digest books in the thirteenth century.[113] One of the first digest magazines in the United States was *Littell's Living Age* in 1844, followed by *Eclectic* in Boston in 1870, *Comfort* in 1888, and *Scrap-Book* in Buffalo in 1889.[114] *Literary Digest*, founded in 1890 by Isaac Kaufmann Funk and Adam Wagnalls of Funk & Wagnalls publishing fame, was an immediate forerunner to *Reader's Digest* and was very popular, with a circulation of more than 1 million in the early 1920s.[115] The *Review of Reviews*, also founded in 1890, summarized material about world affairs.

Yet despite the sight of newspapers and magazines piling up on coffee tables, demand for information remained high during this period. In the business world, the need for a condensed form of business communication increased after World War I as more individuals began investing in the stock market. At the same time, corporations were changing, and a new class of managers craved more analysis about the fast-changing world around them.

Kiplinger was poised to take full advantage of the information desire among business leaders. "We set ourselves up to be those eyes and ears," he wrote.[116]

The concern about information overload led to innovations in journalism production as editors experimented with shorter forms of reporting. "*Liberty* magazine had gone so far as to post, at the head of each article, the reading time," wrote Heidenry. "Soon almost every popular magazine, including the *Saturday Evening Post*, was beginning to shorten its once formidably long short stories and features."[117] Frank Luther Mott observed, "A chief secret of the success of *Reader's Digest* was the brevity of its offerings."[118] Kiplinger shared that obsession with brevity, declaring it an obligation of journalists to help busy readers manage their time. "To achieve brevity in writing takes time, and mental sweat, and more man power, and more expense. Brevity is not the method of cheap cost of production, but the contrary," Kiplinger wrote in a 1936 article for the academic journal *Journalism Quarterly*.[119] The Kiplinger writing style had a primary goal: "It's about saving the reader's valuable time."[120]

Sweep Line

Cognizant of the reader's time, Kiplinger developed a truncated, telegraphic writing style described as "sweep line" writing, designed to help busy business executives quickly scan the news and grasp the most important points. This writing style valued compact information delivery by emphasizing key words and phrases through underlined, bold, and capitalized text. Each line ended on the right margin in hard punctuation and did not wrap to the next line. Kiplinger described the principles behind the sweep line style:

> Sweep-line style, one full line to a statement or thought.
> Brevity, brevity, Essence. Main point. Scant detail. Speed.
> The sweep-line style: A sweep of thought in a single line.
> Your eye moves left to right, to the end, and THERE'S the whole thought.
> The mind is relieved of the burden of carrying over to the next line.
> The mind CAN carry over. The mind CAN do anything you require of it.
> But relieve the mind, and ease the eye. It's a different writing style.

Kiplinger continued: "Impression is enough. No need to fill in tedious detail. Reader does this for himself. Not exact? No. Often no need to be exact." This style was not intended to replace straight news writing "because of the urgencies of speed and mechanical make-up," yet Kiplinger thought it could be used for editorial or policy writing, "as a stimulant, antidote for stodgy style."[121] The sweep line style, for example, was not used in the Kiplinger magazines, such as *Kiplinger's Personal Finance*.

The sweep line concept emerged partly from Kiplinger's early interest in poetry and writing technique. "He respected meter," Austin Kiplinger recalled. "He often recited his sentences out loud, or with his lips, before he wrote them with his typewriter."[122] Mainstream journalism shared the broad goals of efficient, clear information delivery and had adopted a standardized, practical prose style known as the "inverted pyramid," which featured the most salient facts in the beginning of the article and less essential items toward the end, allowing typesetters to trim the article from the bottom as needed to fit a newspaper's layout. The inverted pyramid style evolved from the use of the telegraph in the mid-nineteenth century. The sweep line writing style, which one commentator described as "a crisp, staccato-style of journalism printed in typewriter type on letter-size paper," was influential in the business world.[123] The Kiplinger organization identified twenty-three publications they considered to be imitators from 1942 to 1967, such as *Newsweek*'s "Periscope" column, which attempted to employ the sweep line style of writing to varying degrees. Some journalism organizations, such as the group that published the *Congressional Quarterly*, sought out Kiplinger editors for coaching about this writing style. Apart from newsletters, there's little evidence that the sweep line writing style was widely adopted by other forms of journalism.[124] Yet Kiplinger's big idea of compact information delivery endures today as a goal of many in digital news.

Jakob Nielsen, in summarizing early research on reading habits on the Web, used terminology reminiscent of Kiplinger's sweep line advocacy. "How Users Read on the Web. Summary: They don't. People rarely read Web pages word by word; instead, they scan the page, picking out individual words and sentences. . . . As a result, Web pages have to employ scannable text, using highlighted keywords (hypertext links serve as one form of highlighting; typeface variations and color are others) . . . half the word count (or less) than conventional writing."[125] Arika Okrent argued that the listicle—the much derided article in the form of a list, such as "15 Best Butts in Hollywood"—is a literary form optimized for modern digital news audiences, "compact packages of predictable structure that people enjoy reading."[126] As Jared Spool put it in a 1998 study of website design and usability: "Skimming Is In. . . . [M]ost of the people we tested didn't read all of the information on a page. They scanned the text as they searched for an answer."[127]

CHAPTER 5

A Battle with "Economic Royalists"

THE REVOLUTION OF the New Deal dawned slowly on the US business community. "The business public isn't fully awake yet," Kiplinger reported in May 1933.[1] "The one thing worrying Washington more than anything is that the 'business public-at-large' does not yet quite realize what is coming off."[2] Business leaders initially voiced some acceptance for the general New Deal goals, particularly after Roosevelt's national bank holiday, a bold action that helped stabilize the financial system. "If we are to save our traditional freedom for the future, it is probable that we must make substantial concessions to what we have in the past classified as the more radical school of thought," said P. W. Litchfield, president of Goodyear Tire and Rubber Company.[3] *Business Week* in May 1933 reported, "There is surprising unanimity among business men in favor of the general theory [of the New Deal proposals]."[4]

Yet the honeymoon period ended by the fall of 1933 as business leaders became frustrated over the complexity and uncertainty created by the National Industrial Recovery Act and Roosevelt's chaotic pronouncements on currency and inflation policies. A significant corporate backlash began to emerge, led by the American Liberty League, an interest group headed by former New York governor Al Smith and bankrolled by industrialists like Irénée du Pont. The League's advocacy for free markets and small government would prove influential to later conservative activists such as the Koch brothers, the Club for Growth, and even the Tea Party movement. In addition to the complexity and bureaucracy of the National Recovery Administration, conservative business leaders were concerned about Roosevelt's currency devaluation strategy, aimed at providing debt relief to millions of struggling farmers and other debtors. Business leaders complained that the wide swings in currency values made it difficult to plan their operations.

The fight over currency policy and the gold standard also can be viewed through a broader political and social lens as a proxy in the fight between labor and capital. This tension between creditors and debtors was a central feature of the populist movement and the presidential candidacy of William Jennings Bryan. Creditors, primarily in the Northeast, were "hard money" advocates who resisted inflation since it eroded the value of bonds and other financial assets. The debtors, primarily in farm states, favored inflation and devaluation as a form of debt relief. To conservatives such as the journalist Garet Garrett, Roosevelt's policy of devaluation and inflation was merely a tool to advance wealth redistribution.[5]

This chapter examines the corporate backlash against the New Deal and the news media's coverage of it through the critical formative years 1933–1936. *The Kiplinger Washington Letter* reported the corporate dissent early on and offered important insights on upcoming macroeconomic developments. As a business rebellion built, Kiplinger explicitly advised businesses to sign on with the New Deal industrial codes, appealing to business leaders' sense of patriotism and social duty. Kiplinger also accused industry of playing a role in the dysfunction of the National Recovery Act, citing "greedy and ambitious schemes for government guaranty of their profits, stupid forms of price fixing. Industry in many cases refused to agree to arrangements which would permit collective bargaining, which is specified in the NRA act."[6] In private, Kiplinger had the opportunity to supply critics of the New Deal with bombast and raw meat but declined to do so. When Raymond Moley asked Kiplinger to help write a speech to be delivered before the National Association of Manufacturers, a leading New Deal critic, Kiplinger instead offered a sophisticated defense of the New Deal that addressed key concerns of the business community.

Bank Holiday

As the Depression worsened, some business leaders were willing to consider a larger role for government in the economy to halt self-destructive competition among businesses. *Fortune* was among the news outlets that described a change in the outlook of industrial leaders combating unrestrained competition: "The American business man at this moment is utterly weary of the ruthless competitive struggle.... He is willing, he feels just now, to surrender some part of his freedom of action to achieve a degree of stability."[7] The US Chamber of Commerce "was ready to subscribe to the idea of governmental control of business.... But it was apparent from speeches and from conversations in the lobbies that many business leaders have been converted to the belief that unrestrained individualism had outworn its place in America, and that people as a whole will fare better under a planned economy," *Business Week* reported.[8]

Other top business leaders offered similar sentiments. Alexander Sachs of the Lehman Corporation claimed that the entire Western economic order was threatened "not by the destructive impact of external or natural forces, but by a spontaneous disintegration from within." Industry was suffering from "economic nihilism, which, from a national point of view, cannot he permitted to go on." Bernard Baruch, a leading financier and intellectual influential with many New Deal leaders, described a broad sentiment among business leaders for a bigger role for government regulation: "It is no wonder that the whole of industry seems to have risen en masse to find some way to check it as a matter of stark self-preservation."[9] Roosevelt's first major decision as president, however, acquired some measure of goodwill and respect from the business community.

Upon taking the oath of office, Roosevelt launched perhaps the most intrusive regulatory action of the entire New Deal, a declaration of a national banking holiday to stabilize the financial system. The March 1933 declaration represented a low point in laissez-faire capitalism, evidence that the old economic order had failed to function and a symbol of the loss of public confidence in institutions so critical to the daily functioning of free markets. Roosevelt's decision to shut down all US banks for a week came amid a growing panic. By early March 1933, more than five thousand banks holding some $3 billion in deposits had failed since the beginning of the Depression.[10] During the banking holiday, which stretched from March 5 through March 13, Congress passed the Emergency Banking Act of 1933, and the Federal Reserve pledged unlimited amounts of currency to reopened banks, a combination that "created de facto 100 percent deposit insurance."[11] Moley, describing the drama and consequence of the bank rescue plan, wrote that "capitalism was saved in eight days."[12]

Kiplinger reported closely on the collapse of the US banking system, and like most mainstream media, the newsletter initially played down the notion of an imminent financial crisis. "The bank failure situation is bad enough, but is being held in check by R.F.C.," Kiplinger noted in mid-January 1933, a reference to the Reconstruction Finance Corporation, a government agency that provided business loans and credit.[13] The next week, Kiplinger's tone turned grave: "Banking situation is known to be serious. Many banks must fail. R.F.C. cannot hold them up indefinitely."[14] He then warned in the February 4 issue that a "break-down of private debts early in 1933 . . . marks the beginning of a new phase of the Depression" and estimated that "the crisis is ahead." One severe strain on banking in agricultural states involved the decision of bankers to suspend farm foreclosures, fearing community violence during auctions of bankrupt farms on the courthouse steps. As a result, Kiplinger wrote, "weak banks will be made weaker."[15] The industrial states faced other challenges. A crisis involving the Union Guardian Trust Company of Detroit, whose largest depositor was the automobile magnate Henry Ford, led to a statewide bank holiday in Michigan in February 1933, an event that shocked the financial community and led to a loss of national confidence in the banking system.[16] On February 18 Kiplinger warned that the Michigan bank crisis represented "the worst banking mess of the whole depression" and that readers "should be prepared for further shocks."

Kiplinger's warnings gained urgency with each passing week. On February 25 he wrote, "Banking situation is very grave," noting that the bank runs in Maryland and Michigan "may be duplicated elsewhere." *The Kiplinger Washington Letter* floated the idea of a national bank holiday in its March 4 letter, two days before Roosevelt's announcement. Absent some radical change in public mood, Kiplinger wrote, "there must be a general banking holiday for at least a week." He continued: "Practically this is already in effect, state-by-state, covering all important financial centers. It MAY be made nationally uniform, (a) by Presidential proclamation, which might not be legal but which could be 'gotten away with'; or (b) by 'request' to the state governors." He even reported on the political implications of a bank holiday, describing the move on March 4 as politically dangerous, since the government would be in the position of selecting which banks should be kept open and which should close. Such an insight was not explicit in competing news coverage. *Business Week* referenced the political pressure on state banking officials to reopen banks after the holiday period, noting that "instances of successful wire-pulling apparently are rare."[17] In addition, some depositors would be forced to accept significant losses in a banking system cleanup, Kiplinger wrote. He also predicted a special session of Congress where a federal guarantee of deposits would be debated; the following week, passage of the Emergency Banking Act and the Federal Reserve's pledge to support reopened banks effectively established deposit insurance. Three months later, Congress would pass the Banking Act of 1933, which created the Federal Deposit Insurance Corporation to provide a new deposit insurance system.

Kiplinger's informed and prescient bank holiday coverage stands in contrast to the less detailed coverage from competing news organizations. *Business Week* reported a sense of surprise at the scale of the Roosevelt banking program, which included the national bank holiday. "The President's emergency program is bolder than anyone had predicted," *Business Week* reported.[18] The magazine, oddly enough, described a perception of stability in the banking system on January 4, 1933, even as major problems were about to erupt: "Strength in the banking situation and stability of the securities markets stand in strong contrast to crisis conditions a year ago."[19] Kiplinger painted a starkly different picture. By March 8 *Business Week* had caught up with the sense of impending crisis after Roosevelt's inauguration and declaration of the national banking holiday: "Events of the last 2 weeks have conspired to bring into sharp relief the weakness of the American banking system."[20]

Kiplinger counseled depositors to keep their money in the bank,[21] a call for calm also seen during this period in *New York Times* editorials that solidly backed the president's actions: "High praise for the prompt and intelligent way in which the Roosevelt Administration took hold of the banking situation continues to be heard. It is no doubt deserved."[22] After the bank holiday ended, *Business Week* sought to project a sense of order: "Large deposits, no runs, normal business, attest public confidence in the banks that resume business. . . . Deposits exceeded withdrawals in almost every bank." There was no need for the $2 billion in currency to ward off additional bank runs. "The propaganda against gold hoarding is proving highly effective."[23]

In the edition immediately following the bank holiday announcement, *The Kiplinger Washington Letter* boasted that it had foreshadowed the major events of the week: the weeding out of weak banks, the creation of a single national banking system, a forecast of large losses for some depositors, and financial liability for directors and stockholders of weak banks. The *Letter* focused on macroeconomic questions, such as the implications of the bank holiday on inflation, and arrived at an important insight: "A great expansion of bank CREDIT is in the offing."[24] Banks would be encouraged to extend more loans under certain structural changes to the national banking system, such as allowing borrowers to use government bonds as collateral. The *New York Times* made a more general call for Congress to pass fundamental banking reforms: "It is as true of a nation as it is of an individual, that only a fool will break his leg twice over the same stone."[25]

Business Week offered a sharp observation about the bank holiday, criticizing the Roosevelt plan as "another victory for the big New York banks."[26] The bank bailout formula was based on a bank's liquidity, or cash flow, and so it favored large institutions. This line of criticism continued in subsequent years, particularly from the left. The Methodist Federation of Social Service warned in a February 1935 assessment of the New Deal that "the money changers are back.

"Roosevelt has continued the Hoover policy of seeking to save the debt structure by putting government credit behind the failing credit of big corporations." This action "has intensified the disease of our failing economic order—the piling up a load of debt. The bankers have the money; billions lie idle in their banks. And they can and do call the tune."[27]

American Liberty League

A corporate backlash against the New Deal began to materialize in late 1933 and 1934. Leaders of this backlash included the three du Pont brothers-—Pierre, Irénée, and Lammot—who gathered fellow business leaders in the summer of 1934 to plot strategy against the rise of the new regulatory state. Irénée du Pont's involvement represented a reversal, since his family initially supported Roosevelt's candidacy. Large businesses at first "followed the President in the belief that he was sincere and that experiments which he might initiate would be discarded if they were unsuccessful." As time went on, du Pont lost patience with Roosevelt, declaring, "It must have now become clear to every thinking man that the so-called 'New Deal,' advocated by the Administration, is nothing more or less than the Socialistic doctrine called by another name." The du Ponts' antagonism toward regulation had its origins in the early years of the twentieth century, when the company lost a significant antitrust lawsuit and was the subject of a congressional investigation about its role as a munitions supplier and the US decision to enter World War I.[28] By helping create the American Liberty League in 1934, du Pont helped fill a major void in American

A Battle with "Economic Royalists"

politics at a time when the conservative movement was dispirited and defeated. "There seemed to be nowhere any resistance," columnist Garet Garrett wrote. "The American of old is nowhere to be found. What has become of what he believed? . . . Laissez faire was buried on the mountaintop."[29]

Kim Phillips-Fein observed that by the early 1930s, "a coherent body of conservative thought hardly existed" except for laissez-faire economic philosophy celebrating private enterprise.[30] The League attacked Roosevelt and his policies with great ferocity. "The New Deal represents the attempt in America to set up a totalitarian government, one which recognizes no sphere of individual or business life as immune from governmental authority and which submerges the welfare of the individual to that of the government," said Jouett Shouse of the American Liberty League. "The New Deal has harassed American business and has entered into competition in almost every possible way with private industry."[31] Banker and former McKinley administration treasury official Frank Vanderlip offered a pointed critique of the New Deal and its implications for the future of capitalism: "If the objective of government should prove to be a redistribution of wealth and a sharp restriction of profits, it [1933] might well turn out to be a year which marked the beginning of the end of the capitalistic system in this country."[32]

The League rallied its forces by focusing on the creation of the Securities and Exchange Commission. Irénée du Pont believed that the SEC was "an attempt to change human nature, disrupting the inevitable risks at the heart of life."[33] One irony was that many national Democrats were key forces in the American Liberty League. Former 1924 and 1928 Democratic presidential candidate and onetime New York governor Alfred E. Smith, along with prominent Democrats John J. Raskob, Jouett Shouse, and John W. Davis, became leaders in the American Liberty League.[34]

Amid this industry rebellion, Kiplinger did not emphasize the American Liberty League in his newsletter. In one reference in November 1934, Kiplinger wrote that the League "probably will do a more effective job [of resisting administration policies] than any other single organization, not excepting the Republican Party."[35] Two detailed searches of Kiplinger's personal papers revealed no correspondence with leading figures in the American Liberty League such as duPont, Shouse, Gerard Swope, M. C. Rorty, Raskob, Earl F. Reed, Davis, and R. R. M. Carpenter.[36] Kiplinger did correspond with Shouse's wife, Catherine Filene Shouse, on the death of her father, Lincoln Filene, whose family founded the famous department store empire.

The League enjoyed significant news coverage elsewhere. For example, the *New York Times* carried an extensive page one article in September 1935 citing an American Liberty League–backed study that criticized the National Labor Relations Act, also known as the Wagner Act, as unconstitutional. The *Times* sought to downplay the obvious slant of the study, noting, "The report was offered by the League as an 'unbiased' factual analysis and legal opinion on the National Labor Relations Act." The report was hardly unbiased. It was written by Earl F. Reed, chief counsel of Weirton Steel, a company that had defied the Roosevelt administration's new regulations on union recognition.[37] Roosevelt fought back throughout the 1936 reelection campaign and described the American Liberty League and its supporters as "economic royalists." Democrats joked that the group was the "Millionaires Union," while a Mississippi Democrat excoriated the "American Lobby League" as "apostles of greed."[38]

The Crusaders

Although Kiplinger did not cover the American Liberty League in much detail, he did assist a group affiliated with their cause. In 1934 Kiplinger asked Moley if he wanted to meet with representatives of the Crusaders, a business-backed anti-labor group. Kiplinger described the Crusaders as "midway between the American Liberty League and the President," yet that observation downplayed the reactionary nature of the group. According to Grace Hutchins, a liberal journalist who investigated the American Liberty League, the Crusaders drew from the League's donors and was a close ally. "Started as an anti-prohibition society in 1929, the Crusaders was revived in 1934 as an anti-labor, Red-baiting organization with one of its main aims: 'to stand firm against any drift or drive toward fascism, communism or socialism,'" Hutchins wrote. "It has organized local branches in important centers in nineteen states and is making an effort to give the whole anti-labor campaign a mass basis by securing 1,500,000 members.... [S]everal of the largest contributors to the Liberty League gave also to the Crusaders."[39]

Kiplinger suggested that Moley meet with the group, again providing evidence of his role as a shadow political actor: "There has been some talk of their approaching the President with an advance explanation of their purposes and in this connection your name came up.... I have no special interest in the organization, but I thought I might be a catalytic agent."[40] The meeting idea originated with David Hinshaw, a Kiplinger friend and close friend of Hoover's. Kiplinger urged Moley to meet with Hinshaw to discuss the Crusaders, assuring him, "He [Hinshaw] is a Progressive Republican and at one time would have been secretary of the Republican National Committee except that he was too progressive."[41] Moley asked Hinshaw to schedule a meeting, adding, "I should like to read over Mr. Hinshaw's statement of the purposes and arguments for the Crusaders and perhaps make some editorial comment on it."[42]

Kiplinger's Critical Coverage

By late summer 1933, businesses began waking up to the complex new regulatory world of the National Recovery Administration and the problems with currency policy. Kiplinger's coverage of the New Deal reflected a mix of praise and criticism of the Roosevelt administration's efforts, the sort of balanced approach that established him as a neutral outside party. My review of New Deal business news coverage, which included *Fortune, Business Week,* the *New York Times,* and the *Saturday Evening Post,* showed that Kiplinger turned critical of the Roosevelt administration before most other mainstream journalists. On April 29, 1933, he called for an end to the honeymoon between Roosevelt and Congress, earlier than these other publications.[43] For most media, the honeymoon period with Roosevelt extended until June 1935, when many journalists broke with the administration in the aftermath of the Supreme Court decision invalidating core parts of the New Deal. Journalist Raymond Clapper, writing in June 1934, wrote: "Mr. Roosevelt . . . came to Washington. The correspondents saw him and were conquered. He won them and he has still. Larger proportion of them personally sympathetic than any of his recent predecessors."[44]

Readers of *The Kiplinger Washington Letter* began to learn in April 1933 about discord within the Roosevelt administration over implementing the New Deal, a theme explored in depth throughout Roosevelt's first term. Kiplinger portrayed Roosevelt as a political opportunist with a loose grasp of significant economic issues such as currency policy.[45] The early positive tone of the coverage became much more critical in the fall of 1933 after early promises about employment goals and economic growth went unfulfilled and confusion reigned over implementation of the National Industrial Recovery Act.

In July 1933 article Kiplinger began focusing on the business backlash against the New Deal, writing that the "new passive resistance of industry is serious" and summarizing seven major grievances among the business community.[46] The article also included a point-by-point response from the Roosevelt administration, an explicit attempt to bridge the Wall Street–Washington divide, a theme seen throughout Kiplinger's coverage in the summer of 1933.[47] "Retort: SURE, the new law and system are revolutionary, and the sooner business realizes this, the better for business," Kiplinger wrote. "But there WILL be advantages to neutralize the disadvantages." He discussed how the business community might defy the new law, which "shall and will be administered," adding: "Make no mistake about the seriousness of passive resistance program. There has been very little newspaper publicity on it, but it has been brought to the attention of NRA officials and they are preparing to counteract the influence to it."[48] In the same issue he reminded readers about the key purposes of the National Recovery Act—coordinating industry to put people back to work at decent wages—as if to prod them into obeying the law and getting with the program.

On July 15, 1933, Kiplinger reported on business opposition to new regulations, known as industry codes, to regulate pay and hours. Business groups wanted government action on rules to boost the prices of goods in exchange for raising wages and shortening hours. Kiplinger described the business opposition as a "rebellion" and reported that the administration had responded by threatening to crack down on industry and imposing price regulations without its input. He concluded that NRA administrator Hugh Johnson "IS arbitrary in spirit and manner and methods," but "he is intelligent enough to KNOW that industry control can not be accomplished in this way, and he has picked a good staff of administrators. . . . [H]e has no REAL intention of applying force, or EXCESSIVE force." At the same time, Kiplinger scolded industry for overreacting and wrongly believing the NRA regulations were a temporary piece of "monkey business. . . . This element is blind to the trend of the times,—apart from politics."[49]

In August 1933 *The Kiplinger Washington Letter* provided a clear critique of the New Deal. Overall, the NRA was "less promising than had been hoped or advertised," Kiplinger wrote, adding that the "industry control program is not proceeding satisfactorily" on account of clumsy government administration that harmed small businesses.[50] "NRA is weak in its public relations," Kiplinger reported. Employment had increased, "but how much of it is due to the NRA is not determinable."[51] In the July 22 and August 12 and 19, 1933, issues, Kiplinger warned that social unrest was likely to increase, citing the risk of a business slump and the lack of immediate success of recovery plans, which he said were being oversold to the public through a propaganda campaign. The *Business Week* and *New York Times* critiques, by contrast, involved specific issues with the implementation of the new law but not the sweeping admonition contained in the Kiplinger newsletters.[52]

Business Week began depicting business opposition to the National Industrial Recovery Act with a June 10, 1933, editorial.[53] It reported about ongoing administrative problems, saying that the "National Industrial Recovery Administration ran into its first real troubles when it was one week old" with businesses raising questions about price fixing, production control, and labor. Still, its tone remained optimistic: "A tremendous movement forward is noticeable."[54] *Business Week* also described the business community's opposition. A June 1933 article discussed a report by business leaders, commissioned by Johnson of the NRA, which criticized the SEC act and the proposed Wagner Act as "chief deterrents to the flow of savings into investment in durable goods."[55] On July 21, 1934, *Business Week* led its review of the New Deal policies concerning Wall Street with this sharp rebuke: "The New Deal has had one overshadowing failure. It has been unable to swell the flow of private investment capital into industry above a mere dribble."[56] *Business Week* suggested some fundamental problems in September 1933, asking if the National Recovery Administration's emphasis on collective cooperation could succeed in American business culture. "It symbolized to NRA the whole question of how the individualistic spirit of American industry can be welded with the cooperative ideal held up in the recovery program," it reported.[57] By October, business opposition was a prominent narrative in *Business Week*.[58]

Fortune published a significant profile of Roosevelt in December 1933 with an assessment now reflected in more recent histories of the New Deal: "There are a considerable number of observers who hold that Mr. Roosevelt is a mere improviser, an economic opportunist, a man of action whose passion for movement is so great that he is perfectly capable of mounting the nearest horse and galloping off, like the hero in the fable, in all directions at once." The magazine immediately answered those charges with a sympathetic defense, stating, "The president is conducting an economic offensive on a very wide front and, as always happens in extended maneuvers, he has been obliged to give way on his flank to advance along his center." In the same article, *Fortune* asserted that for the consumer, the New Deal by the end of 1933 had done more harm than good, since increases in the prices of goods had outstripped wage gains. The full reform program had yet to be implemented, *Fortune* continued, and Roosevelt's main goal involved structural change to permanently raise wages and boost consumer buying power.[59]

In other publications, rhetoric about the New Deal was more critical. Garrett claimed that businesses quickly capitulated to Roosevelt and the New Deal: the first one hundred days "was all the time it took to enact a complete temporary dictatorship in the person of the President, standing for the popular will." According to Garrett, "in effect, this act [the National Industrial Recovery Act] declares the President to be the managing partner in all industry." The very concept of relief for workers grated against basic American values, he wrote: "A principle of local responsibility is at stake, together with principles very much deeper, touching the soul of American individualism and the free status of people in relation to the state." Even the concept of unemployment insurance and benefits was problematic according to this line of conservative thinking. "Hitherto, the condition of joblessness was an individual misfortune; now we take unemployment to be the misfortune of society as a whole," Garrett wrote. Noting Henry Ford's high-profile decision not to cooperate with the National Recovery Act, Garrett wrote, "But for the Ford Motor Company, it would have to be written that the surrender of American business to government was unanimous, complete and unconditional."[60]

Kiplinger's critical coverage escalated throughout the fall of 1933 as he reported that the National Industrial Recovery Act had over-promised and failed to put enough people back to work: "Mr. Roosevelt is getting himself surrounded by YES MEN, as did Mr. Hoover. Recent unpublishable incidents suggest that he has not been in close touch with public sentiment out around the country. Examples: NRA, and a growing farmer rebellion. It's hard for a President to get the truth; so many callers feel awed."[61]

Kiplinger reported on the systemic organizational problems at the NRA: "Plenty of generals. colonels, majors but no top sergeants and few privates. No coordination. No real organization. Helter-skelter disorder within the ranks. Conflicting information, conflicting advices, discrepancies in guidance. Urge of speed upon the public, yet no speed within government."[62] By contrast, some coverage in the *New York Times* portrayed Roosevelt as in full command of the process, describing him as "a master of detail."[63] Other articles painted Roosevelt in heroic tones, such as a major retrospective on the first six months of the New Deal by feature writer Robert L. Duffus, which gushed, "Mr. Roosevelt took over the helm with as much assurance as though he had been born to the Presidency rather than elected to it."[64]

On September 2, 1933 Kiplinger published a perceptive report that summarized the impact of the New Deal, saying that the NRA had restricted cutthroat competition and thereby halted the price decline of goods. Business psychology had improved and employment had increased. "Has NRA failed?" he asked two weeks later. "Yes and No, depending on angle of judgement."[65] There were some 2 million people back at work, short of the goal of employing 5 to 6 million by this time. "Unemployment next winter probably will be in neighborhood of 7 or 8 millions." The business community had significant concerns about the program. "The breakdown in confidence in NRA plans is now occurring."[66]

By the end of October 1933, Kiplinger could state, "The time has come to say certain things unequivocally," among them, "The whole NRA program is approaching a break down."[67] In early November he described a significant turning point in the New Deal: "This seems to be the most critical time since last March. The crisis seems to be not a matter of days, but a matter of weeks. . . . There is confusion, turmoil, disagreement and bad feeling within the government. This is a new condition . . . Confidence has been badly shaken, and Washington now knows it."[68]

Further complicating matters was Roosevelt's fraught relationship with business. His 1933 inaugural speech denounced financial interests as "unscrupulous money changers [who] stand indicted in the court of public opinion, rejected by the hearts and minds of men."[69] For many business leaders, the remark still stung months later. Few business leaders were represented in Roosevelt's administration. His team of advisers included few people with major business experience apart from William H. Woodin, his first treasury secretary. In January 1933 *Fortune* published an article featuring fifteen well-known Democrats in senior managerial posts in business, suggesting they would find roles in the new administration. By April 1934, "very, very few of them are now in Washington either physically or in the spirit."[70]

New Currency Policy: Attacking the Heart of Capitalism

Some of the sharpest battles between the business community and New Deal reformers played out in banking and financial policy, particularly management of the US dollar and reduction of the dollar's value relative to gold. Roosevelt's decision to devalue the dollar in 1933 and alter the gold standard was a shock to the domestic and international banking community as well as to large corporations. The economists Barry Eichengreen and Peter Temin wrote in 2000, "The gold standard has become a religion for some of the Boards of Central Banks in Continental Europe, believed in with an emotional fervor which makes them incapable of an unprejudiced and objective examination of possible alternatives." They argued that the Federal Reserve's decision in 1931 to fight inflation by boosting interest rates, thereby defending the value of gold, resulted in depressing domestic prices and led companies to reduce wages. The combination of these forces caused a recession in the economy to metastasize into the Great Depression.[71] These fights over dollar and gold valuation spoke to the ascendancy of the new regulatory state over entrenched capitalistic power, and this was a fight followed closely in the business journalism of the era.

Business Week focused on the tension over monetary and currency policy as Roosevelt was drafting his 1933 inaugural address: "Resisting terrific pressure from New York banking interests, and most of his conservative advisers, President Roosevelt declined to commit himself squarely to gold in his inaugural address."[72] From the inauguration forward, Roosevelt saw that currency devaluation would quickly provide debt relief to millions of struggling farmers and other debtors; devaluation would allow debtors to repay their debts in cheaper dollars, a policy supported by the National Grange and American Farm Bureau Federation.[73] The crushing agricultural debt loads led to strikes by farmers in the Midwest, protests aimed at raising prices and addressing their loan burdens.[74] Other New Deal policies sought to boost prices of commodities and goods, particularly the National Recovery Administration's industry codes and the Agricultural Adjustment Administration's production controls.

Roosevelt's gold and currency policy began to be implemented in March 1933, when he prohibited banks from paying out gold or dealing in foreign currencies. In April, Roosevelt took a major step away from the traditional gold standard to devalue the US dollar relative to foreign currencies, a move that served to boost domestic prices.[75] The plan allowed Roosevelt to reset the value of gold against the dollar in the future. This action led to a decline in the dollar's value internationally, but it allowed more money to become available to Americans, stimulating the economy.[76] Also in April, Roosevelt banned the hoarding of gold and then effectively nationalized the gold market.[77]

World Economic Conference

A low point in Roosevelt's currency and economic policy involved his handling of the World Economic Conference in July 1933. Roosevelt shocked the international community and his own advisers by repudiating any attempt to establish an international agreement to stabilize foreign currency values, believing this would hinder his ability to inflate the dollar's value at home. Roosevelt's emissaries at the London conference, Moley and Secretary of State Hull, were blindsided by the announcement, since they were seeking to reach a stabilization agreement with France, Britain, and Germany.[78] The meeting ended in chaos. Roosevelt's sudden shift allowed him to continue devaluing the US dollar. It was unclear if the World Economic Conference, originally conceived by Hoover in 1932, would have reached any agreement to stabilize currencies on account of disagreements between "sterling bloc" countries such as Great Britain and other countries whose currency was pegged to gold.

Roosevelt's statement represented a harsh denunciation of the banking community. He objected to the "fetishes of international bankers" in reaching a currency stabilization agreement and instead advocated a "commodity dollar" with a purchasing power that would remain stable.[79] French prime minister Pierre-Étienne Flandin, in an interview with the *Times*, described creditor-debtor tension as central to Roosevelt's currency decision: "The main object, as I see it, was to correct a peculiarly American internal disorder by adjusting the enormous load of private debt. Until a balance between the debtor and the creditor is established near a point at which the debtor can pay probably the dollar will not stabilize in relation to world currencies."[80]

According to Kiplinger, the fallout from Roosevelt's currency policy led to declining business confidence and encouraged investors to put their money overseas: "Much of this capital has left the country, making a 'flight from the dollar.'" The business community did not see a clear monetary policy from Roosevelt, and therefore many were worried about the prospect of inflation. These concerns were causing troubles in the US bond market, complicating a source of business financing. Kiplinger also reported that business leaders had continuing doubts about the ultimate success of the National Recovery Act and its related farm program, the Agricultural Adjustment Act.[81] The *Times* reported that Roosevelt had left many in the business community bewildered when he set the dollar at a fixed gold price in September 1933, reporting that his currency actions were an attempt to head off populist political support in Congress while also seeking to rout currency speculators.

Kiplinger described the political dynamics behind Roosevelt's gold devaluation decision. The president wanted to lead on the inflation issue and gain the political upper hand from populists such as Senator Huey Long, the Louisiana Democrat. Populists were finding significant support throughout the nation's Farm Belt and beyond for devaluing the dollar.[82] In July 1933 Kiplinger perceived a "severe test of Roosevelt's policies" amid a flight of American capital overseas as a result of the devaluation of the dollar.[83] He reported on August 5, 1933, that Roosevelt was looking at devaluing the dollar "probably 35% to 40%," offering a level of specificity not seen in other news coverage. Competing news organizations, however, followed the dollar devaluation issue closely. The *New York Times* carried some seventy articles about the dollar drama from spring to summer 1933.[84] In January 1934 Congress passed the Gold Reserve Act, a law that gave Roosevelt power to fix the value of the dollar at fifty to sixty cents in terms of gold, a major step toward further governmental control of the currency.[85] As a result, the dollar was reduced to 59 percent of its former value.[86]

Kiplinger's coverage in the summer of 1933 also emphasized business uncertainty resulting from this policy. The dollar's woes, in turn, affected the labor market. Kiplinger in July described the reluctance of businesses to raise wages and shorten working hours unless there were higher prices for goods.[87] He was offering increasingly blunt warnings by November: "Business feels great alarm at current monetary developments, but from the Washington angle it seems that the alarm is exaggerated." He elaborated on business concerns over monetary policy: "This week's shock to business is due, therefore, not to any new policy, but merely to public discovery that the President really means what he has previously indicated. It is now clearly demonstrated that there is no chance of his backing up, turning toward the conservative right, toward early stabilization, toward forsaking of further inflation, toward permanent stability at this stage of the transition."[88]

The gold and currency policies led the most famous living economist of the time, John Maynard Keynes, to publish a rebuke of Roosevelt in a December 1933 open letter to the *New York Times*. "The recent gyrations of the dollar have looked to me more like a gold standard on the booze than the ideal managed currency of my dreams," Keynes wrote. He went on to wonder "whether there is a confusion of aim, and whether some of the advice you get is not crack-brained and queer." Keynes urged Roosevelt to aggressively extend credit through lower interest rates and government loan programs to stimulate the economy, a classic formulation of his economic philosophy. He wrote about the tension between Roosevelt's twin aims of recovery and reform, warning that the efforts to regulate business might damage business confidence: "Reform may, in some respects, impede and complicate Recovery." Keynes faulted the National Industrial Recovery Act for its hasty implementation, observing that the goal of raising prices to reduce farmers' debt burden was coming at the expense of broader economic growth. "The setback which American recovery experienced this autumn was the predictable consequence of the failure of your administration to organize any material increase in new loan expenditure during your first six months of office," he wrote. Despite this criticism, Keynes offered praise for Roosevelt's overall aims: "You are the only one who sees the necessity of a profound change of methods and is attempting it without intolerance, tyranny or destruction."[89]

Get with the Program

Kiplinger refrained from throwing gasoline on the fire of the growing business rebellion in 1933. While he was critical of the New Deal, Kiplinger repeatedly made the case for businesses to adapt and conform to the New Deal regulatory regime, known as industry codes, arguing it was the best option for society. In July 1933 he wrote: "Should you sign the blanket code? YES, if you can figure your way to do it. Lean toward it. Stretch a point to do it. Have a bit of faith that your joining up will help to put a push in the circle of influences which will return to you material rewards for joining-up."[90]

Kiplinger provided a broader social, economic, and political context to justify the New Deal: "A social argument in the back of official minds is that the dangers of unrest and popular uprisings are not yet past, that popular dissatisfactions (strikes. local riots, etc.) are SURE to develop in the next few months IF a new business slump came along, and IF corporation earnings continued to rise as they have in the recent past, without comparable rise in mass earnings through wages."[91]

Considering all these problems, Kiplinger repeated an overarching message: government regulation was here to stay. Get used to it. "Regardless of mistakes, which must be expected, NRA will stand and government control of industry will be permanent, it seems to us," he wrote in August 1933. "Many of the current experiments will fail, the scheme will be trimmed down. In this more moderate form it will persist, and industry will find that it can not get along without government control. Organized labor will acquire greater power, inevitably."[92]

He again reported on comments by Donald Richberg, general counsel of the National Recovery Administration, who made the big picture arguments for the New Deal: "This is a new opportunity for self-government of business. Enlightened cooperation vs. cannibalistic struggle to survive. If plan fails, it will not be failure of government, but failure of an industrial system."[93] Kiplinger stood by his words and displayed the NRA's "Blue Eagle" emblem, signifying that his business was participating in the broad goals of National Recovery Act.[94] The emblem appeared at the bottom of his newsletters' pages as early as August 5, 1933.

Kiplinger's willingness to criticize business when needed stemmed from a basic principle. "He didn't worship business," Austin Kiplinger said. "Most other business writers, believe it or not, got into a habit of worshipping business and thinking it was a holy cause. He never did. He always retained his objectivity about the business mechanism but he respected it because he said it was effective."[95]

A Bridge to the Manufacturers' Association

In April 1936 Kiplinger was presented with an opportunity to shape a major speech about the New Deal before an audience hostile to Roosevelt: the National Association of Manufacturers. The group had asked Moley to speak at its meeting in New York, an address that would be broadcast nationally on the NBC radio network and would earn coverage in major newspapers. The group was leading the opposition to the New Deal, particularly against the organized labor provisions, and was aligned with the American Liberty League. At Moley's request, Kiplinger provided extensive material for the speech. The address would come at a politically sensitive moment. Roosevelt was facing an upcoming November general election against Kansas governor Alf Landon. The president had recently taken a hard-left political course with endorsement of the Wagner Act and the Revenue Act of 1935, both strongly opposed by the business community. Because of this turn, Moley was emerging as an increasingly vocal opponent of Roosevelt. He would soon break with the president, writing a biting critique of the New Deal in 1939, *After*

A Battle with "Economic Royalists"

Seven Years. Kiplinger's involvement in this episode is revealing on several levels. It shows his influence as a shadow political actor, helping craft an important message before a politically influential business group. The episode also demonstrates a consistency between Kiplinger's writings for public consumption and his private, off-the-record correspondence.

Politically, Kiplinger privately expressed conflicting views about the upcoming presidential election. He admired Landon and considered him a progressive Republican but an underwhelming candidate. Kiplinger soon would develop serious misgivings about Roosevelt's temperament as a leader.[96] Kiplinger thought the election would be close, but Roosevelt won easily. This speech potentially offered Kiplinger an opportunity to advocate a case against Roosevelt, to throw red meat to conservative business leaders without leaving any public fingerprints. But he did not do so.

Instead, Kiplinger's advice was remarkable. He urged Moley to describe how businesses could adapt to the New Deal. In a three-page letter elaborating themes for the speech, Kiplinger suggested that Moley "indulge in some criticism of the New Deal, if you wish," which would appeal to this audience, but the balance of the speech should be a defense of the New Deal. In a handwritten note at the bottom, Kiplinger warned that the newspapers would focus on any criticism of the New Deal "especially now that you are acquiring the reputation of being critical."[97]

Kiplinger further suggested that Moley explore what Roosevelt would do in a second term and provided some important political advice: "Incidentally it is apt to be well received by the President and the Democratic politicians, especially if you happen to think and say that Roosevelt in a second term is not going to be 'anarchistic' or 'communistic' or 'socialistic' or 'radical' or 'wild.' This would be welcomed by those of your auditors who are primarily business men. It would be unwelcome to those whose dominating passion is to get rid of Roosevelt." Kiplinger urged that Moley use the speech to emphasize how business could advance broader social goals:

> A secondary theme—means of improving the social and economic welfare of the masses with emphasis on what this means in purchasing power, therefore welfare of manufacturers. You know how to develop this theme. Try to show that the welfare of the masses is translated quickly into the welfare of the manufacturers as a class. Suggest that there is no inconsistency between Roosevelt's catering to the masses and the other extreme of catering to manufacturers and business men. They are one and the same thing.

In past times the subject has been approached from the angle of business men, with the assumption that what was good for them would ultimately be good for the masses. Perhaps Roosevelt says the same thing with reverse English,—what is good for the masses is good for the business men. This is an old line, and you may think it is hackneyed, but it is sufficiently important to hammer home again and again.[98]

News coverage of the Moley speech focused, predictably, on his criticism of the New Deal, particularly Roosevelt's housing policy.[99] Yet some elements of Kiplinger's themes were present. Speaking from a ballroom at the Waldorf Astoria Hotel in New York, Moley told the business leaders they can help eliminate poverty by paying "wages and dividends large enough to make consumption possible." In essence, Moley was encouraging executives at General Motors, McGraw Hill, and others in attendance to raise workers' wages. Moley offered an anecdote of a banker who considered his business "primarily an institution for public service rather than as a profit-making enterprise." During the banking panic, this bank stayed open because his customers trusted the institution and didn't make excessive withdrawals. "You successful business men might well make an analysis of why you are successful. You are successful only because your industry is serving a social and economic need," he said. "Business is of society—in health and disease, in life and in death."[100]

The Jews in Government Narrative

Some critics used anti-Semitic rumors as a weapon to discredit the New Deal. Father Charles Coughlin, the influential radio commentator and reactionary, raised the specter of a Jewish cabal taking over the government as a way of attacking the administration and its policies. Other conservatives believed the "Brains Trust" of college professors were pushing a pro-socialist and pro-labor agenda that sought to weaken the business sector. How did business journalists such as Kiplinger address these narratives? Kiplinger was offended by the anti-Semitism and sought to debunk the myth of the Jewish cabal in his newsletter in 1933 and again in 1942 in a book and a *Reader's Digest* article that was condensed from a chapter in the book. The blunt manner in which he tackled the sensitive topic led to significant criticism. The episode spoke to Kiplinger's influence in the public debate and his underlying idealism in the belief that issues of racial and religious discrimination should be confronted directly and publicly. It also revealed that he could be headstrong and tone-deaf.

Kiplinger first addressed the myth of Jewish influence in the July 1, 1933, issue of *The Kiplinger Washington Letter*: "Do they gang together? Do they form any single coordinated sphere of influence? No. . . . Significance of Jewish influence in Roosevelt administration: we see none; perhaps you can." Kiplinger acknowledged the reader backlash to this article in the July 22 issue: "Jewish influence within government. We dealt factually with this whispered question in Letter of July l, naming names, arriving at conclusion that there's nothing significant, except that Jews drawn into Roosevelt government are doing exceedingly good jobs. A few nationally prominent Jews thanked us for bringing issue into open, out of the realm of whisper. Many of our Jewish friends criticized us."

Fortune raised a similar question in its 1934 profile of the Roosevelt administration that highlighted the Jewish faith of advisers Jerome Frank and Mordecai Ezekiel. Concerning Frank, *Fortune* reported, "He has the warm, sympathetic nature of the Jewish enthusiast. . . . He suffers from the insensitiveness to physical reality which is characteristic of his race and his profession. He is secretive and suspicious," language that represented a highly anti-Semitic stereotype. *Fortune* used similar Jewish stereotypes when describing Ezekiel.[101]

Kiplinger returned to the issue again in 1942 in his book *Washington Is Like That*, devoting an entire chapter to the subject. "It's an artificial issue—this issue of 'Jews in Government'—but it does exist and so it should be discussed factually, not hushed," Kiplinger wrote. "Jews have become concentrated in a few government agencies where they *are* disproportionate, and where they are conspicuous for their numbers, and where they have close and intimate contact with the public, and where they tend to create the public impression that Jews are ascendant in government." He singled out the Securities and Exchange Commission, Department of Labor, National Labor Relations Board, Social Security Board, and some offices in the Justice Department as agencies with some offices where "the Jews are so numerous that the public which deals with them gets the idea that Jews are quite as numerous in the whole government.

"By any standards of administration, public or private, this is an error, and it needs to be remedied by the reduction of the proportion of Jews in these offices. Inherently it may not be wrong, but it looks wrong to have any public offices manned by people of any particular group."[102] Kiplinger's proposal of identifying and managing government employment by race or religion drew sharp public criticism, particularly after this book chapter was squeezed down and published in *Reader's Digest*.

Reader's Digest already had drawn criticism from liberals for its nationalistic and anticommunist editorial views.[103] According to a biographer of founders Lila and DeWitt Wallace, *Reader's Digest* had adopted an "inconsistent attitude toward Jews."[104] The Kiplinger article drew a public attack from the novelist Pearl Buck, the first American woman to win the Nobel Prize in literature and a prominent civil rights advocate. "'Lie low,' Mr. Kiplinger advises the Jews in effect, 'for your own good, stay in your 4 per cent ghetto,'" Buck wrote. "The truth is that America has nothing to do with percentages of race and sex and religion and national origin.... When anyone here begins inquiring into whether a person is a Jew or Gentile, he is helping Hitler."[105] Congressman Emanuel Celler, a New York Democrat, then issued a statement also condemning the Kiplinger article. In a letter to Buck, Kiplinger argued that her commentary "twisted, distorted, and played fast and loose with fine points of emphasis in my original writings." At the same time, he said he agreed with Buck's basic goals of fighting discrimination:

> In my own way I am as passionately devoted to that cause as you are.... I wish you could see some of the letters which have poured in upon me from outright anti-Semites who denounce my chapter and the digest of it as "pro-Jewish." It is with these people that I am doing most of my fighting, and doing it with relish. I wish, too, that you could see some of the many letters from thoughtful Jews expressing tremendous appreciation for my reporting job which they call "fair" and "constructive."[106]

Leftists in the Cabinet

One consistent theme in the business backlash against the New Deal involved claims that there was a leftist influence in the Roosevelt cabinet and that the president was pursuing a socialist agenda. The prospect of men and women who were college professors, social workers, and economists from nontraditional backgrounds being elevated to top government ranks was a novel one that drew ongoing media fascination and suspicion. *Business Week* and *Fortune* downplayed the notion that Roosevelt's Brains Trust would lead some sort of socialist revolution, and Kiplinger warned of a socialist turn in some respects. "Many of these proposals [from Roosevelt's advisers] will be frankly socialistic," Kiplinger wrote in February 1933, while observing a few months later that the Roosevelt "program is regarded frankly as experimental. No one feels SURENESS in the results."[107]

Kiplinger's coverage of Roosevelt's cabinet was detailed, with insights and rumors assessing the influence of the various secretaries and providing context for their public pronouncements. His detailed media coverage about the Roosevelt cabinet began in January 1933 and would build, with more detail and insight as the years progressed. Overall, coverage of the cabinet was done very thoroughly by competing business news organizations, so Kiplinger's coverage didn't offer a clear advantage in this area except for its frequency.

The Roosevelt cabinet included a range of voices across the political spectrum, from conservatives such as Secretary of State Cordell Hull to leftists such as Rexford Tugwell, an early member of the Brains Trust. The conflicting visions of these advisers was a major undercurrent in the media coverage of Roosevelt's first term. An examination of the coverage of Tugwell, for example, illustrates the broader theme of how Kiplinger covered the ideological splits within the Roosevelt administration. Kiplinger described two spheres of influence: the reformers such as Tugwell and a group influenced by Roosevelt adviser and future Supreme Court justice Felix Frankfurter. Frankfurter's allies included SEC chairman James Landis, Public Works Administration attorneys Thomas Corcoran and Benjamin Cohen, Reconstruction Finance Corporation counsel Jerome Frank, and Treasury Undersecretary Dean Acheson. "The Frankfurter idea is to take capitalism-as-is and build on it with a series of police regulations, leaving a sphere in which individual initiative has free play," Kiplinger wrote, whereas Tugwell represented a systemic threat to capitalism, a "new system government dictation of business policies and methods, something akin to 'fascism.'"[108]

In December 1933 Kiplinger began to report on Tugwell's domination of the Agriculture Department, claiming that he was performing end runs around Secretary Henry Wallace, whom he described as overburdened and a poor executive. Kiplinger charged that Tugwell was pursuing an agenda of radical change through collectivist and socialist politics. "Tugwell is the most conspicuous radical," Kiplinger declared in March 1934. "Tugwell group in Agriculture contains the best examples of radicals, or extreme social controllers, experimenting on a big scale."[109] Kiplinger flagged Tugwell's June 24, 1933, speech to the American Bar Association as significant for his business readers, particularly the assertion that "competition is no longer necessary."[110] Kiplinger noted that Tugwell and Eleanor Roosevelt were intellectual allies and that some of Tugwell's influence in the cabinet could be credited to this relationship.[111] President Roosevelt "must ride both horses within his administration," Tugwell wrote. "But he leans to the left."[112]

Business Week sought to put the Brains Trust and its influence into context: "Roosevelt's classroom cabinet of economists comes to Washington with ideas that startle conservatives and methods that annoy politicians. They command the President's ear but not his decisions." The article noted that all of the main Brains Trust advisers were Columbia University professors with "a decided leaning to the left. . . . All of them berate the concentration of national wealth in a few hands, are determined to increase the buying power of the masses. Application of their ideas probably will mean higher taxes on big incomes, an increase in federal power, more and more government in business."[113]

Fortune, in a July 1933 article, observed that "the most striking fact about the present Administration is its domination by intellectuals," although "it is also true that no one knows as yet precisely where the Roosevelt intellectuals propose to take us." While raising the specter of intellectuals leading revolutions, *Fortune* used the rest of the article to debunk the idea. The *Fortune* article sought to normalize the New Deal within existing structures and personalities by saying it didn't represent a major revolution, except for the banking system, and emphasized the number of mainstream business officials in the cabinet who would serve as counterweights to the leftists. Agriculture Secretary Wallace was described as "the only young intellectual in the Cabinet" and an author of the far-reaching farm bill, which should make him "an object of suspicion to all revolution hunters." The article then normalized Wallace squarely within contemporary WASP culture, noting he was a "lay reader in the Episcopal Church" and a former farm newspaper editor whose motto was "Good Farming, Clean Living, Right Thinking." At the same time, the article discussed some of the foundational fears of intellectuals in American culture as a way of understanding public wariness of the notion of a Brains Trust: "A professor is a figure of fun. . . . But an intellectual is sinister. Intellectuals are associated with revolution as ducks are associated with wild rice."[114]

Other news coverage generally portrayed Tugwell as one of the most influential leftists in the Roosevelt cabinet. The focus on Tugwell was partly due to the sweeping nature of the farm programs under Roosevelt, which involved major government interventions to cut production, centralize credit, and boost prices. *Business Week* raised the prospect of a dictatorship in agricultural policy in articles titled "Farm Dictator, Too?" on March 22, 1933, and "Farm Dictator?" on March 29. Kiplinger had concluded that Wallace, a veteran farm journalist, and his aides had American farmers' best interest at heart. Similarly, *Business Week* spelled out the Tugwell vision of centralized economic planning: "the encouragement of industrial development along socially useful lines, based on the recognition that the social utility of an industry can not always be determined by its ability to yield private profits. Planning involves public participation through government in the distribution of capital among industries, by means of taxation, regulation of profits and in various other ways."[115] The magazine reported on the tensions between the reformer wing led by Tugwell and the more conservative forces, and described setbacks for the reformers in the spring of 1934. *Business Week* also portrayed Tugwell as a leading leftist, whose proposals for giving $5 billion in direct relief to the unemployed and using semi-public enterprises to clear slums represented a sharp break from the corporatist agendas of Hoover and Coolidge. The magazine reported: "He [Tugwell] is sure that the machine has created a new economy which our age has yet to accept. The Hoover policies of rugged individualism, he attacks as protecting 'privilege' at the expense of the country as a whole."[116]

Government by Amateurs

Fortune provided a central insight about the new Roosevelt administration: it was filled with amateurs, and this was good for democracy since it elevated new voices to power. The Hoover administration had been filled with professional civil servants who attended to the regular business of government, but the extraordinary nature of the Great Depression forced Roosevelt to recruit "from classes which have not before served government and from classes which have not before directed great industrial and financial undertakings." He drew from the ranks of economists, social workers, professors, some businessmen, a few politicians, and a great many lawyers.

> [The amateur nature of the government] gives its peculiar tone and character to the entire Administration. It accounts for the extraordinary fervor and idealism and honesty and devotion of the members of the government.... And it accounts as well for the administrative inefficiency and the too frequent excesses of zeal and misdirection of enthusiasm which are characteristic of Washington in the year 1934.... [I]t explains the frequently noticed recurrent

conflicts which cancel one recovery effort against another and leave the entire program shaky and confused.

Fortune viewed the new administration in a sinister historical context: "The Administration of Mr. Roosevelt has proved that it is possible for a democratic government retaining at least the democratic forms to act more rapidly and decisively than either Hitler or Lenin was able to act at the moment of assuming power."[117]

The *Kiplinger Washington Letter* also described the Roosevelt cabinet members as amateurs in November 1933 but did not explore the democratic implications of this concept as did *Fortune*. Instead, Kiplinger addressed the more practical effects of elevating amateurs into top government positions, noting that inexperienced managers contributed to poor government administration and caused disproportionate harm to small businesses. In addition, he faulted the amateur economic policy that resulted in consumer prices rising faster than incomes.[118]

Business and a Self-Inflicted Wound

Kiplinger could also be critical of the business sector itself, decrying the greed, parochialism, and stubbornness of industry leaders, especially trade industry officials. "Do industries have the 'nerve' to do their own 'cracking down' on their business associates who violate?" he asked in November 1933. "Are industries 'honest'? Can they be trusted to conduct themselves in the public interest?"[119] In doing so, Kiplinger was playing a classic role in the trade press as an overseer of industry, pointing out its faults in the hope that such criticism would lead to socially beneficial improvements.

Kiplinger's reporting revealed a deeper issue within the business community. Laissez-faire capitalism had been so ingrained in business culture that many businesses and their trade associations were ill-equipped to coordinate to the degree that would be necessary for the success of the New Deal. This theme is evident in his late summer and early fall 1933 reporting about the inability of businesses and their trade associations to reach agreement on price and production questions: "In the beginning it was thought to be a quick and relatively simple job to get industries to agree on codes. Then it developed that most industries were not organized well within themselves and could not agree quickly on codes. Furthermore industries began to balk on raising wage costs without opportunity for compensatory increase of selling prices. So delay, no speed."[120] General Motors presents a useful illustration. In March 1935, GM president Alfred P. Sloan Jr. complained that increased labor costs resulting from New Deal regulations had bitten into profits. Still, GM's reported net profit was $94.8 million in 1934, up 14 percent from a year earlier, as sales had risen 48 percent.[121] Despite double-digit gains in profits, Sloan was still complaining about the National Recovery Act.

Six months later, Kiplinger pointed out the inherent weakness in trade associations: "A FEW trade associations will be the enforcing agencies. But many trade associations aren't adequate, aren't strong enough, must degenerate into mere cooperative agencies."[122] Furthermore, "the abilities of industries to organize themselves and compose their own internal rivalries within a few months were overestimated."[123] He openly questioned the intelligence of some leading trade association figures: "American Bankers Association showed its usual stupidity on matters of public and political relations by asking abandonment of deposit insurance at this late date. Bankers as credit technicians are all right: bankers as economic statesmen are questionable; bankers as judges of popular and political sentiment are total losses—more inept than any other single class of business men."[124]

Kiplinger offered some sharp criticism of the US Chamber of Commerce and a nationwide poll of member sentiment on the New Deal, arguing that the questions were "phrased in such a way to suggest obvious answers—answers hostile to New Deal." As a result, many businesses were refraining from answering the survey: "Seems major tactical blunder by Ch. of Com."[125] Garet Garrett expanded on the theme of a self-inflicted wound in a 1934 letter to Hoover: "Almost I am persuaded that business itself has done more harm to capitalism and to its principles of liberty than all the demagogues."[126] Other national conservative figures expressed similar views. Senator Lester J. Dickinson, an Iowa Republican, said that "the lack of social mindedness and the short-sightedness of business men who permitted manifest weakness and abuses to creep into the economic system were in part to blame for the current trend toward more stringent regulation and control of industry by the government."[127] This was a sentiment reflected by some in the business community. As one Texas businessman noted, "The capitalist system can be destroyed more effectively by having men of means defend it than by importing a million Reds from Moscow to attack it."[128]

CHAPTER 6

"They SEEM Reasonable"

A CENTRAL FIGURE IN the New Deal was Senator Robert Wagner of New York, a Roosevelt confidant and architect of key labor and social safety net legislation, such as the Social Security Act, making him one of the most influential US senators of the twentieth century. A tragedy at the Triangle Shirtwaist Factory in New York City in 1911 proved foundational in Wagner's worldview and was a force in advancing major legal and political gains for organized labor in the New Deal some two decades later. Events arising from this sweatshop fire served as a crucial foundation for advancing workers' rights in 1933 under the National Industrial Recovery Act, and in 1935 under the National Labor Relations Act, named the Wagner Act for the New York senator's energetic and persistent work on behalf of its passage. To understand labor's victories in the New Deal, and to understand Wagner's power and influence in the Roosevelt administration, you have to understand the Triangle Shirtwaist Factory disaster.

The Triangle Shirtwaist Factory occupied the top three floors of the ten-story Asch Building in the New York City neighborhood of Greenwich Village. Conditions for the garment workers inside were deplorable. Rows of mostly teenage girls and young women, many new immigrants who couldn't speak English, labored over sewing machines every day in twelve-hour-shifts for as little as $6 a week in 1911.[1] For working an eighty-four-hour week, their paycheck would have equaled $172 at $2 an hour in current dollars.[2]

The owners of the Triangle Shirtwaist Factory, Max Blanck and Isaac Harris, had not installed basic safety precautions such as sprinkler systems in this sweatshop even though fires had broken out in their other factories. The Triangle Factory itself experienced two fires in 1902. And then on March 25,

1911, a fire broke out and tore through the Asch Building. The young women tried to flee on one of the four elevators, but only one was operational. A door to one of the two stairways leading to the street was locked from the outside to prevent theft. The narrow fire escapes could not handle the hundreds of workers.

In the end, 146 workers died in the Triangle Shirtwaist Factory fire, described as "one of the most infamous incidents in American industrial history."[3] The event outraged the public and caught the attention of two politicians in the Tammany Hall Democratic machine: Al Smith, who would later become governor of New York, and Wagner, then a New York state senator. Wagner chaired a state Senate investigation into the sweatshop disaster. The tragedy was a catalyst for dozens of worker safety laws Wagner helped pass in Albany, laws that helped the working class and immigrants struggling with the hard edges of capitalism: low wages and the lack of pensions, health care, and other social benefits. Wagner and Smith found inspiration for their social safety net legislation in the essential social services provided by the Tammany Hall political machine. J. Joseph Huthmacher, in his biography of Wagner, argued that the reforms that evolved from the Triangle Shirtwaist disaster led to local and state governments' adopting a formalized social safety net: "In effect, the laws that they passed helped transfer the Welfare State responsibilities, formerly shouldered by Tammany Hall on the neighborhood level, upward to the municipal and statewide levels. And that marked a large step in the alteration of the 'Old American Creed' and the growth of a new brand of modern urban liberalism. One step remained, and that would be to make the Welfare State a national-level responsibility."[4]

In Wagner's words, Tammany Hall "may justly claim the title of the cradle of modern liberalism in America."[5] The biggest setback for business in the New Deal involved the expansion of organized labor's power, and Wagner was at the center of this fight. He was the primary author of Section 7(a) of the National Industrial Recovery Act, which offered new federal protections for unions and their attempts to organize at steel plants, auto factories, and other businesses through collective bargaining agreements. Section 7(a) was weak in several key aspects, yet it represented a revolution in the US business world by greatly expanding the power of labor unions. *Fortune* magazine declared in 1934 that Wagner's expansion of organized labor's right to collective bargaining was "without exaggeration . . . the greatest concession to labor in American history. For the first time, the employer has been compelled to deal with whatever unions his employees may set up."[6] Arthur Schlesinger Jr. observed that Section 7(a) "greatly circumscribed the legal right of business to exterminate trade unionism."[7] Passage of the pro-labor provisions became a focal point and a rallying cry for conservative business opposition and played a central role in the rise of the American Liberty League, a free-market advocacy group that would influence other groups down to the present day. The conservative critic Garet Garrett described Section 7(a) as "the most slippery, unmanageable piece of writing that, perhaps, ever went into a law."[8]

Wagner had a close relationship with Roosevelt and was once considered for labor secretary. Wagner was to the left of Roosevelt politically, pushing for greater power for unions. Roosevelt expressed ambivalence about expanding labor's rights at first, although he was more willing to regulate banks and Wall Street. He allowed Hugh Johnson, head of the National Recovery Administration, to weaken the collective bargaining enforcement at several turns to accommodate business objections.[9] Section 7(a) lacked important enforcement powers, and companies such as Weirton Steel openly defied this centerpiece of the New Deal by refusing to recognize worker elections. By 1935, organized labor was suffering major defeats between the reinvigorated business lobby and Roosevelt's reluctance to back his National Labor Board, as we shall see in greater detail later in this chapter. Wagner pushed a new bill to enhance labor protections and to improve the weak enforcement of Section 7(a), legislation that set off what the *New York Times* described as "an industrial 'battle of a century.' Organized industry, as represented by chambers of commerce and manufactures' associations, and supported by unorganized employers in many sections of the country, has almost literally drowned legislators with appeals to head off the bill on the ground that it would foment industrial strife."[10] The political dynamic shifted in June 1935, when the US Supreme Court invalidated key aspects of the New Deal and Roosevelt responded by turning left politically and endorsing the much more aggressive labor protections that Wagner had been pushing all along.

This chapter examines how journalists covered this epic battle among business, labor, and government, a fight that spawned hundreds of strikes and lawsuits and resulted in significant violence and property damage. This chapter analyzes Kiplinger's labor coverage and personal correspondence involving labor. Sifting through this drama, Kiplinger balanced criticism of the labor movement with a plea to the business community to engage with the unions as more of a coequal force. The chapter also examines Raymond

Moley's break with Roosevelt as the president turned leftward with the Second New Deal, which emphasized class rhetoric and condemned the business community.

Coverage of Labor in the First Hundred Days

Labor issues were not a prominent theme in the media coverage of the first one hundred days of the Roosevelt administration. The administration didn't begin working on the National Industrial Recovery Act until April 1933, having been preoccupied with bank and agriculture rescues. *The Kiplinger Washington Letter* in the spring of 1933 similarly was consumed by the banking and credit crisis, but Kiplinger took the cause of mainstream organized labor seriously and told his readership, primarily business executives, that labor was a major force. Kiplinger's reporting on labor focused on broad thematic developments and foundational issues as opposed to topical spot news coverage of individual labor disputes, coverage that typically focused on picket line violence. Kiplinger's treatment reflected a deeper understanding about the long-term goals of labor to gain direct participation in management, a departure from standard news media coverage in which management-labor relations were painted in a more binary fashion. Furthermore, the radical labor press closely read *The Kiplinger Washington Letter* for insights into business perception of labor issues.

Yet there were limits to Kiplinger's coverage of labor. The work of communist and socialist organizers was not portrayed in a favorable light, despite their considerable success in organizing workplaces. Such negative portrayals of radical labor leaders were prevalent in mainstream media at the time. Kiplinger's reporting sought to normalize mainstream labor organizations such as the AFL, discussing how the labor movement could stabilize and advance the economy. In that respect, Kiplinger aimed to reform and refine capitalism but not overthrow it. Still, the Kiplinger coverage stands out in an era when mainstream newspapers, owned by business interests hostile to organized labor, were often critical of unions. Philip Glende's study of labor coverage in the 1930s found that "the bulk of labor reporting reflected poorly on unions, because institutional forces, including entrenched practices and what was deemed newsworthy, shaped the body of labor news." The sociologist C. Wright Mills once observed that the mass media "are not kind to unions or labor leaders.... [V]iolence is the meat and gravy of labor news."[11]

Labor Market Dynamics

To understand the context of labor news coverage during the New Deal, it's important to review the changing dynamics in the labor market in the period leading up to the Great Depression. Technology was transforming the workplace and industry had seen major advances in mechanization, leading to a point where a "radical change in hours worked and a corresponding alteration in hourly wages paid" was needed for further gains in production.[12] Workers had few benefits enshrined in law. This was an era prior to widespread adoption of employer-provided health care: one survey showed just 13 percent of companies provided health insurance. There were few social insurance schemes for retired workers outside of private pension plans, and these gave limited coverage since many required twenty years' service at a firm, impractical given the migratory nature of the American labor force then as now. States had regulations on work hours, but the lowest limit was forty-four hours a week.[13]

Despite these problems, organized labor saw significant declines in membership through the boom years of the 1920s, starting at 19.4 percent of the workforce in 1920, falling to 10.2 percent by 1930.[14] The labor movement was suffering its own divisions that pitted the old-line craft unions, representing primarily skilled workers such as carpenters, against industrial unions, such as the United Mine Workers, which covered many unskilled workers and entire workplaces. The split also presented differences in politics and strategy; craft union leaders were far more conservative than industrial unionists, whose ranks included some communists and other radical elements. Conditions in some industries, such as coal mining, were brutal; worker objections were met with violence, often by local police or state troopers. For example, a coal strike in Harlan County, Kentucky, that began in 1931 led to the deaths of twelve miners and four deputies by the end of 1933.

The dynamics of the labor-management relationship were shifting amid the enormous human suffering from the Great Depression, with nearly 25 percent unemployment in 1932 and a partial breakdown in charitable relief. Wealth inequality was significant: the two hundred largest non-financial corporations controlled some 22 percent of the wealth of the entire nation.[15] This disparity drove populist politicians such as Senator Huey Long, the Louisiana Democrat, to push for wealth redistribution. The combination of technological displacement, patchwork unemployment benefits, and renewal of labor contracts would lead to "the likelihood of an active labor campaign as soon as industrial expansion begins," *Fortune* observed.[16] These predictions proved true. The American Federation of Labor's membership doubled under the NRA from 2 million in 1932 to about 4 million by the end of 1933. Kiplinger began noting the union progress in June 1933, and a month later he reported that organized labor's gains were "going like wildfire."[17]

While the Roosevelt administration sought to boost the rights of organized labor, a major uprising was happening throughout the country in the summer of 1933. In June there were 137 new strikes, rising to 240 in July and 246 in August. By September, some 300,000 workers were out on strike, ranging from Pennsylvania coal miners to Pacific Coast longshoremen.[18] By September 2, 1933, Kiplinger was predicting "a tremendous increase in strikes" because organized labor had expressed disapproval of the modest benefits in the National Recovery Act.[19] In October *Business Week* editorialized, "Strikes and fear of strikes, and the forecast of turbulent times with labor are largely responsible for such slowing up of business as there has been in recent weeks."[20] The labor unrest continued in 1934 as some 337,000 members of the United Textile Workers struck cotton mills in various states in September and 100,000 walked out during a general strike in San Francisco.[21] Other walkouts involved some 35,000 building trades workers and five thousand truck drivers in Minneapolis in May 1934. In the spring of 1934 *Business Week* began framing the labor unrest as a threat to the economic recovery. For example, it described a strike of Cleveland gasoline attendants in May 1934 as a "New Deal strike." Some of this activity arose from disaffected rank-and-file workers, who organized sit-down strikes and pressed for confrontations with management, an approach more aggressive than that of their more conservative union leaders.[22]

Kiplinger's Coverage of the National Recovery Act

In early February 1933 Kiplinger began reporting on the conceptual outlines of the New Deal, but he lacked details about the major labor provisions that were to be part of the National Industrial Recovery Act.[23] The lack of detail was understandable since Roosevelt had yet to be inaugurated. Moley and other administration officials were still debating the contours of the program and had not settled on a final course of action. On February 4, 1933, Kiplinger provided the following preview of the new regulatory order: "Liberalization of anti-trust laws under Roosevelt, letting industries agree on fundamentals of working hours and minimum wages, as well as the superficials of ordinary trade practices." He referenced moves toward a unified national banking system, long-range farm policies to control production and boost prices, a loosening of federal antitrust laws, and "favorable labor concessions," a theme that would be developed in greater detail over the next three years. "There IS a Roosevelt program. Taken as a whole it will sound good, although particular parts of it will be highly disturbing to many," Kiplinger wrote.[24] The *New York Times* also began to piece together the elements of the National Recovery Act, reporting on April 14 the broad outlines of a new federal agency, akin to the War Industries Board in the Wilson administration, that would direct expansion of industrial production.[25]

As the National Recovery Act was being drafted in subsequent weeks, Kiplinger sketched out what was at stake. "Organized labor now has the chance of a generation to fix wages into the general scheme of production costs and to promote collective bargaining," he stated in March.[26] The next month Kiplinger reported that labor was close to winning collective bargaining powers, which would be a major victory. The path to these new labor rights was indirect at best. In April 1933 the White House was jolted into action on labor policy when the US Senate passed thirty-hour workweek legislation, sponsored by Senator Hugo Black, an Alabama Democrat. The Black bill, supported by the American Federation of Labor, would share the work among a larger number of workers but wouldn't increase consumer purchasing power, a key Roosevelt goal.[27] The business community strongly opposed the Black bill and was surprised to see it advance so quickly through the Senate. *Business Week*, in the April 19, 1933, edition, reported, "Business is rubbing its eyes, wondering how the Black thirty-hour bill got through the Senate without anyone's seeing it coming."[28] Kiplinger correctly predicted the bill wouldn't be enacted, forecasting instead that labor leaders would use the bill as political leverage to pursue a more profound goal of gaining a voice in managerial decisions. "The TACTICS behind 30-hour legislation are important," Kiplinger wrote. "It will be used as a threat, a real threat, in order to get other concessions." Labor leaders, the article continued, did not trust the Roosevelt administration, even with its pro-labor orientation, to look out for labor's rights and felt the National Recovery Act was biased toward business. Therefore labor was going to push for direct participation in management. "Thus NRA will continue between two fires, industrialists on one side claiming NRA is squeezing them too hard, leaning too far toward labor; labor on the other side claiming NRA is controlled by industrialists, is favoring management, is perpetuating feudal system. To understand NRA you must understand these powerful forces which are pushing it."[29] This episode demonstrates how Kiplinger was teaching his readers the way government works by addressing the structural forces and hidden tactics in policymaking.

By May 1933, two draft industrial recovery bills surfaced in Congress, including an ambitious proposal to incorporate trade associations, spearheaded by Hugh Johnson. The legislation, designed to stabilize prices and limit overproduction, allowed various industry and business groups to write the rules of competition and production. The National Recovery Act essentially waived antitrust laws in order to permit industries to craft such agreements; critics said it enabled the creation of corporate cartels.[30] The bill enjoyed support from Gerard Swope, then head of General Electric, and Charles M. Schwab, chairman of Bethlehem Steel, among other industrial leaders.[31] US Chamber of Commerce president Henry I. Harriman said that the National Recovery Act marked "a most important step in our progress toward business rehabilitation." Business supported the bill in part because it followed a familiar framework, that of the War Industries Board in World War I, which used trade associations as a means to prevent harmful competition during the war. According to Cabell Phillips, "The NIRA was a bold break with the traditional doctrine of laissez-faire, yet it fell considerably short of the genuinely controlled economy sought by the more radical planners."[32]

Purchasing Power and Economic Theory

One of the driving aspirations behind the New Deal labor provisions involved boosting the growth of consumer spending through expansion of workers' purchasing power. A main advocate of this economic concept was Marriner S. Eccles, a Utah banker whom Roosevelt would appoint as Federal Reserve chairman in 1934. Eccles's economic policy emphasized growth of consumer income and spending to boost aggregate spending, and thus increase demand in the broader business world. His ideas represented a shift away from nineteenth-century economic theories that focused on production of capital goods, ideas he blamed for the economic disaster. "By taking purchasing power out of the hands of mass consumers, the savers denied to themselves the kind of effective demand for their products that would justify a reinvestment of their capital accumulation in new plants," he wrote.[33]

Wagner echoed a similar theme in his labor relations legislation in 1934, arguing that the nation faced significant wealth inequality and that unions would address that imbalance by ensuring that workers got a proper share of the economic pie.[34] Some businessmen such as Cyrus Ching at US Rubber and Gerard Swope at General Electric saw the benefits of the New Deal and unionization and signed union contracts that were influential in their industries.[35] They viewed organized labor as a force to stabilize industrial relations, standardize labor costs across industries, police competitors, and block new entrants.[36] Myron Taylor of US Steel sat down with John L. Lewis of the United Mine Workers and agreed to sign a contract with the CIO under the condition that Lewis would organize Taylor's competitors and get them to sign contracts, thereby stabilizing the labor market.

Section 7(a)

A flashpoint in the congressional debate over the National Industrial Recovery Act involved a portion of the legislation known as Section 7(a), which allowed workers to engage in collective bargaining with unions of their own choosing. This could mean joining an outside union, such as the United Mine Workers, or a "company union," established by individual companies to thwart outside labor organizing. Section 7(a) was drafted by a group led by Senator Wagner and would prove to be a boon to organized labor, especially innovators like Lewis, who used the provision as a major recruitment tool. At the time there was no national standard to govern collective bargaining agreements. The principles of Section 7(a) drew from precedent in World War I with the National War Labor Board, which "developed the doctrine that workers were entitled to choose their own representatives by majority vote," Schlesinger observed.[37] Roosevelt had served on this board. The New Deal architects also borrowed collective bargaining language found in the Railway Labor Act of 1926 and the Norris–LaGuardia Act of 1932.[38] Other precedents for the Section 7(a) provision could be found in labor's sporadic victories at the state level, particularly the April 1933 passage of minimum wage legislation in New York.

Fortune magazine devoted its December 1933 edition to an extensive profile of the American Federation of Labor. It claimed that Section 7(a) had "opened a Pandora's box of strikes and labor unrest." *Fortune* reported that the United States ranked sixteenth on the list of nations with a unionized workforce, placing it in the league of Estonia, Latvia, and Spain. Major European nations had long ago adopted labor unions "as an integral part of the economic structure," *Fortune* noted. "The battle now being fought over Section 7 of the NRA was fought years ago in most European countries."[39]

Business Week published little labor coverage until Roosevelt signed the National Industrial Recovery Act in June 1933, when it declared, "Continued flashes of opposition failed to blind astute observers to the fact that the program was going into operation with few essential changes."[40] *Business Week* expended considerable energy, however, following specific company challenges to the NIRA, ranging from Henry Ford's refusal to abide by industry competition agreements to the Weirton Steel challenge of the National Labor Board. Both were highly significant corporate stories that Kiplinger covered in far less detail. *Business Week*, for example, fully grasped the enormity of the Weirton Steel challenge in late 1933, devoting several long analytical articles to the drama.[41] By contrast, Kiplinger mentioned the Weirton case only in passing as he sought to make a broader point about the dispute: that the Weirton case would provide the impetus for stronger labor legislation sponsored by Senator Wagner.

Kiplinger counseled his business executive readers to understand the mindset of labor leaders and their desire for a direct voice in a company's entire operations, not just in labor relations. This is why labor officials were pushing for representation in the development of industry competition codes within the NRA. Such a move "is part of labor's long-time program to work toward direct participation in management. The issue should be taken seriously, for it will be a major plank in labor's legislative platform in the coming season of Congress."[42]

Portrayal of Organized Labor

The *Kiplinger Letter*, like other mainstream media publications, offered a blunt critique of the labor movement, describing the leadership of the American Federation of Labor as entrenched and more concerned with their own personal welfare than with that of the broader labor movement. In the April 29, 1933, edition, amid the drafting of the NIRA, Kiplinger wrote that labor was being handed "the chance of a generation" to win collective bargaining and lift wages. "Labor leaders do not seem to see it, however. You, as employer, seem safe in assuming continuing stupidity of labor." This comment drew some press coverage, such as an item in an Oklahoma City socialist newspaper, *American Guardian*: "The widely used *Kiplinger Washington* letter, very popular among business men, dated April 29, contains some amazing advice to labor. It is not less important because it ends with an insult."[43] While this and similar passages portrayed labor leaders harshly, Kiplinger could also be as critical of the banking industry.[44]

Other mainstream media offered a tough assessment of labor leadership. *Fortune* described an irony in the labor movement. Inept, entrenched leaders were being handed a historic opportunity to expand: "It is true that the Federation is stupidly reactionary, run by machine bosses, lacking courageous leadership. It is also true that it has managed to survive and even progress as no other American labor body has done." Although the AFL faced a "golden opportunity" under the NRA, it was bungling it by "failing to give the labor movement an aggressive effective leadership" and "refusing to revise its outworn craft unionism so as to include the masses of unskilled workers." As evidence of labor's lack of political power, *Fortune* noted that no labor leaders, including the AFL leaders, were present when Section 7(a) of the NRA was drafted, which the magazine portrayed as a sign of the weakness and lack of leadership in the organization and the US labor movement in general. The *Fortune* article carried several unflattering photos of labor bosses in candid settings, drinking, carousing, and slouching at meetings, with captions that commented unfavorably about the leaders' weight or age. A map pinpointing labor strikes nationwide defined areas of labor unrest as "the infected area."[45]

Overall, Kiplinger adopted a more moderate tone toward mainstream labor leadership. He reported on conversations with nationally known labor leaders in the early summer of 1933, stating: "We find them soberly conscious of their grave responsibilities. They aren't belligerent. They don't use portentous 'warfare terms.' They aren't 'mad,' as they were a few months ago. They say they've got a big job of 'educating labor' and 'sitting on troublemaking recalcitrant.' They say this is their 'big chance' and they 'mustn't demand too much.' . . . They SEEM reasonable."[46] On some occasions, however, his reporting portrayed strikers as irrational and unproductive, for example: "Strikes. Impartial review of the fragmentary reports on circumstances behind strikes suggests that many of them have been unwarranted, have been precipitated by labor leaders who are irresponsible and who may be racketeers. Some are under wing of A.F. of L., some aren't." Yet he followed this up with a more moderate view of organized labor trends: "Employers' attitude toward unions. Seems to us independently that there's no way to stop the rapid extension of trade unions, and no way to avoid the gradual extension of recognition of unions by employers. Pleas of industrialists that the government ask labor to suspend unionization activities (just for the emergency) seem incompatible with industrialists' activity in organizing themselves under associations and codes. Government MUST let both sides organize, then control and restrain BOTH."[47]

Fortune, in line with other contemporary media coverage, praised Lewis, the United Mine Workers president, for his strategy and his intellect. *Fortune* also praised Frances Perkins, the Roosevelt administration's labor secretary, and described her as "labor's ablest champion," a view not shared by all in the labor movement. At the same time, *Fortune* criticized the AFL leadership as "machine bosses who are as inept at directing a militant labor movement as they are skillful at keeping their jobs."[48] Media coverage of labor unrest focused on how it was harming business confidence, which in turn was accused of slowing the economic recovery. "Strikes and fear of strikes, and the forecast of turbulent times with labor are largely responsible for such slowing up of business as there has been in recent weeks," *Business Week* argued.[49]

Alan Dawley described the summer of 1934 as "a turning point in U.S. labor relations" because of a series of major, violent strikes, including a longshoremen's strike along the West Coast in which eight people died and dozens were injured amid a series of police clashes.[50] Violence also marred strikes in Minneapolis and Toledo. "Over the course of the year, there would be more than 1,800 work stoppages involving more than 1.4 million workers—everyone from the southern garment workers striking for the most basic questions of union recognition and wage increases," wrote Kim Phillips-Fein.[51] *Business Week* in July 1934 framed the failure of the San Francisco general strike as an outgrowth of long-simmering tensions between radical unionists and old school labor leaders "It is common opinion in Washington that the A.F. of L. has lost ground as a result of the San Francisco fiasco, and dire predictions are being made as to what this means in a 'turn to the left' in labor control."[52] *Business Week* minimized the concerns of Goodyear, Goodrich, and Firestone plant workers in Akron, Ohio, dismissing a pending strike by some 35,000 people as part of "the spring strike season" in an article titled

"Labor Puts on a Show." It described AFL organizing efforts in Detroit as labor leaders "trying to stir up trouble (and union dues)." One of the article's subheadings read "Union Against Union," which falsely placed on equal footing AFL organizing efforts and company unions, which were devices used by management to thwart outside labor organizing.[53] Even reporting about outright union victories, such as the General Motors workers' win in Toledo in May 1935, included passages that denigrated the work of the AFL, saying, for example, that "whatever the A.F. of L. got was practically handed to it by its left-wing leaders and rank-and-file following at Toledo."[54] The general strike in San Francisco caused worry for establishment labor leaders. According to a *Fortune* article, leaders such as Lewis of the United Mine Workers "realize that strikes endanger the NRA and they do their best to prevent them."[55]

Weak White House Backing

Roosevelt gave mixed signals to organized labor. While the new Section 7(a) powers in the National Industrial Recovery Act allowed for collective bargaining, the Roosevelt administration waffled on enforcement of the provisions and emboldened businesses to defy the newly appointed National Labor Board, created to mediate labor disputes. The president allowed Johnson, the NRA administrator, to weaken the Section 7(a) collective bargaining provisions through a series of contradictory decisions that undermined the labor board.

In September 1933 Johnson handed automobile manufacturers a major victory when he intervened in a protracted labor dispute, citing his role as coordinator of industrial cooperation agreements. One highly controversial move was his approval of a "merit clause" in the auto industry's labor and pricing agreement with the NRA, a concession to industry that allowed companies to continue to fire, hire, and demote. The move effectively weakened majority rule in labor elections.[56] Once this agreement was signed between the auto industry and the National Recovery Administration, some fifty other industries quickly adopted the same language, further weakening the new National Labor Board. Roosevelt, in a significant move against organized labor, in March 1934 removed automobile firms from the jurisdiction of the National Labor Board and placed them under a special Automobile Board, a panel that lacked direct union participation. "President Roosevelt delivered an almost fatal blow to Wagner and labor," Melvyn Dubofsky wrote of the episode. "The settlement ruled out exclusive majority representation and legitimated both proportional representation and company unions. It established a diluted form of job seniority, which scarcely protected union militants, and no basis for effective collective bargaining."[57] Donald Richberg, general counsel of the National Recovery Administration, complained that the National Labor Board was "powerless to enforce its decisions."[58]

Schlesinger painted a grim picture for organized labor: "Defeat, indeed, was the keynote for labor in 1934. There were local successes as in Minneapolis, San Francisco, and Toledo; but the main story was failure, and, most crucial of all, failure in the mass production industries. Labor failed in textiles, failed in the automobile industry, failed in steel, failed in rubber." By June 1934, the National Labor Board was on the verge of collapse, facing the Weirton challenge and the end-run actions by Johnson. By late October, the situation had become untenable and Roosevelt intervened to kill the merit clause. Under pressure from Wagner, Roosevelt signed an executive order that set up a new National Labor Relations Board and appointed Lloyd K. Garrison, dean of the Wisconsin Law School, as chairman.[59]

In the wake of these developments, some outside religious groups pressured Roosevelt to act. The Methodist Federation of Social Service in February 1935 complained that a crucial pro-labor section of the National Recovery Act had been almost completely nullified and the current federal regulations on minimum wages were not effective.[60] Senator Wagner in early 1935 introduced a new and tougher organized labor bill to essentially allow for enforcement of Section 7(a), but Roosevelt held off on endorsing it at first. He reversed course in early summer 1935 when it became politically expedient.

Kiplinger focused on the conflicting forces concerning labor policy within the White House. In June 1933 he told readers the "new law gives lip service to collective bargaining, but administrative policy will be pretty much 'hands off' on unionization.... Government wants wages raised, but doesn't want to get all tangled up with rows over unions, union recognition, and theoretical rights of bargaining. Government will curb industry with one hand, curb labor with other hand. "[61] He also described a significant shift in the focus on the Department of Labor, saying that under Labor Secretary Perkins, the agency "is going through a metamorphosis. Formerly it was (theoretically) an agency FOR labor. Now it is becoming an agency for labor in labor's position as a broad social factor. New emphasis is on public interest with reference to labor, rather than just on 'labor's rights.'"[62]

A few high-profile business challenges revealed that the Labor Relations Board lacked enforcement powers. In the fall of 1933, businesses began to defy the board by refusing to show up at hearings over recognition of outside unions. The fights occurred as industries negotiated to alter their own specific wage and price agreements, known as industrial codes, to modify the broader Section 7(a) labor provisions, especially in the automobile, cotton, and coal industries. By the end of 1933, the conservative opposition had begun to articulate its case that the National Recovery Act was unconstitutional. The initial business opposition focused on the collective bargaining requirements as well as issues involving industry price-fixing and production controls. Criticism escalated through the summer and fall. Writing in *Fortune*, US Representative James M. Beck, a Pennsylvania Republican, argued that the government had responded to the economic disaster by violating the Constitution.[63] "Criticism of the Administration policies and acts becomes vigorous. Business morale droops. How the President meets the situation will be highly significant," *Business Week* reported. "The Administration finds itself on the defensive for the first time."[64]

The Weirton Steel Corporation openly defied a National Labor Board decision ordering a union election for representation by the Amalgamated Association of Iron, Steel, and Tin Workers. In December 1933, Weirton refused to permit its workers to participate in a secret election for union representation, marking the boldest corporate challenge to the New Deal and its labor provisions. The National Labor Board settled a strike by ordering an election, which the company rejected. The next month, the H. C. Frick Company, a mining unit of US Steel, also defied the Labor Board's ruling on collective bargaining. Another act of business defiance came in September 1934, when Houde Engineering Corporation refused to obey a proportional representation ruling by the Labor Board. The National Association of Manufacturers stepped into the fray and urged its members to disregard the board's decision.[65] Budd Manufacturing in Philadelphia posed a similar challenge to an NLB ruling ordering a union election. Other businesses involved in significant opposition to labor rulings included cotton garment manufacturers, who fought requirements to shorten hours and raise wages, and the American Institute of Steel Construction, which refused to accept an NRA industry agreement. Goodrich Tire began taking out advertisements stating industry's view on labor relations and wages.[66] "NRA is facing rebellion," *Business Week* proclaimed in July 1934.[67]

Roosevelt declined to back the National Labor Board when it came under attack. "Spectacular fights are breaking out in all kinds of industries," *Business Week* reported.[68] Roosevelt used a labor speech in October 1933 to scold unions: "This is no time to seek special privilege, undue advantage or personal gain because of the fact of a crisis."[69]

Although Roosevelt sent the labor movement conflicting signals in the First New Deal, he delivered an important message in the 1934 labor uprising, which included the San Francisco general strike and major clashes in Minneapolis and Toledo. Departing from past practice during major strikes, Roosevelt "did not call in the Army to break up the strikes and force people back to work. This time, the unions were winning strikes."[70] The strikes of the summer of 1934 were intense enough that Roosevelt devoted his Fireside Chat radio broadcast on September 30, 1934, to the subject of government, capitalism, and labor relations. "During the last twelve months our industrial recovery has been to some extent retarded by strikes, including a few of major importance," Roosevelt said. He announced his intention to meet with representatives of both labor and large businesses in the coming weeks to seek "industrial peace" and recognized the limits of government interference in business affairs.[71]

Wagner Act

Amid Roosevelt's vacillations on labor policy, Senator Wagner introduced a new and strengthened labor bill in the spring of 1934 to give the NLB the power to order union elections, prohibit unfair labor practices, and enforce its orders. This was a step toward the landmark labor legislation known as the Wagner Act, or the National Labor Relations Act of 1935, a major victory for organized labor and a defeat for business interests. The bill created a new independent agency, the National Labor Board, to enforce employee rights. Workers could choose to form and join unions, and employers were required to bargain collectively with unions selected by a majority of employees.[72] The new law covered most workers whose operations affected interstate commerce. It is considered one of the most important legislative protections for worker and union rights.[73]

Roosevelt's eventual endorsement of the Wagner Act can be viewed as a sharp leftward break in the New Deal, since the president was taking a stand that was highly unpopular with both business and some of his advisers, such as Moley. Roosevelt's decision also can be viewed as a continuation of the basic framework set forth in the 1933 National Industrial Recovery Act, since it allowed for full implementation and enforcement of existing laws calling for collective bargaining. Wagner's legislation codified key rulings from the old National Labor Board, such as the "Reading formula," which resolved a hosiery workers strike in the summer of 1934 in Reading, Pennsylvania. This formula, as described by Dubofsky, required all parties to declare a truce in hostilities pending the labor board's investigation; required employers to rehire strikers without discrimination; allowed workers secret ballot elections to choose labor representatives of their choice; and ordered employers to bargain collectively with the elected representatives.[74]

Wagner believed that the path out of the Great Depression involved unionization of the workforce, which would expand the purchasing power of workers, which in turn would stimulate consumer spending and demand in the economy. By March 1935, purchasing power of individual employees working full-time was less than it had been a year earlier. He wanted a better balance between workers and corporations. After all, the National Industrial Recovery Act had increased the power of businesses as they united in trade associations, where they could pool their information and address systemic problems within the economy. The united strength of businesses, however, "is fraught with great danger to workers and consumers if it is not counterbalanced by the equal organization and equal bargaining power of employees," Wagner said in 1934. "It is necessary to ensure a wise distribution of wealth between management and labor, to maintain a full flow of purchasing power, and to prevent recurrent depressions.... It can be remedied only when there is genuine cooperation between employers and employees, on a basis of equal bargaining power."[75]

Kiplinger's Coverage of the Wagner Act

At first, *The Kiplinger Washington Letter* predicted on March 9 that passage of the Wagner Act was "very doubtful." As the year evolved, Kiplinger came to believe that the fate of the Wagner Act was inversely tied to the survival of the National Recovery Act, then up for renewal in Congress and under review by the US Supreme Court. Invalidation of the NRA would boost prospects for the labor bill. "If NRA is extended, the force behind Wagner bill will be lessened, it may fail," Kiplinger wrote. "If NRA is not extended, Wagner bill will pass."[76] The *New York Times* offered a similar analysis on May 29 and June 5.[77] By late May, Kiplinger was predicting the Wagner bill would be enacted after all despite industry's opposition.[78]

Kiplinger's coverage of the Wagner Act and its implementation was very different from his reporting on the National Recovery Act, in which he explicitly made the case for businesses to get on board: "Wagner bill a drag on business recovery? Seems so but lawyers of opponents feel sure the law will be invalidated by Supreme Court."[79] Kiplinger offered plenty of criticism of the Wagner Act but leavened that with a call for business executives to take labor seriously and understand its views. "It is practically desirable for employers to know labor's aims, methods and philosophy," he wrote.[80]

Business Opposition: Revolt

The American Liberty League and its leaders had an important role in opposing the Roosevelt labor policies. Earl F. Reed, counsel for the Weirton Steel company and a leader in the business rebellion against the New Deal, was a central player in the League.[81] The American Liberty League argued that the Wagner Act violated employees' freedom under the Fifth Amendment of the US Constitution. "The National Labor Relations Act constitutes a severe threat to that freedom in more ways than one," the group warned, arguing that "it is unconstitutional and that it constitutes a complete departure from our constitutional and traditional theories of government."[82] The National Association of Manufacturers joined the American Liberty League to fight the New Deal labor provisions, urging businesses to oppose the law and wait for it to be overturned by the courts since it violated the Constitution.[83] Robert L. Lund, president of the National Association of Manufacturers, claimed that the bill could "destroy the welfare organizations for sickness insurance, group life insurance, and such things now common in industry and might further serve to force employers to deal with communistic or racketeering organizations."[84] The National Association of Manufacturers launched a propaganda effort against the New Deal in 1934, a fifteen-minute radio show called *American Family Robinson*, which criticized the New Deal and the labor movement. The group recorded seventy-three programs between 1934 and 1938 and flooded the airwaves: some 229 radio stations nationwide requested the programs.[85] Employers fought the changes by boosting company unions, which grew by 170 percent to 1.2 million members in 1933 from the previous year.[86] Weirton's strategy for undermining the NRA was to use an employer-controlled company "union," which many steel companies and other industrial businesses had created to ward off independent unionization efforts by the AFL and others.[87] They sought to have company union election rules established to allow proportional representation and then to allow workers who selected a company union to avoid joining an outside union, such as one sponsored by the AFL.

As the business backlash grew through 1935, Kiplinger continued to report about broader economic improvements resulting from the New Deal. "Administration's most effective answer to business opposition will be that business IS better, that the trend is up, that recovery is definitely indicated. Forecasts of unbiased Washington analysts predict about 10% business improvement in 1936 over 1935," Kiplinger wrote in August 1935.[88] A month later he noted: "Business prospects continue to brighten. Our heavy incoming correspondence from business men in all lines, all parts of country, shows more consistent good tone than at any time since mid-1933. Gradual rise in business volume is expected from now to next spring."[89]

Amid Roosevelt's equivocation on labor, some business leaders were taking steps on their own to expand worker pay and benefits. *Fortune* described a far more nuanced and complex labor situation than the one suggested by general newspaper narratives of a labor-management war. For example, Henry Ford supported paying high wages at Ford Motor Company. Other business leaders attempted some conciliatory steps toward labor. The business community had varying opinions on the New Deal labor provisions, with divisions based on regional location, the type of industry, and business strategy.[90] Walter C. Teagle of Standard Oil of New Jersey, Alfred Sloan of General Motors, and Owen Young and Cyrus Ching of US Rubber supported the AFL's call for a five-day workweek. A Cornell University survey of 1,200 large and small industrial plants in 1933 revealed some moderate opinions about labor regulation, such as the recognition by manufacturers that they could implement a shorter workday and still produce an adequate supply of goods. The survey also revealed some support for a universal minimum wage.[91] Significantly, *Fortune* reported greater worker efficiency in companies that instituted the five-day workweek. Even within certain factions of the Republican Party there was some consensus about labor reforms. The Association of New York State Young Republican Clubs adopted a platform in 1935 calling for minimum wage compacts, maximum hours, and abolition of child labor.[92]

The *New York Times* emphasized industry opposition in its coverage leading up to the passage of the Wagner Act from March to July 1935, with ten articles focused on opposition to the act and eight articles supporting it.[93] The American Liberty League and representatives from clothing, steel, and retail industries all assailed the bill in separate articles during the congressional debate in the spring of 1935. Members of the Underwear Institute, a clothing manufacturers' trade group, feared that the Wagner bill "would interfere with friendly relations between employer and employee and lead to industrial strife."[94] Newspaper publishers also opposed the Wagner bill, along with the extension of the National Industrial Recovery Act, arguing it would "place regulatory control over the press in the hands of the government."[95]

A February 1935 *Business Week* editorial continued the magazine's critical coverage of organized labor, suggesting that a split between the AFL and Roosevelt was due to the union leadership's incompetence: "The American Federation of Labor had the greatest opportunity in its history. NIRA was not merely a labor bill; it was a union labor bill. The federation had powerful friends in NRA, in the Department of Labor, and in the White House itself. It has disappointed and alienated them." In perhaps an expression of wishful thinking, the editorial observed, "Astute observers here and there are saying the twilight is descending upon the A.F. of L."[96]

Auto Unrest

Media coverage of labor fights in the automobile industry provides a good example of the complex forces at work in implementing the New Deal. Before Roosevelt's inauguration, Briggs Manufacturing Company workers in Detroit struck in January 1933. Briggs was a key supplier of auto bodies to Ford and other automakers; therefore the strike shut down Ford's operations. *Business Week* described the Briggs walkout as the first "Depression-Era strike."[97] Organized labor, emboldened by the New Deal, saw the auto industry as prime ground for expansion. "Greenest of fields in the eyes of the labor organizer is Detroit, where the Administration's hands-off policy spells trouble for the defenders of the automobile industry's historic open-shop policy," *Business Week* declared.[98] Kiplinger had made a similar point about the NRA in general but did not address the significance of the Briggs strike or examine brewing labor unrest in the automobile sector in 1933.

Some press coverage became stridently anti-union in March 1934, when workers at Hudson, Fisher Body, and Buick threatened to strike over collective bargaining and AFL recognition. The March 31, 1934, cover of *Business Week* featured an image of a mass strike. The workers' affiliation was left ambiguous but the message was clear: "RECOVERY TROUBLE."[99] The image represented a disconnect from the week's events, since Roosevelt acted to avert a major strike with the settlement on collective bargaining issues. The next week, a *Business Week* editorial used anti-union rhetoric not seen in *The Kiplinger Washington Letter*: "The people of this country will rightly be indignant with any group that precipitates industrial warfare at this critical time, attempting to advance its special interests at peril to the general welfare."[100] It condemned the AFL for calling the strike to enforce Section 7(a), not for explicitly advancing better pay and working conditions. *Business Week*, however, didn't acknowledge the open defiance of the law by Weirton Steel and others. It later described how "the radical fringe of the Brain Trust is enthusiastic for the Federation of Labor's effort to dominate the automobile industry."[101] Writing about automobile labor unrest in March 1934, Kiplinger predicted that a strike would occur and that the automobile industry, "with its demonstrable claim of having treated labor fairly on wages and hours, will appear to be the victor."[102]

The news media showed some fascination with Henry Ford, "the Sphinx of Dearborn," because of his influence in both the business and political realms.[103] *The Kiplinger Washington Letter* offered little coverage of Ford compared to *Business Week* or the *New York Times*. Partly because of its anonymous sourcing policy, the *Letter* lacked the interviews with political and business industry leaders that were the hallmark of *Fortune* and, to some extent, *Business Week*. The role of Ford in the New Deal was significant because he never signed on to any industry regulatory agreements, arguing that he was already paying above-market wages. The automobile icon claimed that the NRA had not materially increased purchasing power because the wage raises had been too small for the industries. Ford's lack of cooperation with the New Deal proved to be a vexing problem for the Roosevelt administration.

The *Schechter* Decision

The prospects for the Wagner Act, and the entire New Deal, changed in May 1935, when the US Supreme Court declared that the heart and soul of the NRA was unconstitutional.[104] The case, *Schechter Poultry Corp. v. United*

States, involved a Brooklyn, New York, firm that sold chickens to butchers and was found to have violated an NRA industry code. The court ruled that Congress had delegated too much authority to the executive branch without adequate standards and that the Roosevelt administration's codes of fair competition represented a violation of the Commerce Clause.[105]

Kiplinger alerted his readers to the case's significance and warned of an early erosion of the New Deal through other Supreme Court decisions. A January 1935 decision, known as the "hot oil" case, found that Congress had delegated excessive powers to the president to regulate domestic and international oil shipments. On the basis of this precedent, Kiplinger argued, the New Deal would be curtailed significantly: "It is doubted that any major emergency laws will be wholly invalidated but a good many specific features of individual codes may be invalidated."[106] In addition, Kiplinger said, a recent railway case decision suggested that the "Supreme Court will wallop NRA specifically in Schechter poultry case."[107]

Anticipation was running high in the business community. Concerned that uncertainty in federal policy was slowing down commerce, business leaders in March 1935 were expecting that the Supreme Court would invalidate the National Recovery Act. Kiplinger observed: "Many manufacturers are reported to be preparing to curtail production in next few months, thinking they can produce more cheaply after June, if NRA expires."[108]

After warning about the implications and previewing the impact of the *Schechter* decision, Kiplinger spent little time discussing the actual Supreme Court decision after its release. Instead, he focused on its impact: "We shall not analyze Supreme Court decision, for it has already been done.... We shall comment on anticipated effects, distinguishing between those which seem certain, and those uncertain."[109] One likely outcome was an increase in strikes and other labor troubles, as well as improved prospects for the Wagner Act, he wrote. Initially, Kiplinger saw a silver lining: "Longer range view is that something has happened which business hasn't yet clearly discerned, but which will look good later. Supreme Court has dampened the spirit of New Deal experimentalism. Hereafter the administration will be forced to trim sails, to allow business greater leeway to work out its own policies." Assessing the political fallout, Kiplinger felt that conservative prestige had risen and the prestige of the New Deal was diminished. He described Roosevelt's style of governing as "government by bluff.... New Deal methods are to stretch its powers beyond legal limit, by subterfuge, by bluff. Thus reformers, by overplaying their hand, have endangered their reforms."[110]

Despite Roosevelt's defeat in this case, Kiplinger clearly warned his readers that the overall trend toward increased regulation remained in force:

> Will Roosevelt "draw in his horns" or "turn right"? NO. He will try to develop new methods to accomplish same results as in past.... Federal control, regulation, supervision of industry, of the "economic life of the nation,"—this still is the Roosevelt program. He is getting ready to make bigger issue of it in future than in past. He wants to dim lines as between intrastate and interstate commerce, making all or most economic activities interstate or "national."[111]

Political Impact

The *Schechter* decision marked the end of the First New Deal in two ways. It invalidated the core national economic planning experiment that was the National Recovery Administration. And politically, it marked a new phase of the Roosevelt administration that included an explicit attack on business and a strong embrace of labor, which proved to be a major ally in the 1936 presidential campaign. As Roosevelt began to position himself for reelection, he found rising unhappiness with the New Deal. A *Literary Digest* poll reported that 55 percent of Americans opposed the New Deal, while 45 percent supported it, results that Kiplinger said were "having a sobering influence in Washington."[112] In April 1935 Kiplinger predicted that the growing unpopularity of the New Deal and a belief that it was hindering the economic recovery could cloud Roosevelt's reelection chances, writing, "President Roosevelt's reelection is no longer taken for granted."[113] What remained unknown was the role of a third-party challenge and the emergence of a strong Republican challenger.

Kiplinger observed how the president's anti-business rhetoric sharpened in the wake of the 1935 *Schechter* decision: "[Roosevelt] thinks a good deal in terms of political power VERSUS business power, as if they were antagonistic." Even though Roosevelt revived an advisory council of business leaders, "beneath the surface there's bad feeling," Kiplinger wrote. Roosevelt "seeks advice but doesn't really want it."[114]

Roosevelt's decision to attack big business was a centerpiece of a newly formed coalition of big-city political machines, labor unions, African Americans, and Catholics and other religious minorities. Roosevelt's new direction was partly due to political necessity. An attack on business would allow him to harness the energy whipped up by populists such as Senator Long of Louisiana and socialists such as Upton Sinclair. Movements led by Long, Sinclair, Dr. Frances Townsend, and Father Charles Coughlin "are gaining far bigger followings than the communists," observed Kiplinger. He said that some of the New Deal legislation, such as Social Security, was necessary to ward off broader socialistic or populist movements in the country, inspired by demagoguery such as Long's attacks on wealth: "Social insurance buttresses the capitalistic system, although it is a socialistic approach. . . . Demagoguery: Social insurance, if wisely planned and administered, will take wind out of sails of share-the-wealth movement. This movement is growing rapidly."[115]

As he viewed the upcoming election, Roosevelt had taken business opposition for granted, Kiplinger wrote, and "he has cast his lot with the numerically large classes of direct beneficiaries of New Deal's pro-labor, pro-farmer, pro-unemployed policies."[116] John L. Lewis, the Mine Workers leader who by 1936 was head of the new Congress of Industrial Organizations, became a significant force in the fall 1936 election, coordinating with the Roosevelt reelection campaign to supply cash and turn out workers. Lewis and Roosevelt appeared at a campaign rally together in October, where the president, speaking before 35,000 people, endorsed the labor agenda in explicit terms: "Today we aim to make the public conscious that the welfare of labor is the welfare for all."[117]

For Moley, the attack on business and embrace of populism marked a significant turn in the direction of the Democratic Party. Of Roosevelt's new political coalition Moley observed, "It was possible to unite all schools of radical change by making his cause a crusade with a good wide target to hit at, and that proved to be big business and the rich."[118] At this point Moley broke with Roosevelt. "I didn't regard the social order as being divided between business, on the one side, and some mythical 'us' on the other. I had no class-struggle concept of the reforms that were going on in Washington," Moley wrote.[119] Years later he recalled, "I could not remain a Democrat when the nature and objectives of that party had so completely departed from its earlier faith." Moley declined Roosevelt's request to be his speechwriter in the fall 1936 campaign and the two men parted amicably. "There was no sharp 'break' between us," Moley wrote. "The ties had deteriorated over so long a span that there was no argument or bitterness or, so far as I knew, diminution of personal warmth."[120]

Internal Labor Rift

A key narrative in news media coverage of labor during this period involved the tension between skilled craftsmen, covered by the American Federation of Labor, and the unskilled labor and semiskilled workers who generally lacked union representation. Generally speaking, organized labor prior to 1933 was strong in a handful of industries, such as coal mining, railroads, and the needle trades, and among highly skilled craft workers such as machinists and carpenters. The AFL's failure to organize both skilled and unskilled workers, noted *Fortune*, "means that the great mass of American labor, which the machine age is reducing more and more to an unskilled status, is locked outside the Federation's doors."[121]

Fortune in 1934 provided a comprehensive overview of the fight between the AFL and more activist insurgents, describing AFL leaders as conservative in that they were "unwaveringly opposed to the extension of governmental control over private business, which it brands 'Socialism.'" According to *Fortune*, the AFL opposed minimum wage legislation, arguing that a minimum wage might wind up being a maximum wage. This was evidence of the pervasiveness of liberalism in society, even in organized labor. To make the point about the conservative leanings of labor leaders, *Fortune* noted that Lewis of the United Mine Workers had been a Republican in 1932 who backed Herbert Hoover in the presidential election.[122] *Fortune* described the AFL as "bourgeois to the core.... [It has] always been ultraconservative in its social point of view."[123] Workers prized not revolution but instead stable employment and the continuing profitability of their employers.

This divide between skilled and unskilled labor was further illustrated by the influence and success of communist and radical union organizers, who played important roles in organizing the auto and coal industries. Anthony Badger observed, "Above all, Communists gained prestige by their willingness to enter the most forbidding territory in an effort to represent the most unpromising groups of unorganized workers: Harlan County coal miners, California farm laborers, Alabama sharecroppers." The radical organizers were striking a chord with workers, who would launch sit-down strikes that caused production to grind to a halt, at times catching AFL leaders by surprise.[124]

Kiplinger explored the internal labor divisions on numerous occasions. Reporting on a March 4, 1934, forum about the National Recovery Act, he described harsh criticism of AFL leadership. "A majority of the labor speakers attacked A.F. of L. almost as vigorously as they did NRA," he said. "Industrialists attending the meetings were impressed by the hostility toward A.F. of L. by the more radical labor spokesmen, and there was some quiet talk among industrialists of A.F. of L. as the 'lesser of two evils.'"[125] Kiplinger's special report on the labor movement, a dispatch from the October 1935 AFL convention in Atlantic City, explored the active communist opposition to the AFL leadership: "Communists hate AFofL. They call it 'tool of capitalism.' They call its leaders 'reactionary.'" Kiplinger reported that communism was opposed by 90 percent or more of AFL members: "Labor leaders urge businesses to support 'responsible labor unions' as against 'dangerous communists.'"[126]

Kiplinger still attempted to bridge the gap between executives and labor leaders, which was notable since labor disputes were a dominant business and political story, and labor was getting some amount of negative press for widespread strikes that were disrupting the economy. To discuss the state of the labor movement and report on the 1935 Atlantic City conference, he created an entire special issue on October 12, 1935, one of his "Brown Letters." He described the differing political dynamics involving business and labor:

> In the aggregate, industry probably has much more political power than labor. But labor is better organized for purposes of political pressure,—right down to the individual workman. One average labor leader has more political drag with officials or candidates for office than ten average business men. Labor is our most powerful "organized minority"—even better than farmers or veterans. Zeal, cause fervor, social and humanitarian viewpoint: Many business men have these qualities en masse but they don't talk about them. Labor puts them always to the fore. Thus they give labor movements a certain virility which business movements often lack.[127]

Kiplinger also examined the split between the AFL and the new Congress of Industrial Organizations, led by Lewis. His reporting delved into the internal dynamics of the labor movement, such as the organizing strength and momentum of the United Mine Workers and union organizing campaigns for the steel industry.[128]

The radical labor press cited passages from *The Kiplinger Washington Letter* to disparage AFL leaders, particularly John L. Lewis and William Green, and accuse them of being in league with corporate interests. An April 11, 1931, article in the *Daily Worker* mentioned Kiplinger's reporting as evidence that businesses were pushing the wage cuts and the AFL leadership was going along: "It shows that big business and the office of President Green of the A. F. L. are just two offices of the same concern."[129] The *Daily Worker* also pointed to Kiplinger's economic forecasts as evidence that the labor market was suffering more than official forecasts indicated: "That unemployment will grow infinitely worse and that the federal government plans no relief is admitted in a confidential circular issued by the Kiplinger agency here which privately circulates 'The Kiplinger Washington Letter,' containing information for the bosses which usually does not reach the capitalist newspapers."[130] The *Montana Labor News* cited Kiplinger's commentary as evidence that labor's wage demands were reasonable: "And Kiplinger Washington letter adds that the pay increases workers are now demanding 'are normal in ANY period of rising prosperity, rising profits, and rising costs of living.'"[131] Although the *Daily Worker* quoted from Kiplinger's reporting some twenty-two times between 1931 and 1935, it often disparaged *The Kiplinger Washington Letter,* describing it in 1932 as "one of the instruments of finance capital to direct the lower ranks of the bourgeoisie."[132]

Tax Bill

One immediate manifestation of Roosevelt's populist turn was the passage of the 1935 Revenue Act, which increased taxes on corporations, wealthy individuals, and inherited wealth. In many ways it was more radical than the Wagner Act because it represented an explicit attack on concentrated wealth in America. With this bill Roosevelt targeted the heart of laissez-faire capitalism and advanced the evolution of the regulatory state. The 1935 Revenue Act increased taxes on inheritances and gifts, as well as on higher incomes and on corporations. It reversed long-standing revenue laws that had favored America's wealthiest elite. The 1935 tax legislation represented a major leftward turn in the New Deal with the explicit goal of income redistribution. Roosevelt, in a June 20, 1935, message to Congress, spelled out the justification for the tax bill, citing wealth inequality and the inequity of the current corporate taxation regime, which put the burden on smaller companies. He also said that wealth accumulation by elite families was not translating into new capital for businesses to expand and create jobs.[133]

Industry opposition to the tax bill was intense. According to the *New York Times,* Fred H. Clausen, president of the Van Brunt Manufacturing Company and chairman of the Chamber of Commerce's federal finance committee, claimed that a new tax on excess profits was "'tantamount to confiscation' and 'highly discouraging to enterprise'" and that the bill amounted to a form of class warfare.[134] Kiplinger told the business community the tax bill was starting off as a politically driven exercise to redistribute wealth and to better position Roosevelt in the 1936 election with the party's progressive wing. One aim was to head off challenges from Senator Long: "This is a way to out-hooey Huey: it is definitely on the President's mind."[135]

Kiplinger wrote that Roosevelt's main goals with the tax bill were "(a) to discourage Bigness in Business, to encourage smallness, or at least independents rather that 'trusts.' (b) To redistribute wealth; to hamper creation of big private fortunes; to whittle down big fortunes already established; to tax the rich, the near-rich and the upper middle classes who have substantial incomes. (c) To steal the political thunder of the Long-Coughlin-Townsend, et al. (d) To raise taxes to pay off the depression debts." While critical of the tax bill and its political origins, Kiplinger still offered a fair explanation of the bill's underlying philosophy, such as the rationale for new inheritance taxes: "Persons should not be allowed to transmit big fortunes from generation to generation. They are as bad in a democracy as inherited kingship. They don't help the recipients. They don't encourage creative enterprise."[136]

Kiplinger described the tax bill as a fait accompli even before Roosevelt signed the measure. Roosevelt is "trying to make political power ascendant over the power of large accumulations of capital in the hands of other individuals or corporations," he wrote. "Practical attitude: Like or dislike these political influences all you individually wish, but recognize them for what they ARE, and adjust your business policies to make the most of them."[137] Once the bill passed, Kiplinger was unsparing in his analysis of the tax law: "It soaks a few big rich at top of pyramid; takes up to 79% of income, up to 70% of estates at death. . . . It establishes the principle of penalizing bigness, and also inter-corporate ownership relations. Practically it does not serve to break down big corporations but it lays the ground work. Practically it does not hurt business. All in all, it's a political gesture by a tired Congress. It is grotesque."[138]

Utilities Battle

Another direct battle between the New Deal and big business involved Roosevelt's attempt to break up and regulate electric utilities. Roosevelt's fight with the utilities via the Public Utilities Holding Company Act represented one of the major attacks on capitalism in the New Deal. "The Act was among the most controversial pieces of legislation in American history, and it produced a violent reaction among utility companies," Thomas McCraw wrote in his examination of business regulation in the New Deal.[139] Passage of the act represented the third major blow to corporate interests in the summer of 1935, coupled with the Wagner Act and the Revenue Act of 1935. Kiplinger followed the utility battle closely and described its broader impact on the business world: "In attacking holding companies, President has a broader idea than just to 'get' utility holding companies which have been 'bad.' He is moving into new phase of New Deal philosophy—against 'bigness.'"[140]

The origins of the battle lay in Roosevelt's desire to eradicate poverty and extend modern services to rural America, especially farms. He criticized utilities for failing to expand electric service to rural areas and to keep rates low enough for farmers and other non-urban dwellers to reap the benefits of electric power. Roosevelt's broader goal was to force the utilities to provide rural electrification, with the Tennessee Valley Authority symbolizing his efforts to promote jobs and economic development along with flood control and expansion of electrification to farms and small towns. Roosevelt and Brains Trust adviser Tugwell, a key force in centralized economic planning as assistant secretary of agriculture, essentially held classic Jeffersonian views in their approach to rural development. Kiplinger spelled out the rationale for the bill in a November 10, 1934, report: "[Public utility] holding companies can serve useful economic purpose, but many have committed abuses, and these must be prevented by federal regulation. This will reduce costs for operating companies and lower rates to consumers."[141]

Roosevelt had noted the opportunity for rural development when, as governor of New York, he saw lower prices for electricity and higher levels of household electric consumption in neighboring Canada.[142] Morris Cooke, the first director of the Rural Electrification Administration, argued that utility companies "discriminated against small and domestic consumers, especially farmers, and he believed that rural electrification would remedy the economic imbalance between the country and the city, thereby correcting what he called the 'uneven progress of industry and agriculture.'"[143] Roosevelt believed that rural development and electrification were winning political messages too. "During the 1932 presidential campaign," wrote

William M. Emmons, "Franklin D. Roosevelt lashed out repeatedly at the nation's investor-owned electric utility industry, accusing it of exploiting ratepayers and slowing national economic development through monopoly pricing practices, facilitated by ineffective state-level regulation."[144] Emboldened by the Democratic victories in the 1934 midterm elections, Roosevelt pushed ahead with a plan to break up large utility holding companies. In 1935 he won passage of the Public Utility Holding Company Act, which gave the Securities and Exchange Commission power to regulate, license, and, if necessary, break up interstate public utility holding companies. The law contained a "death sentence" to eliminate any holding company that controlled power systems in more than one geographic area.[145]

In February, Kiplinger observed that the public utility dispute had yet to draw much attention but would prove to be a major issue. By July he was framing the utility dispute in clear terms that didn't adopt the demagoguery of competing publications: "Government fears Bigness in Business, seeks to abolish billion$ combines. Business fears Bigness in Government .... Both claim to serve the public interest. Who's to check both big powers? Obviously, Congress. President has more pull with it than business has."[146] He described an intense political battle over the bill, citing an investigation that said utilities "spent a lot of effort and money—probably more than was ever spent on any single bill by any single industry."[147] He wasn't shy about calling out the industry for its mistakes: "Lobby tactics of utilities: Stupid, dirty,—fake telegrams." One congressman reported receiving more than eight hundred telegrams opposing the bill; all of the messages came from a small town in his district and were generated from a phone book or a list of utility customers.[148] *Business Week* took the telegram onslaught at face value, reporting that the utilities drew investor support and "went at Congress through the 'people back home' who own utility shares, and in which thousands of investors protested voluntarily."[149] According to Kiplinger, Roosevelt and his allies in Congress were delaying progress on the bill so that more dirt on utility lobby tactics would surface and allow them to further discredit the opposition.[150] Kiplinger's coverage for the rest of the year focused on the SEC's implementation of the new law and the prospects for court challenges.

The *New York Times* focused on Roosevelt's utilities proposals in late 1934 in "two militant speeches" advocating expansion of the Tennessee Valley Authority model nationwide.[151] The newspaper covered the utility bill fight closely in March and followed the legislation as it moved through Congress. *Business Week* also covered the utility fight closely but with a more critical view of Roosevelt's position, at one point describing it as an attempt to "Sovietize that industry."[152] The magazine editorialized, "Every business organization and every business man has an acute interest in the battle of the utilities against this radical encroachment."[153] In a March 16, 1935, editorial, *Business Week* observed that the president's harsh anti-utility rhetoric should be viewed against the political challenges he faced on the left: "It may have seemed to Mr. Roosevelt that it was necessary at this time that he manifest a belligerently liberal attitude about something," and the utilities seemed like a politically expedient target.[154]

Second New Deal

Following passage of the tax bill, Kiplinger warned business readers that the New Deal had not ended: "Things have gone too far for such a backdown." He predicted that upcoming Second New Deal initiatives would feature "further attacks on bigness: in the areas of agriculture, rural resettlement, government lending and labor relations, all of which point to steady progress toward larger measure of national social control and economic planning."[155] He later noted, "Everything points to ultimate proposal of some sort of new gov't scheme for regulation or direction of business."[156]

As dire as this outlook would be for large companies, Kiplinger offered some balance: "Shocks to business from Washington? Yes, some severe perhaps. But stimulants to business too. Business will withstand the shocks.... There will be annoyances. No close embrace of White House and business. But administration knows the need for business rise, more private jobs. Stimulants will follow New Deal lines,—not orthodox business lines."[157] His warning came with a dose of constructive criticism: "Trend in Congress will be TOWARD govt' regulation of business. Trend will be generally PRO-LABOR.... Moral: Business and trade associations must get a move on."[158]

By 1936, however, Kiplinger had become alarmed that Roosevelt was moving on to the Second New Deal and its more forceful regulation of businesses. Following Roosevelt's 1936 State of the Union address, which sharply criticized business, Kiplinger told his readers to expect "further ascendancy of political over business power. Further regulation of business by government.

Further curbing of gov't of industrial and financial 'autocracy.'" Kiplinger's annoyance with Roosevelt's populist turn was evident: "The assumption is, of course, that only the government at Washington can be trusted to look after the 'public interest.' Business can not be trusted. State and local governments can not be trusted. Federal power, federal paternalism."[159]

CHAPTER 7

The Promise of Independent Journalism

WILLARD KIPLINGER LEFT many legacies, some of which provide hope for the troubled and fragmented world of modern journalism. Kiplinger offered a strong, well-reported, and independent view of the business and economic landscape, a perspective sometimes out of sync with the conventional wisdom of the time. William Grimes, editor of the *Wall Street Journal* from 1941 to 1958, considered Kiplinger "a nut." The two men "would work with the same information and the result was entirely different," recalled George Bryant, who worked for both Grimes and Kiplinger.[1]

Perhaps we need more nuts like Kiplinger, journalists willing to push against the corporate conventional wisdom. An important example of Kiplinger's journalistic independence involves his coverage of the American Liberty League and the National Association of Manufacturers. The American Liberty League, with its wealthy benefactors and affiliated organizations, was at the forefront of the rise of neoconservatism. Its opposition to the New Deal and advocacy of free markets would be echoed later in the work of the economists Friedrich Hayek and Milton Friedman and would shape the broad contours of the modern conservative movement.

Generally speaking, Kiplinger resisted the propaganda of these groups and urged these corporate extremists to work with Roosevelt and help advance society as a whole, as illustrated by his 1936 correspondence with Raymond Moley over the latter's speech that year to the National Association of Manufacturers. As a ghostwriter, Kiplinger could have pandered to business executives, but he declined to do so. Instead, he counseled Moley to articulate a defense of the New Deal and explain how business could be more socially responsible. Kiplinger's coverage of controversial figures in the Roosevelt administration offers another example of his independence. An ideologically driven journalist could have campaigned to denigrate leftists in Roosevelt's cabinet, such as Rexford Tugwell. Kiplinger, like other journalists, noted how Tugwell's arrogance had damaged his political effectiveness. Yet Kiplinger's coverage of Tugwell, as well as Hugh Johnson, showed he had a basic sense of fairness. In private correspondence Kiplinger sought to find a more effective role for Tugwell and acknowledged his significant intellectual and professional achievements. While he disagreed with Tugwell's style and viewpoint, Kiplinger praised him in the newsletter on occasion.[2] Kiplinger would still praise Johnson's work on occasion too, even after Johnson sought to shut down the journalist's access to the National Recovery Administration. The two men resumed their correspondence after Johnson left the Roosevelt administration.

Kiplinger's decision to remain largely independent from the American Liberty League represented an important lesson for trade journalism and journalism in general. The American Liberty League, like the National Association of Manufacturers, flooded newsrooms with speeches and position papers critical of the New Deal. It was an onslaught similar to what think tanks such as the American Enterprise Institute, the Heritage Foundation, and the Cato Institute unleash on today's newsrooms. The Liberty League's talking points turned up as lead articles in the *New York Times* or as grist for editorials in *Business Week*. Those corporate forces have only grown more powerful over time, as journalist Jane Mayer has shown in her work on the Koch brothers.[3] The prevalence of business reporters relying on corporate handouts for news remains a worrisome trend.[4]

Business journalism historically has been a product of its culture and its times, which makes journalistic independence unusual in the face of powerful corporate interests.[5] Culture plays a critical role in news selection and reflects a set of enduring values, as Herbert Gans wrote. News is selected and produced by journalists "who, for a variety of reasons, look at America in much the same way."[6] Playing to its audience of conservative readers, *Forbes* magazine adopted the motto that the magazine was a "capitalist tool" and framed its news through a free-market lens. Kiplinger's business reporting, rooted in the editorial tradition of the Associated Press, was a contrast to corporate-centric coverage of labor and economic issues.[7] Kiplinger, by urging the business community to cooperate with the New Deal, was swimming against the tide of dominant business views. This decision also presented some commercial risk since these views were held by his subscribers and potential customers. To publish unpopular material during the New Deal and to see circulation expand so rapidly was a notable achievement.

Kiplinger struck an important balance as a business journalist. He was not awed by the corporate sector. "He was not over-reverent toward business, but he was appreciative of it as a mechanism for getting things done," Austin Kiplinger said. "But that isn't to say that it can't be greatly improved and that isn't to say that it won't make a lot of mistakes along the way. I think this kind of cool appraisal of the American business system, tempered by his interest in people as people, was a very large part of the philosophical, ideological background of the Kiplinger Letter."[8]

Ownership

The Insider illustrates the importance of having a professional journalist as an owner of a publication. My study of the trade press in *The Enforcers* showed innovation and independence in news organizations where journalists either were owners or shared an ownership stake. Stan Strachan, publisher and co-owner of *National Thrift News*, a mortgage industry newspaper, was able to produce innovative journalism during the savings and loan crisis in the 1980s and was among the first to uncover the political machinations of developer Charles Keating and his influence with five US senators. Having a journalist as owner shapes the way foundational decisions are made about allocation of resources, such as expanding the number of reporting jobs or spending on longer-form articles. According to Austin Kiplinger, his family's ownership of the publication guided important strategic decisions about their journalism. "I think we want to cover our expenses and make a reasonable amount for our efforts but we're not run by a group of financiers," he said. "Had we been owned by a group of hard-nosed investors, a lot of things we do in this organization we wouldn't do."[9] The company probably would not have had such a generous profit-sharing plan, for example. It's also likely that Kiplinger's personal finance magazine never would have been launched or at least sustained for years afterwards, since the magazine lost millions of dollars in its startup phase from 1947 through 1960. Former managing editor Herbert Brown estimated that the magazine lost "probably six or seven million dollars over a period of 10 or 12 years before it broke even. This does not happen very often. He [Kiplinger] had tremendous patience." Several employees recalled the journalistic independence they enjoyed and how Kiplinger would support them even when they wrote articles critical of powerful businesses. "It did not matter how much hell was raised about an article, if we could persuade him that it was an honest piece of research and writing, no matter who raised hell about it, we would be protected," said Brown.[10]

The Kiplinger tale also points to the professional compromises, commercial imperatives, and personal sacrifices faced by young start-up publications. *The Kiplinger Washington Letter* was not a profitable enterprise at first—subscriptions grew by some 2,100 between 1925 and 1930—so Kiplinger supplemented his earnings and supported the business through various outside sources of income. Some of this came from legitimate journalism, such as freelance writing for the *New York Times,* while other work was ethically more problematic for a journalist, such as lobbying for passage of the McFadden Act in 1927, a major banking bill, or doing private research for Cordell Hull when he was a congressman. Eventually the journalistic start-up became profitable, and Kiplinger was able to drop the lobbying and other controversial sources of outside income.

These commercial trade-offs remain tricky for the current generation of media entrepreneurs. What sort of advertising does a publisher accept to sustain the publication? What agreements, implicit or not, are embedded when a publication sponsors an industry conference and recruits prominent politicians or corporate sources as speakers? Lastly, there is the issue of Kiplinger's personal sacrifice to launch and sustain *The Kiplinger Washington Letter.* His workaholic habits factored into the breakup of two marriages. He rarely took vacations and had few personal hobbies. "He devoted himself to this, his career, to the detriment of a lot of other elements in his life.... [H]e put his work above everything else in his life," Austin Kiplinger said.[11] While we celebrate Kiplinger's journalistic achievements and influence, this raises the inevitable question: At what cost?

Trust

At a time when journalism followed the objectivity norm, Kiplinger produced a style of journalism that reflected his individual voice and outlook. He made no apologies for imbuing his newsletter with opinion. "That violated all the rules of news writing," Kiplinger told the *Washington Evening Star* in 1960. "But I felt a reporter couldn't tell everything if he were restricted to the facts, and I still think so."[12] Kiplinger certainly saw the value of a personal brand as a journalist and cultivated this identity through his freelance journalism, speeches, and voluminous correspondence. "He wasn't afraid to be predictive, analytical and personal," said Al Warren, editor of *Television Digest* and a past president of the Independent Newsletter Association. "Newsletters seem to be the last outpost of personalized journalism. And Kip did it best."[13]

This legacy of personalized and opinionated journalism poses a dilemma for modern journalism, which faces significant distrust problems with the public. A 2020 survey by the Pew Research Center examined trust in thirty news sources and found that none of these news outlets won the trust of more than 50 percent of US adults. It found political polarization so extreme that "Republicans and Democrats place their trust in two nearly inverse news media environments."[14]

Kiplinger was well aware of audience trust issues in the 1930s, and his solution was to demystify his reporting process for the public. He spelled out the newsletter's work process and the qualifications and training of his reporters. He articulated a clear vision to serve his readers, which included critical writing that didn't necessarily fit the preconceived ideas of businesspeople: "Situations reported as they ARE, not as writers WISH THEY WERE."[15] In the 1930s, Kiplinger asked his readers to trust his professional credentials. This is a much tougher sell today, when some portray journalists as liberal villains who fabricate material to smear conservatives. Even before the era of Donald Trump, trust in the news media was declining, and readership of mainstream newspapers was on a multi-decade decline. Think of the challenges facing modern-day policy forecasters in the mold of Kiplinger—like Ezra Klein or Nate Silver—when they ask a politically diverse readership to trust their analysis. That request to "trust me" is even more difficult when a journalist doesn't identify sources or quote anyone by name. As the Pew survey suggests, regaining public trust is a difficult task, yet Kiplinger's approach certainly is an important first step: describing your reporting methods, tackling issues of bias directly, and staying in constant dialog with your readers. In today's environment, Kiplinger would need to rethink the no-source quotation policy in order to promote transparency for readers about the quality of the journalist's sources. Certainly the no-quotation policy is well out of the mainstream at the *Wall Street Journal* or Bloomberg News, which emphasize source transparency to allow readers to judge the quality of the information themselves.

One of Kiplinger's legacies helped shape the format of modern digital journalism: the emphasis on brevity and compact information delivery. While the "sweep line" writing style was not adopted by other publications, the concepts of tightly edited, insightful, and engaging writing can be seen daily in Axios, Politico, and similar specialized news outlets. In this way Kiplinger was a pioneer in a format that is now widely used in mainstream journalism at publications ranging from the *Wall Street Journal* to the *New York Times*. "I think of W. M. Kiplinger as being kind of the Henry Ford of the newsletter field. He didn't invent the device but he perfected it," observed Austin Kiplinger.[16]

Kiplinger's Wealth

Kiplinger's decision to share such a significant amount of wealth with his employees and community serves as a window into his complex personality. By many accounts, he was personally generous. Margaret Rodgers, a longtime Kiplinger office staff member and supervisor, remembered that the newsletter was struggling to meet payroll in the early 1930s. Kiplinger had just received a $1,200 check from *Reader's Digest* for a freelance article, and he gave the check to eight women handling subscriptions and other business duties. "That was the happiest group of girls you ever saw in your life," Rodgers recalled. "I know he needed the money but he gave it to us just the same."[17] On a basic level, Kiplinger's generosity rewarded a staff that worked long hours and sacrificed personal time to make the Kiplinger organization a success. The generosity made him popular among his employees, without a doubt, but it also served to establish him as a paternal presence in their lives.

This provides insight into another aspect of Kiplinger's personality, a hard-edged side seen primarily by senior editors. "Kip didn't want you to get too important when he was around," said John Hazard, a longtime Kiplinger magazine editor and author of an unpublished company history. "He was in my opinion quite an egoist. I think he really thought well of his own abilities and his abilities were great, no question about it."[18]

How are we to understand these two aspects of Kiplinger, the generosity and the need for control? In one respect, these traits are elements of welfare capitalism, a movement in the nineteenth century through the mid-twentieth century. Many employers in this movement would supply generous benefits to employees ranging from recreation to profit sharing and health care. This trend was inspired by progressivism. It served to increase employee loyalty and advance productivity; examples would include Henry Ford's generous pay scale in 1914 and Western Electric's employee benefits in that era "to win the hearts and minds" of workers.[19] The free food, generous benefits, and lavish company parties at Bloomberg News or at tech firms would be modern parallels.

Another perspective for understanding Kiplinger's use of his wealth come from his writings about corporate power and social responsibility. He had fundamentally unconventional ideas about business, and those ideas flowed through the way he ran his company. As he told his readers in 1935: "It is socially too dangerous to allow concentration of economic power in the hands of a few. It is socially safer to have the business structure rest on many small pegs, rather than on a few big piles."[20] He saw the value of organized labor as a counterforce to major corporate power and trade associations as a means to promote social good.

Enforcers Thesis

In this book I have shown how the example of *The Kiplinger Washington Letter* advances and expands the Enforcers Thesis about trade journalism's potential social impact and its ability to influence business conduct. The Enforcers Thesis emerged from my study of trade journalism and the essential role it can play in holding companies accountable for socially desirable conduct. Trade journals tend to center their watchdog reporting on violations of industry norms, such as when bankers take excessive risks or shipbuilders build leaky vessels. By reporting on violations of behavior, these journalists are enforcing standards of ethical conduct in an industry and are thereby helping promote harmony between business and society. It is a type of classic watchdog journalism but one applied to the specifics of trade industry reporting.

The case of *The Kiplinger Washington Letter* during the First New Deal shows the broader promise of trade and specialized journalism to serve society. By urging businesses to transform their conduct and cooperate with the New Deal, Kiplinger was suggesting a significant change in business behavior and the economy at large. In a sense, he was part of a movement that was seeking to rescue capitalism. His solution involved the Hoover ideal of associationalism, whereby businesses voluntarily work with government to become more socially responsible and blunt the sharp edges of free-market capitalism. "I think Kiplinger's attitude at the time was, 'All right, whether we like this or not, this is something we're going to have to live with awhile' and his message to business was 'All right, you've got it, now you'd better make the best of it,'" Bryant said.[21]

This book is perhaps the first attempt to examine how newsletters and trade journalism shape public policy and frame discourse. It shows the vital functionalist role that Kiplinger played as a bridge between the business community and the government. "We try to give our readers the judgment that they can put to use," Austin Kiplinger said.[22] This functionalist role found the sweet spot of a journalistic moment and commercial opportunity in the New Deal; Kiplinger's circulation exploded fivefold from 1929 to 1933. His success was due to a tight relationship with his readers, a personalized voice, and a focus on the unmet information needs of his readers.

One important lesson from the Kiplinger coverage of the New Deal involves how business journalists can emphasize social responsibility as a priority in their coverage. "To him it was very important that businessmen represented their responsibilities on their side and took a broader view of things than just the dollars and cents profit thing," said Herb Brown. "He was very eager to disseminate the philosophy that business concerned everybody and that the public in general should reciprocate by being open and sympathetic to what the free enterprise system could offer."[23]

The genre of specialized reporting also carries significant risks and problems of advancing antidemocratic goals. There are forms of specialized reporting that are the foundations of the modern corporate lobbying infrastructure in Washington, a system fueled by information, in which insider analysis and insight give companies a leg up on how to best engage with government overseers. Bloomberg Government and *Politico Pro* are examples of the "paywall journalism" that helps elites advance corporate power in Washington. These tools ultimately weaken democracy. Kiplinger resisted this trend in several ways, keeping the price of his newsletter affordable and envisioning a middle America business and general readership. "We are conscious that we are not just writing to the 'captains of industry,'" Austin Kiplinger said.[24]

The Insider has focused on Kiplinger's work in the First New Deal, the period that made him nationally famous. There's another significant chapter to the Kiplinger story that I intend to examine in the future: how Kiplinger pioneered personal finance journalism, empowering individual consumers in the rapidly expanding post–World War II economy. He created the first such magazine in 1947, now known as *Kiplinger's Personal Finance* magazine. While Sylvia Porter was the first personal finance journalist, Kiplinger was an important force in this new journalistic genre, helping democratize the financial markets by providing consumers with critical information on how to invest effectively and avoid costly scams. In the process, Kiplinger and his organization found considerable financial success and expanded his offerings in new media through books, films, and, after his death, videos and tax preparation software. This multiplatform content production and distribution strategy offers an example for other media companies seeking to survive in a turbulent media climate.

Kiplinger's vision of providing affordable analysis of business and political events through multiple media platforms increased readers' sense of agency in the democratic process. While popular with businesses, the Kiplinger newsletter sought to engage a broader public to learn about the inner workings of Washington and the business community and help expand the public voice in the business and economic sphere. He wrote to inform broader audiences with his freelance journalism in the *New York Times* and his best-selling book *Washington Is Like That,* which aimed to demystify the intersection of business and politics, a realm previously confined to elites. Everett Dennis, director of the Freedom Forum Media Studies Center, described Kiplinger's journalism in these terms: "It's a connector, a great sense maker. And there's not enough of that around."[25] According to Austin Kiplinger, his father approached Washington journalism from a fundamentally different perspective from that of his peers: "The fact that he was not an economist or a specialist probably was a benefit in his whole career, because he always viewed the subject from the other end of the telescope—the user's end, the businessmen's end, the reader's end.... This made him 'reader-minded,' and he always edited that way. He regarded himself as the reader's representative."[26]

Kiplinger was part of a broader push of business journalism in this era that included the emergence of publications such as *Fortune* and *Business Week,* all of which brought fresh attention to the conduct and social impact of businesses. Rather than just reporting on the New Deal, Kiplinger told businesses how to prepare for regulatory hearings, how to communicate effectively with the new team of bureaucrats, and how to act in a socially responsible manner. "This letter has always kept its eye on the ball—how can you help the subscriber make a decision, get something done, help himself," said Austin Kiplinger. "And I really think that is the essence of democratic society."[27]

Notes

Abbreviations
KA   Kiplinger Personal Papers, Seneca, MD
KWL   *The Kiplinger Washington Letter*
MP   box 28, folder 16, Raymond Moley papers, Hoover Institution Archives, Stanford

Notes on Sources

My research for this book included access to Kiplinger's personal and corporate records, which hold business and personal correspondence, photographs, books, and other media documenting the company and family history since the early 1900s. No academic researchers previously had access to this resource, which includes Kiplinger's correspondence with presidents and senior political and business leaders in the United States and abroad. Knight Kiplinger, grandson of the newsletter's founder and former editor in chief and CEO at Kiplinger, granted extensive interviews and provided access to unpublished manuscripts, including Willard Kiplinger's 228-page unpublished autobiography and a 224-page unpublished company history prepared by longtime Kiplinger magazine editor John Hazard, as well as his grandfather's voluminous scrapbooks (W. M. Kiplinger, "W.M.K. Autobiography. Unpublished"; John Hazard, "Hazard Draft—KWE History—Unpublished," chap. 11). The author reviewed extensive portions of *The Kiplinger Washington Letter*, including a close reading of the New Deal coverage from 1932 through 1936. Other research included the correspondence between Kiplinger and the Roosevelt aide Raymond Moley, obtained from the Hoover Institution at Stanford University; the correspondence with Hoover, obtained from the Hoover Presidential Library and Museum West Branch, Iowa; correspondence with former Republican presidential candidate Alf Landon, obtained from the Kansas Historical Society; publications of the National Association of Manufacturers, obtained from Cornell University; and publications of the American Liberty League, obtained from the University of Kentucky.

Database Searches

The following news databases and collections were searched for a content analysis of New Deal business journalism.

    Search terms for *New York Times* general news coverage of business and Roosevelt's policies

    FDR Employ-Economy 1933
    Searched for: pubid(45545) AND Roosevelt AND economy AND employment AND pd(19330401–19331001)
    Limited by: Date: see below

Databases:
ProQuest Historical Newspapers: *New York Times* with index
Saved: January 01 2020
—Jan. 1–Dec. 31 1933 = 184 results
—Jan. 1–Dec. 31 1934 = 208 results
—Jan. 1–Dec. 31 1935 = 105 results, 69 articles without ads

Search terms for *New York Times* editorials on New Deal and economy

((Roosevelt AND economy AND employment OR jobs) AND nysub.exact ("unemployment" OR "politics and government" OR "budget and appropriations" OR "economic conditions and policies" OR "finances")) NOT (nygeo.exact("germany" OR "great britain" OR "canada" OR "spain") AND nysub.exact("unemployment" OR "politics and government" OR "economic conditions and policies" OR "finances" OR "employment" OR "labor"))
Jan. 1, 1933–Jan. 1, 1937
119 results

Search terms for *New York Times* editorials on the bank holiday

Search terms for *New York Times* editorials on New Deal and economy

(Roosevelt AND banks) Jan. 1, 1933–May 1, 1933
37 results

Search for "Wagner Labor Relations" in New York Times Historical Newspapers, Jan. 1, 1935–Sept. 1, 1935. Author reviewed 26 articles for pro- and anti-Wagner Act emphasis.

—26 articles, 18 were categorized.

Business Week was reviewed from 1932 to 1936 and relevant New Deal articles were scanned.

Fortune was reviewed from 1932 to 1936 and relevant New Deal articles were scanned.

Editorials from *Saturday Evening Post* and writings of Garet Garrett were reviewed from 1932 to 1936 and relevant New Deal articles were scanned.

The Library of Congress online database of Historic American Newspapers, Chronicling America, was searched using terms "Kiplinger" and "Willard M. Kiplinger," 1922–1940. Searches were conducted in June and July 2021. Articles in *The Daily Worker, Montana Labor News, Producers News,* and the *Evening Star* (Washington, DC) were reviewed. The *Daily Worker* and other radical papers quoted the *Kiplinger Washington Letter* in twenty-six separate issues from 1931 through 1940 (https://chroniclingamerica.loc.gov/lccn/sn84020097/1933-03-01/ed-1/).

Much of this material, along with issues of *The Kiplinger Washington Letter,* was loaded into the MaxQDA content analysis software, where articles were coded for business, labor, and political narratives. Metadata from the *New York Times* article was analyzed in Excel spreadsheets. This allowed the author to discern narrative trends in the news coverage over time and construct simple data visualizations using Tableau and Flourish software.

Introduction

1. W. M. Kiplinger, "W.M.K. Autobiography, Unpublished," Washington, DC, 1960, chap. 12, 154, KA.
2. Raymond Moley, "A Journalist's Journalist," *Ohio News*, August 21, 1967.
3. "Brains Trust," plural, is how Moley and other Roosevelt aides referred to the group; newspaper writers referred to it in the singular, "Brain Trust."
4. Rexford Guy Tugwell quoted in Raymond Moley, *The First New Deal* (New York: Harcourt Brace & World, 1966), 238.
5. Raymond Moley, *After Seven Years* (New York: Harper & Brothers, 1939), 147.
6. Moley, "A Journalist's Journalist."
7. Kiplinger named Woodrow Wilson as a significant political influence. Former *Kiplinger* editor Herbert Brown described him as a "Wilsonian Democrat." W. M. Kiplinger to Bonnie Kiplinger, July 22, 1960, KA; Herbert L. Brown, "Company History—Herbert L. Brown," October 14, 1976, KA.
8. John Hazard, "Hazard Draft—KWE History—Unpublished," May 1978, chap. 11, Kiplinger Personal Papers, Seneca, MD.
9. W. E. Wietzel to the Kiplinger Washington Agency, January 7, 1935, KA.
10. Moley, "A Journalist's Journalist."
11. Milton Friedman and Anna Schwartz, *Monetary History of the United States, 1867–1960* (Princeton: Princeton University Press, 1963), 299.
12. Peter Temin, "The Great Depression," *National Bureau of Economic Research Historical Working Paper* 45, no. 62 (1994): 1:49. , http://www.nber.org/papers/h0062.pdf; "National Bureau of Economic Research, Unemployment Rate for United States," Federal Reserve Bank of St. Louis, *FRED* (blog), https://fred.stlouisfed.org/series/M0892AUSM156SNBR.
13. David E. Hamilton, "Herbert Hoover: Domestic Affairs," Miller Center, UVA blog, https://millercenter.org/president/hoover/domestic-affairs.
14. Temin, "The Great Depression," 3.
15. Hazard, "Hazard Draft," chap. 11.
16. "It Started with Kip," *Newsweek*, August 21, 1967, 63.
17. "Industrial Control Postscript," *KWL*, August 5, 1933.
18. Kathy Roberts Forde and Sid Bedingfield, eds., *Journalism and Jim Crow: White Supremacy and the Black Struggle for a New America* (Champaign: University of Illinois Press, 2021); Sid Bedingfield, *Newspaper Wars: Civil Rights and White Resistance in South Carolina, 1935–1965* (Champaign: University of Illinois Press, 2017); Kathy Roberts Forde, "An Editor and His Newspaper Helped Build White Supremacy in Georgia," *The Conversation*, February 19, 2019, https://theconversation.com/an-editor-and-his-newspaper-helped-build-white-supremacy-in-georgia-111030.
19. Kiplinger to Raymond Moley, October 6, 1934, MP.
20. Kiplinger to Raymond Moley," September 18, 1934, MP.
21. Kiplinger, "W.M.K. Autobiography, Unpublished," chap. 4, 36, 54.
22. "Industrial Control Postscript," *KWL*, August 19, 1933.
23. Kiplinger to Raymond Moley, January 6, 1934, MP.
24. Alan Betten, book review, "The Brandeis/Frankfurter Connection: The Secret Political Activities of Two Supreme Court Justices," *University of Baltimore Law Review* 12, no. 2 (1983): 386–96.

25. Kiplinger to Raymond Moley, November 5, 1935, KA.
26. Kiplinger to Raymond Moley, January 6, 1934.
27. Kiplinger to Raymond Moley, August 3, 1934, MP.
28. *KWL*, May 20, 1933.
29. *KWL*, April 1, 1933.
30. Arthur M. Schlesinger Jr., *The Age of Roosevelt: The Coming of the New Deal*, 7th ed. (Boston: Houghton Mifflin Company, 1958), 91.
31. Ellis W. Hawley, *The New Deal and the Problem of Monopoly* (Princeton: Princeton University Press, 1966), 7.
32. Hawley, *The New Deal*, 14.
33. Schlesinger, *The Age of Roosevelt*, 22.
34. Angus Burgin, *The Great Persuasion: Reinventing Free Markets since the Great Depression* (Cambridge: Harvard University Press, 2012), 4.
35. Nancy Cohen, *The Reconstruction of American Liberalism, 1865–1914* (Chapel Hill: University of North Carolina Press, 2002).
36. "Kiplinger Washington Letter," *KWL*, May 20, 1933.
37. "Kiplinger Washington Letter," *KWL*, May 5, 1933.
38. "Industrial Control Postscript," *KWL*, June 22, 1935.
39. *KWL*, August 19, 1933.
40. "Industrial Control Postscript," *KWL*, December 2, 1933.
41. "Industrial Control Postscript," *KWL*, October 12, 1935.
42. "Industrial Control Postscript," October 12, 1935.
43. "Chamber for Change," *Business Week*, May 17, 1933, 3.
44. W. M. Kiplinger, "Why Business Men Fear Washington," *Scribner's*, October 1934, 207.
45. *KWL*, May 20, 1933.
46. Howard Penn Hudson, *Publishing Newsletters*, 3rd ed. (Rhinebeck, NY: H&M Publishers, 1997), 1.
47. For example, see Kevin Reilly, "Dilettantes at the Gate: *Fortune* Magazine and the Cultural Politics of Business Journalism in the 1930s," *Business and Economic History* 2 (December 1, 1999): 213–22.
48. "Industrial Control Postscript," *KWL*, July 1, 1933.
49. "Industrial Control Postscript," *KWL*, August 5, 1933.
50. Alfred D. Chandler Jr., "The Beginnings of 'Big Business' in American Industry," *Business History Review* 33, no. 1 (April 1, 1959): 27.
51. Alfred D. Chandler Jr., *The Visible Hand: The Managerial Revolution in American Business* (Cambridge: Belknap Press, 1977).
52. *KWL*, December 30, 1933.
53. Ellis W. Hawley, "Herbert Hoover, the Commerce Secretariat, and the Vision of an 'Associative State,' 1921–1928," *Journal of American History* 61, no. 1 (June 1974): 116–40; Alan Dawley, *Struggles for Justice: Social Responsibility and the Liberal State* (Cambridge: Belknap Press of Harvard University Press, 1991), 319; Louis Galambos and Joseph Pratt, *The Rise of the Corporate Commonwealth* (New York: Basic Books, 1988).
54. *KWL*, February 18, 1933.
55. *KWL*, April 29, 1933.
56. Kiplinger, "W.M.K. Autobiography. Unpublished," chap. 3, 18–24.

Notes to Pages 20–24

57. *KWL*, December 23, 1933.
58. Hazard, "Hazard Draft," chap. 13, 7.
59. Hazard, "Hazard Draft," chap. 13, 7.
60. *KWL*, September 19, 1936.
61. Austin Kiplinger and Knight Kiplinger, "70 Years of Looking Ahead," 1993, xvi.
62. "KWL Circulation, 1925–1976," circa 1977, KA.
63. Michael Schudson, *Discovering the News: A Social History of Newspapers* (New York: Basic Books, 1978), 148.
64. Kathy Roberts Forde, "Discovering the Explanatory Report in American Newspapers," *Journalism Practice* 1, no. 2 (2007): 227–44.
65. W. M. Kiplinger, "Interpret the News," *Journalism Quarterly* 13, no. 3 (1936): 289–94; W. M. Kiplinger, "The Political Role of Labor," *Annals of the American Academy of Political and Social Science* 184 (1936): 124–29.
66. Yates Cook, "Company History—Yates Cook," May 24, 1977, KA.
67. Cohen, *Reconstruction of American Liberalism*, 13.
68. Paul Starr, *The Creation of the Media: Political Origins of Modern Communications* (New York: Basic Books, 2004), 401.
69. Earl Browder, "Report by Comrade Earl Browder for the Central Committee to the 8th National Convention, Communist Party, U. S. A," *Daily Worker*, April 14, 1934.
70. Wayne Parsons, *The Power of the Financial Press* (New Brunswick: Rutgers University Press, 1990), 48.
71. Knight Kiplinger, telephone interview with the author, May 29, 2020. Overall, the employment drop was more severe than the revenue drop when one looks at the parent company and not just the publishing operations between these two time periods. The Kiplinger Washington Editors, Inc., the parent company of the publishing concern, employed 109 people in 2017. In 2018 it reported annual revenues of $33.1 million, down from $90 million in revenue and 836 employees in 1986. (Standard & Poor's reported the company's 2017 revenue as $23 million, which the company disputes.) The steep employment and revenue drop from 1986 was due to two back-office subsidiaries that were later sold. Knight Kiplinger to Rob Wells, October 5, 2021, which includes internal accounting documents. The 1986 data are from Sandra Sugawara, "Kiplinger's Formula Stays in Place Despite Changing Times," *Los Angeles Times*, June 22, 1987. See also "The Kiplinger Washington Editors Inc Private Company Profile," Standard & Poor's NetAdvantage, 2019, https://www-capitaliq-com.eu1.proxy.openathens.net/CIQDotNet/company.aspx?companyId=7755419.
72. Cory Schouten, "(News) Letter Perfect," *Quill*, Spring 2020.
73. Sarah Perez, "TheSkimm Closes Its $12M Series C with Big Names Shonda Rhimes and Tyra Banks on Board," *Tech Crunch* (blog), May 21, 2018, https://techcrunch.com/2018/05/21/theskimm-closes-its-12m-series-c-with-big-names-shonda-rhimes-and-tyra-banks-on-board/.
74. Matt Kinsman, "Revenue Up 5.4% for B2B Media & Information Industry in 2017," *SIIA* (blog), August 30, 2018, https://www.siia.net/blog/index/Post/76816/Revenue-Up-5-4-for-B2B-Media-Information-Industry-in-2017.
75. For combined annual 2017 revenue for Fox News, CNN, MSNBC, CNBC, Fox Business, and Bloomberg of $6.29 billion, see Pew Research Center Journalism & Media, "Cable News Fact Sheet," June 25, 2019, https://www.journalism.org/fact-sheet/cable-news/. For ad spending for morning and evening network news of $1.64

billion, see Pew Research Center Journalism & Media, "Network News Fact Sheet," June 25, 2019, https://www.journalism.org/fact-sheet/network-news/.
76. "About Kiplinger," *Kiplinger* (blog), July 22, 2021, https://www.kiplinger.com/about-us#:~:text=With%20a%20paid%20circulation%2C%20in,forecasting%20periodical%20in%20the%20world.
77. "The TJFR Group/MasterCard International Business News Luminaries of the Century," *TJFR Business News Reporter*, 2000.
78. Kiplinger Programs, "Who We Are, W. M. Kiplinger, Program Founder," http://www.kiplingerprogram.org/kiplinger/about_us.html.
79. "It Started with Kip," 63.
80. Quoted in "Who We Are, W. M. Kiplinger, Program Founder."
81. *KWL*, December 23, 1933.
82. Kiplinger, "W.M.K. Autobiography. Unpublished," chap. 1, 2.
83. Kiplinger, "To Each Member of the Kiplinger Organization," December 1, 1948, KA.
84. The *Kiplinger* Washington Editors, "Dear Kip," January 8, 1966, KA.
85. George Kennedy, "Company History—George Kennedy," July 12, 1976, KA; Oeveste Granducci, "Company History—Oeveste Granducci," October 13, 1977, KA.
86. Austin Kiplinger, "Company History Interview—Austin Kiplinger," April 21, 1977, KA.
87. "The Kiplinger Washington Letter Can Help You," circa late 1940s, KA.
88. "Kip Dies—An Assessment—A Tribute," *The Newsletter on Newsletters*, August 1967.
89. Austin Kiplinger, "To: All Members" (Kiplinger obituary), August 9, 1967, retrieved from https://www.harvardsquarelibrary.org/biographies/w-m-kiplinger/.
90. Rob Wells, *The Enforcers: How Little-Known Trade Reporters Exposed the Keating Five and Advanced Business Journalism* (Champaign: University of Illinois Press, 2019), 45–59.

Chapter 1: "Pound My Beat and My Typewriter"

1. W. M. Kiplinger, "W.M.K. Autobiography, Unpublished," Washington, DC, 1960, chap. 3, unnumbered page, KA.
2. The fact that meat was served regularly for dinner was a marker of wealth. "A neighbor boy eating supper at our house boasted that his family had meat sometimes, too." Kiplinger, "W.M.K. Autobiography," chaps. 1, 7, and 1a, 1.
3. Austin Kiplinger, "Company History Interview—Austin Kiplinger," April 21, 1977, KA.
4. Knight Kiplinger, telephone interview with the author, July 12, 2019.
5. Austin Kiplinger, "Company History Interview."
6. World War I Draft Registration Cards, 1917–1918, National Archives and Records Administration, June 5, 1917, District of Columbia no. 10, image 2805 of 5802.
7. George Bryant, "Company History—George Bryant," October 4, 1976, KA.
8. Knight Kiplinger, telephone interview with the author.
9. "W. M. Kiplinger Is Dead at 76," *New York Times*, August 7, 1967; Kiplinger Programs, "Who We Are, W. M. Kiplinger, Program Founder," http://www.kiplingerprogram.org/kiplinger/about_us.html.
10. John Hazard, "Hazard Draft—KWE History—Unpublished," Washington, DC, May 1978.

11. "Who We Are"; Hazard, "Hazard Draft."
12. "W. M. Kiplinger Is Dead at 76."
13. Austin Kiplinger and Knight Kiplinger, "70 Years of Looking Ahead," 1993, x, xi.
14. "W. M. Kiplinger Is Dead at 76."
15. W. M. Kiplinger, "Speech Given by W.M. Kiplinger, Sigma Delta Chi Dinner," National Press Club, Washington, DC, June 17, 1966.
16. Kenneth Crawford, "Want to Tell You about Kiplinger," *Saturday Evening Post*, January 25, 1947, 25, 65–69.
17. "In Memoriam: Willard M. Kiplinger," *Ohio State Lantern*, August 10, 1967.
18. Austin Kiplinger, "Company History Interview."
19. Clarence Gale Kiplinger, "Company History—Clarence Gale Kiplinger," July 29, 1976, KA.
20. Margaret Rodgers, "Company History—Margaret Rodgers," July 10, 1976, KA.
21. Austin Kiplinger, "Company History Interview."
22. Knight Kiplinger, telephone interview.
23. George Kennedy, "Company History—George Kennedy," July 12, 1976, KA.
24. Oeveste Granducci, "Company History—Oeveste Granducci," October 13, 1977, KA.
25. Kennedy, "Company History."
26. Bryant, "Company History."
27. Robert Marshall, "Company History—Robert Marshall," July 21, 1977, KA.
28. John Hazard, "Company History—Sally Almquist," circa 1977, KA.
29. Granducci, "Company History."
30. Kennedy, "Company History."
31. Austin Kiplinger, "Notes for JWH Interview," April 18, 1977, Kiplinger Personal Papers, Seneca, MD.
32. Knight Kiplinger, "The Kiplinger Way: Sharing the Wealth with Employees and Community," July 6, 2021, 25.
33. Austin Kiplinger, "Company History Interview."
34. Bob Levey, "Austin H. Kiplinger, D.C. Publisher and Philanthropist, Dies at 97," *Washington Post*, November 21, 2015.
35. Austin Kiplinger, "Company History Interview."
36. Kiplinger to Bonnie Kiplinger, July 22, 1960.
37. Austin Kiplinger, "Company History Interview," 32.
38. Knight Kiplinger, telephone interview.
39. Austin Kiplinger, "Notes for JWH Interview," April 18, 1977.
40. Austin Kiplinger, ed., *Every Monday Morning for Sixty Years: The Past Sixty Years as Reporter in the Kiplinger Washington Letters* (Washington, DC: The Kiplinger Washington Editors, 1983), 4.
41. Kiplinger, "W.M.K. Autobiography," 69.
42. Knight Kiplinger, "The Kiplinger Way," 44.
43. "KWL Milestones," 1963[?], KA.
44. "W. M. Kiplinger Is Dead at 76; Created Capital News Letter," *New York Times*, August 7, 1967.
45. "Pricing for a POLITICO Pro subscription starts in the high-four figure range, but depends on a range of factors like the plan selected (Plus or Premium), users and subscription credits." "Politico Pro Plans," *Politico Pro*, July 30, 2021, https://www.politicopro.com/plans.

46. Joel Whitaker, telephone interview with the author, February 14, 2020.
47. Knight Kiplinger, "The Kiplinger Way," 40.
48. Austin Kiplinger, "Company History Interview."
49. Knight Kiplinger, "The Kiplinger Way," 15.
50. Kiplinger, "W.M.K. Autobiography," chap. 4, 36.
51. Mary M. Cronin, "Pronouncements and Denunciations: An Analysis of State Press Association Ethics Codes from the 1920s," *Journalism & Mass Communication Quarterly* 72, no. 4 (1995): 893.
52. Kiplinger, "W.M.K. Autobiography," chap. 7, 69.
53. Kiplinger, "W.M.K. Autobiography," chap. 6, 54, 57a.
54. Kiplinger to Thomas Corcoran, June 15, 1934, MP.
55. Kiplinger to Raymond Moley, June 19, 1934, MP.
56. Austin Kiplinger, "Company History Interview."
57. Bryant, "Company History."
58. Lew Garrison Coit, "Company History—Lew Garrison Coit," circa 1977, KA.
59. Austin Kiplinger, "Company History Interview."
60. Coit, "Company History."
61. Bryant, "Company History."
62. Austin Kiplinger, *Every Monday Morning for Sixty Years*, 8.
63. "It Started with Kip," *Newsweek*, August 21, 1967, 63.
64. Frank Luther Mott, *American Journalism—A History: 1690–1960*, 3rd ed. (New York: Macmillan, 1966), 675.
65. Arthur M. Schlesinger Jr., *The Age of Roosevelt: The Coming of the New Deal*, 7th ed. (Boston: Houghton Mifflin, 1958), 87.
66. Robert R. Nathan, "Estimates of Unemployment in the United States, 1929–1935," *International Labour Review* 33, no. 1 (January 1936): 49.
67. Peter Temin, "The Great Depression," *National Bureau of Economic Research Historical Working Paper* 45, no. 62 (1994): 1–49.
68. Peter Temin and Barry Eichengreen, "The Gold Standard and the Great Depression," *Contemporary European History* 9, no. 2 (July 2000): 195.
69. Milton Friedman, *Capitalism and Freedom* (Chicago: University of Chicago Press, 1962); 50; Temin and Eichengreen, "The Gold Standard and the Great Depression," 195.
70. Howard Carswell, "Business News Coverage," *Public Opinion Quarterly* 2, no. 4 (1938): 616.
71. John Kenneth Galbraith, *The Great Crash, 1929* (Boston: Houghton Mifflin, 1972), 74.
72. Charles Merz, "Recovery Tide Swinging Strongly Upward," *New York Times*, November 3, 1935.
73. "Chronological Survey of the Outstanding Financial Events of the Past Year," *New York Times*, January 2, 1934.
74. "Bryan! Bryan!! Bryan!!! Bryan!!!!" *Fortune*, January 1934. A 1965 research article reached similar conclusions about the limited political impact of the farm strikes and the Farmers' Holiday Association. John L. Shover, "The Farmers' Holiday Association Strike, August 1932," *Agricultural History* 39, no. 4 (1965): 196–203.
75. John Quirt, *The Press and the World of Money: How the News Media Cover Business and Finance, Panic and Prosperity, and the Pursuit of the American Dream* (Byron, CA: Anton/California-Courier, 1993), 62.

Notes to Pages 46–51

76. Kevin S. Reilly, "Dilettantes at the Gate: *Fortune* Magazine and the Cultural Politics of Business Journalism in the 1930s," *Business and Economic History* 2 (December 1, 1999): 213–22.
77. James L. Aucoin, *The Evolution of American Investigative Journalism* (Columbia: University of Missouri Press, 2005), 37.
78. Herbert Hoover, *The Memoirs of Herbert Hoover: The Great Depression, 1929–1941* (New York: Macmillan, 1952), 17, 19.
79. Galbraith, *The Great Crash*, 80.
80. Galbraith, *The Great Crash*, 72.
81. Quirt, *The Press and the World of Money*, 34, 35.
82. John Hazard. "Hazard Draft," chap. 8, 2.
83. Austin Kiplinger, *Every Monday Morning for Sixty Years*, 4.
84. Kiplinger, "W.M.K. Autobiography," chap. 9, 91.
85. Hazard. "Hazard Draft," chap. 8, 3.
86. Galbraith, *The Great Crash*, 76.
87. Galbraith, *The Great Crash*, 73.
88. Quirt, *The Press and the World of Money*, 46; see also Galbraith, *The Great Crash*, 73.
89. US Senate, Committee on Banking and Currency, *Stock Exchange Practices: Hearings before the Committee on Banking and Currency, U.S. Senate*, Washington, DC, June 1932, 603–4.
90. Maury Klein, *Rainbow's End : The Crash of 1929* (New York: Oxford University Press, 2001), 151.
91. Quirt, *The Press and the World of Money*, 39.
92. Galbraith, *The Great Crash*, 73.
93. Quirt, *The Press and the World of Money*, 40.
94. Raymond Moley to Kiplinger, October 27, 1934, MP.
95. *The Kiplinger Washington Letter*'s 1932 circulation of seven thousand grew to thirty thousand by 1940. Hazard, "Hazard Draft," chap. 11; Ferdinand Lundberg, "News-Letters: A Revolution in Journalism," *Harper's Magazine*, 1940, 464–73.
96. Letter to Kiplinger from Shawmut National Bank President Walter Bucklin, November 12, 1936, KA.
97. Search of Library of Congress online database of Historic American Newspapers, Chronicling America, using search terms "Kiplinger" and "Willard M. Kiplinger," 1922–1940, https://chroniclingamerica.loc.gov/..
98. "'Confidential' News Agency Says All Talk of Wage Cuts," *Daily Worker*, April 30, 1931.
99. Howard Penn Hudson, *Publishing Newsletters*, 3rd ed. (Rhinebeck, NY: H&M Publishers, 1997), 2.
100. "The TJFR Group/MasterCard International Business News Luminaries of the Century," *TJFR Business News Reporter* (2000), 42.
101. A 1940 *Harper's* article about the newsletter industry mentioned other notable publications such as *Congressional Intelligence, Manufacturers News Letter,* the *Labor Letter* produced by Chester Wright, a newsletter produced by the Babson financial service, a newsletter produced by David Lawrence, *Week by Week* by Frankling Roudybush, the *Weekly Foreign Letter* by investment banker Lawrence Dennis, and *The Insider* by Johannes Steel and Charles Hedges. Lundberg, "News-Letters," 466.
102. *Tomorrow* was published as early as March 20, 1942.

103. "New Concept in Journalism Graduate Education," *Ohio State University Monthly* (April 1966), 21.
104. Knight Kiplinger, "The Kiplinger Way," 23.
105. Austin Kiplinger, "Notes for JWH Interview."
106. Yates Cook, "Company History—Yates Cook," May 24, 1977, KA.
107. Raymond Moley, *The First New Deal* (New York: Harcourt Brace & World, 1966), 293.
108. *KWL*, August 26, 1933.
109. *KWL*, August 5, 1933.
110. *KWL*, July 29, 1933.
111. "Industrial Control Postscript," *KWL*, September 2, 1933.
112. See Schlesinger, *The Age of Roosevelt*, 152: "When life became too much for him, as it did increasingly, he [Johnson] took to drink. Sometimes he disappeared for a day or two to return sheepishly with bloodshot eyes behind heavy lids, his face splotched and his hair plastered down, while [Johnson's secretary] Frances Robinson, to the irritation of the staff, tried to run NRA in his absence."
113. Paul Mallon, "What's What Behind News in Capital," *Washington Star*, October 19, 1933.
114. "Legitimate Criticism," *Today*, December 16, 1933. Moley sent an advance copy of the editorial to Kiplinger.
115. W. M. Kiplinger, "Statement by W. M. Kiplinger, Washington Business Writer," October 16, 1933, KA.
116. Kiplinger, "W.M.K. Autobiography," chap. 12, 166, 167.
117. "Industrial Control Postscript," *KWL*, October 14, 1933.
118. *KWL*, December 2, 1933.
119. "General of Industry," *Business Week*, May 31, 1933, 6.
120. "Turning the Tables," *Business Week*, July 7, 1934, 24.
121. Kiplinger to Raymond Moley, August 3, 1934, MP.
122. Kiplinger, "W.M.K. Autobiography," chap. 14, 196.
123. Crawford, "Want to Tell You about Kiplinger," .
124. Knight Kiplinger, "The Kiplinger Way"; "US Inflation Calculator," 2021, https://www.usinflationcalculator.com/.
125. "Current Population Reports, Consumer Income," Bureau of Census, US Department of Commerce, January 28, 1948, https://www2.census.gov/prod2/popscan/p60-001.pdf.
126. Knight Kiplinger, "The Kiplinger Way," citing figures from Willard Kiplinger's 1967 estate tax form and LaVerne Kiplinger's 1999 estate tax form.
127. Knight Kiplinger, "The Kiplinger Way," 36, 35.
128. Kiplinger Foundation, Inc., Form 990 Tax Return, 2018, Internal Revenue Service, April 26, 2019, https://projects.propublica.org/nonprofits/display_990/520792570/06_2019_prefixes_51-56%2F520792570_201812_990PF_2019060316371319.
129. Kiplinger Foundation, Inc., Form 990 Tax Return, 2017, Internal Revenue Service, September 25, 2018, 14, https://pdf.guidestar.org/PDF_Images/2017/520/792/2017-520792570-0fc770ec-F.pdf.
130. "Collection by Suggestion—and a Little (Very Little) Persuasion," *Financial Executive*, October 1991.
131. Norman Rockwell and Mary Rockwell to Kiplinger, August 30, 1954, KA.
132. Knight Kiplinger, "The Kiplinger Way," 31.

Notes to Pages 58–62

133. Knight Kiplinger to Rob Wells, October 5, 2021.
134. Knight Kiplinger, telephone interview.
135. Knight Kiplinger, "The Kiplinger Way," 40.
136. Knight Kiplinger, "The Kiplinger Way," 45, 50.
137. Knight Kiplinger, telephone interview.
138. W. M. Kiplinger, "To Each Member of the Kiplinger Organization," December 1, 1948, KA.
139. Knight Kiplinger, "The Kiplinger Way"; Sandra Sugawara, "Kiplinger's Formula Stays in Place Despite Changing Times," *Washington Post*, June 22, 1987.
140. W. M. Kiplinger, "Memorandum to Employees on Our New Profit-Sharing Plan," December 30, 1952, KA (details about historical returns were noted in the margins by Knight Kiplinger, May 2021); "Employee Costs Fact Sheets, 1969, 1971, 1975," Kiplinger Washington Editors, Inc., undated, KA.
141. Austin Kiplinger, holiday bonus letter, December 1968, KA.
142. W. M. Kiplinger, LaVerne Kiplinger holiday bonus letter, December 1954, KA. Similar bonus letters were sent to every employee, according to Knight Kiplinger. Her total compensation of $12,317 is worth $122,279 in 2021 dollars.
143. Knight Kiplinger, "The Kiplinger Way," 15, 16.
144. Knight Kiplinger, telephone interview; Linden Dalecki, "Kiplinger Washington Editors' Bay Tree Lodge: An Old Florida Dream," *Journal of Florida Studies* 1, no. 8 (2019): 5.
145. Plan Sponsor Council of America, "PSCA Releases 34th Annual Survey," *Employee Benefit Plan Review*, December 1991. A 2006 survey showed that profit-sharing contributions ranged from 8.1 percent of payroll in 2001 to 9.4 percent in 2005, according to the Profit-Sharing/401(k) Council of America. See "Profit-Sharing Plans Tend to Offer the Most Generous Company Contributions," *Pension Benefits*, January 2007.
146. According to Knight Kiplinger in a telephone interview, with the addition of year-end and deferred payments, distributions often exceeded 25 percent of salary.
147. Knight Kiplinger, telephone interview; Knight Kiplinger, "The Kiplinger Way," 13, 15.
148. Kiplinger, to Members of the Kiplinger Employees' Profit Sharing Plan, March 17, 1955, KA.
149. Austin Kiplinger, "Report to Members of the Kiplinger Employees Profit Sharing Plan," March 17, 1961, KA.
150. "The Kiplinger Employees' Pension Plan Form 5500, 2016," Employee Benefits Security Administration, October 12, 2017, https://s3.amazonaws.com/filings5500/2010/11/12/C51ABBB76E4592206D920FF226D5152B08797E1A.zip; "The Kiplinger Employees' Pension Plan Financial Statements and Supplementary Information," December 31, 2016, and 2015," Employee Benefits Security Administration, October 9, 2017, 4.
151. "The Kiplinger 401(k) Savings Plan Form 5500, 2019," Employee Benefits Security Administration, October 2, 2020, https://s3.amazonaws.com/filings5500/2020/10/02/2833F4EBEB81CC03EF241117D15ACF9DAD3F2096.zip.
152. Kiplinger, "W.M.K. Autobiography," chap. 4, 38.
153. Austin Kiplinger, "Company History Interview."
154. Clifford Christians, "Community Epistemology and Mass Media Ethics," *Journalism History* 5, no. 2 (1978): 38.

155. Sally S. Almquist, letter to the editor, "W. M. Kiplinger," *Washington Post*, August 19, 1967.
156. James O'Connor, "American Welfare Capitalism, 1880–1940: Stuart D. Brandes," *American Journal of Sociology* 82, no. 5 (March 1, 1977): 1107–9.
157. W. M. Kiplinger "What's Behind Profit Sharing," April 26, 1966, KA.
158. "Dennis Acquires Kiplinger," *Business Wire*, February 28, 2019.
159. Knight Kiplinger to Rob Wells, October 5, 2021; Dalecki, "Kiplinger Washington Editors' Bay Tree Lodge."
160. Dalecki, "Kiplinger Washington Editors' Bay Tree Lodge," 7.
161. According to Kiplinger's brother Clarence, "Willard was flush [with money] but a lot of times he was broke or darn nearly so. . . . He gave it away too easily." Clarence Gale Kiplinger, "Company History—Clarence Gale Kiplinger," July 29, 1976, KA. John Hazard remarked, on Kiplinger's purchase of three streetcars, "Things would catch his fancy." Irv Brooke, "Company History—Irv Brooke," July 21, 1976, KA.
162. Rodgers, "Company History."
163. Hazard, "Company History—Sally Almquist."
164. Clarence Kiplinger, "Company History—Clarence Gale Kiplinger."
165. Coit, "Company History."
166. Knight Kiplinger, "The Kiplinger Way," 29.
167. Hazard, "Company History—Clarence Gale Kiplinger."
168. Knight Kiplinger, "The Kiplinger Way."
169. Irv Brooke, "Company History—Irv Brooke," July 21, 1976, KA.
170. Bryant, "Company History," 8.
171. Brooke, "Company History."

Chapter 2: A Bridge between Wall Street and Washington

1. Dow-Jones Industrial Stock Price Index for United States, FRED Economic Data, St. Louis Federal Reserve Bank (accessed December 20, 2020), https://fred.stlouisfed.org/graph/?g=yX7g.
2. Thomas F. Schwartz, "Parodies of the New Deal," National Archives, *Hoover Heads* (blog), August 21, 2019, https://hoover.blogs.archives.gov/2019/08/21/parodies-of-the-new-deal/.
3. David E. Hamilton, "Herbert Hoover: Domestic Affairs," Miller Center, University of Virginia, US Presidents, October 4, 2016, https://millercenter.org/president/hoover/domestic-affairs; Donald A. Ritchie, *Reporting from Washington: The History of the Washington Press Corps* (New York: Oxford University Press, 2005), 3.
4. Kiplinger to Herbert Hoover, February 27, 1933.
5. Herbert Hoover to Kiplinger, February 28, 1933, KA.
6. *KWL*, March 4, 1933.
7. Ritchie, *Reporting from Washington*, 5.
8. Franklin D. Roosevelt to Kiplinger, November 6, 1931.
9. Kiplinger to Raymond Moley, August 5, 1959, Raymond Moley file, KA.
10. Louis Galambos and Joseph Pratt, *The Rise of the Corporate Commonwealth* (New York: Basic Books, 1988), 93.
11. Joan Hoff Wilson, *Herbert Hoover, Forgotten Progressive* (Boston: Little, Brown & Co., 1975), 6.

Notes to Pages 68–73

12. John Hazard, "Hazard Draft—KWE History—Unpublished," Washington, DC, May 1978, chap. 9.
13. Some journalists had hailed Hoover as a "superman." Ritchie, *Reporting from Washington*, 2. Even Drew Pearson and Robert Sharon Allen's scathing critique of the Hoover presidency begins with a celebration of his relief work during World War I and his reign as commerce secretary. Robert Sharon Allen and Drew Pearson, *Washington Merry-Go-Round* (New York: Horace Liveright, 1931).
14. Ellis W. Hawley, "Herbert Hoover, the Commerce Secretariat, and the Vision of an 'Associative State,' 1921–1928," *Journal of American History* 61, no. 1 (June 1974): 117, 138.
15. Galambos and Pratt, *Corporate Commonwealth*, 97.
16. Laura Phillips Sawyer, "Trade Associations, State Building, and the Sherman Act: The U.S. Chamber of Commerce, 1912–25," in *Capital Gains: Business and Politics in Twentieth-Century America*, ed. Richard R. John and Kim Phillips-Fein (Philadelphia: University of Pennsylvania Press, 2017), 33.
17. Alexis de Tocqueville, *Democracy in America*, trans. Gerald Bevan (London: Penguin Books, 2003), 597.
18. Richard John, "Introduction: Adversarial Relations? Business and Politics in Twentieth-Century America," in John and Phillips-Fein, *Capital Gains*, 15. See also Kerman Krooss and Charles Gilbert, *American Business History* (Englewood Cliffs, NJ: Prentice-Hall, 1972), 256, stating that trade associations "intentionally or unintentionally were designed to circumvent the Sherman Act by restricting competition." Also, Sawyer writes that during and after World War I, trade associations such as the US Chamber of Commerce "became an embedded intermediary capable of coordinating business practices and regulatory prerogatives." Sawyer, "Trade Associations," 42.
19. James Weinstein, *The Corporate Ideal in the Liberal State, 1900–1918*, (Boston: Beacon Press, 1968), xv.
20. Alan Dawley, *Struggles for Justice: Social Responsibility and the Liberal State* (Cambridge: Belknap Press of Harvard University Press, 1991), 319.
21. Hawley, "Herbert Hoover, the Commerce Secretariat," 139.
22. Frank Freidel and Hugh Sidey, "Herbert Hoover," *The Presidents of the United States of America* (blog), 2006, https://www.whitehouse.gov/about-the-white-house/presidents/herbert-hoover/; French Strother, "Four Years of Hoover: An Interpretation," *New York Times*, February 26, 1933.
23. Fred Siebert viewed economic functionalism as a key role of the press. Fred Siebert, *Four Theories of the Press: The Authoritarian, Libertarian, Social Responsibility, and Soviet Communist Concepts of What the Press Should Be and Do* (Champaign: University of Illinois Press, 1956).
24. *KWL*, July 8, 1933.
25. *KWL*, September 2, 1933.
26. George Bryant, "Company History—George Bryant," October 4, 1976, KA.
27. "DuPont," *Fortune*, November 1934.
28. Kevin S. Reilly, "Dilettantes at the Gate: *Fortune* Magazine and the Cultural Politics of Business Journalism in the 1930s," *Business and Economic History* 2 (December 1, 1999): 213–22.
29. *KWL*, July 1, 1933.
30. "Lessons of Leadership," *Nation's Business*, August 1966.

31. "Lessons of Leadership." A review of correspondence between Kiplinger and Hoover shows a significant uptick after Hoover left office in 1933.
32. Herbert Hoover letter to Kiplinger, July 14, 1930, Herbert Hoover Papers, Post-Presidential Correspondence, Herbert Hoover Presidential Library and Museum, West Branch, IA.
33. Kiplinger to Herbert Hoover, July 15, 1930.
34. *KWL*, July 19, 1930.
35. W. M. Kiplinger, "W.M.K. Autobiography, Unpublished," Washington, DC, 1960, chap. 3, 24.
36. John, "Introduction: Adversarial Relations?" 11.
37. John, "Introduction: Adversarial Relations?"
38. "These changes in economic and political institutions led businesses to pay more attention to public relations, labor relations and government relations." Krooss and Gilbert, *American Business History*, 247.
39. Robert Griffith, "Dwight D. Eisenhower and the Corporate Commonwealth," *American Historical Review* 87, no. 1 (1982): 98.
40. Gerald F. Davis, *Managed by the Markets: How Finance Reshaped America* (New York: Oxford University Press, 2009), 75.
41. Weinstein, *The Corporate Ideal*.
42. James O'Connor, "American Welfare Capitalism, 1880–1940: Stuart D. Brandes," *American Journal of Sociology* 82, no. 5 (March 1, 1977): 1107–9.
43. Davis, *Managed by the Markets*, 75.
44. Garet Garrett, *Salvos against the New Deal: Selections from the Saturday Evening Post, 1933–1940*, ed. Bruce Ramsey (Caldwell, ID: Caxton Press, 2002), 23 and Ramsey's introduction, ix. See also Weinstein, *The Corporate Ideal*, ix; Weinstein argued, "The political ideology now dominant in the U.S. and broad programmatic outlines of the liberal state had been worked out and tried by the end of WWI."
45. Galambos and Pratt, *Corporate Commonwealth*, 13, 14; Krooss and Gilbert, *American Business History*, 167.
46. Galambos and Pratt, *Corporate Commonwealth*, 92.
47. Krooss and Gilbert, *American Business History*, 255, 167.
48. Alfred D. Chandler, "Government versus Business: An American Phenomenon," in *Business and Public Policy*, ed. John T. Dunlop (Cambridge: Harvard University Press, 1980), 7.
49. Weinstein, *The Corporate Ideal*, xiii.
50. Chandler, "Government versus Business" 5.
51. "The desire for economic protection was the one and only unifying force among those who supported regulation." Krooss and Gilbert, *American Business History*, 167, citing Edward A. Purcell, "Ideas and Interests: Businessmen and the Interstate Commerce Act," *Journal of American History* (December 1967): 561–78. See also John, "Introduction: Adversarial Relations?" 10. Passage of these business reforms would not have been possible without the guidance or at least tacit approval of large corporations. See Weinstein, *The Corporate Ideal*, ix.
52. "After the NRA—the NRA?" *Fortune*, June 1934, 92.
53. Colin Gordon, *New Deals: Business, Labor and Politics in America, 1920–1935* (Cambridge: Cambridge University Press, 1994), 86.
54. Thomas McCraw, "Regulation in America: A Review Essay," *Business History Review*,

Notes to Pages 78–82

49 (Summer 1975): 165. McCraw cites Gabriel Kolko, *The Triumph of Conservatism: A Re-interpretation of American History, 1900–1916* (New York: Free Press, 1977): "In the case of the Interstate Commerce Commission, the railroad executives "were the most important single advocates of federal regulation from 1877 to 1916. . . . [T]he Interstate Commerce Commission entered into a condition of dependency on the railroads."
55. "Du Pont," *Fortune*, November 1934.
56. Chris Roush, *Profits and Losses: Business Journalism and Its Role in Society* (Portland, OR: Marion Street Press, 2006).
57. Roush, *Profits and Losses*, 43.
58. Krooss and Gilbert, *American Business History*, 164.
59. Ron Chernow, *The House of Morgan: An American Banking Dynasty and the Rise of Modern Finance* (New York: Atlantic Monthly Press, 1990), 151.
60. Michael Schudson, *Discovering the News: A Social History of Newspapers* (New York: Basic Books, 1978), 134.
61. Cayce Myers, "Regulating Public Relations: How U.S. Legal Policies and Regulations Shaped Early Corporate Public Relations," *American Journalism* 37, no. 2 (April 2, 2020): 148.
62. Galambos and Pratt, *Corporate Commonwealth*, 97.
63. Franklin D. Roosevelt, "Commonwealth Club Address," San Francisco, September 23, 1932, https://teachingamericanhistory.org/library/document/commonwealth-club-address/.
64. Phillips-Fein writes that the New Deal represented a rejection of the old order of laissez-faire economics. Kim Phillips-Fein, *Invisible Hands: The Businessmen's Crusade against the New Deal* (New York: W. W. Norton, 2010), 25.
65. *KWL*, January 28, 1933.
66. *KWL*, April 1, 1933.
67. *KWL*, April 15, 1933.
68. *KWL*, May 5, 1933.
69. *KWL*, April 22, 1933.
70. "Mr. Roosevelt's Men," *Fortune*, April 1934, 95.
71. "Resolutions Adopted by the National Chamber of Commerce," *New York Times*, May 5, 1934.
72. "Securities Act Called a Damper," *New York Times*, October 16, 1933.
73. Thomas K. McCraw, "With the Consent of the Governed: SEC's Formative Years," *Journal of Policy Analysis and Management* 1, no. 3 (Spring 1982): 352.
74. "What's to Become of Us?" *Fortune*, December 1933, 118.
75. Phillips-Fein, *Invisible Hands*, 24.
76. Francis Brown, "The Storm Centre of the Banking Bill," *New York Times*, May 5, 1935.
77. "Marriner Stoddard Eccles," *Fortune*, February 1935, 65; Richard Timberlake, "The Tale of Another Chairman," *The Region*, June 1, 1999, https://www.minneapolisfed.org/article/1999/the-tale-of-another-chairman. John Maynard Keynes advanced his "General Theory" in 1936 to address the global economic crisis by arguing "that an economy could settle in equilibrium with high levels of unemployment and that government spending might be necessary to stimulate consumption. . . . Great Britain—like the United States—began to experiment with deficit financing and building a welfare state." Phillips-Fein, *Invisible Hands*, 51.

78. Marriner Eccles, *Beckoning Frontiers: Public and Personal Recollections*, ed. Sidney Hyman (New York: Alfred A. Knopf, 1951), 76.
79. Timberlake, "Tale of Another Chairman."
80. Kiplinger, "W.M.K. Autobiography," chap. 13, 187.
81. William S. Hopkins, "*The Industrial Discipline and the Governmental Arts*, by Rexford G. Tugwell," *Economic Journal* 43, no. 171 (1933): 500–502.
82. Kiplinger, "W.M.K. Autobiography," chap. 13, 186.
83. "Aid to 24,000,000 Reported by NRA," *New York Times*, January 1, 1934.
84. "Mayor Predicts Move to Change Basic Law to Widen Power of Congress," *New York Times*, May 29, 1935.
85. Phillips-Fein, *Invisible Hands*, 22.
86. Angus Burgin, *The Great Persuasion: Reinventing Free Markets since the Great Depression* (Cambridge: Harvard University Press, 2012), 4. Burgin also observed, "After the onset of the Great Depression at the decade's end, the remaining popular support for free markets rapidly dissipated" (4).
87. "Industrial Control Postscript," *KWL*, August 19, 1933.
88. *KWL*, January 26, 1935.
89. *KWL*, April 29, 1933.
90. "What's in the Recovery Act," *Business Week*, June 17, 1933, 4.
91. "What's to Become of Us?" 30, 112.
92. George David Smith and Richard Eugene Sylla, *The Transformation of Financial Capitalism: An Essay on the History of American Capital Markets* (Cambridge: Blackwell, 1993), 33.
93. "Industrial Control Postscript," *KWL*, May 27, 1933.
94. *Business Week*, June 7, 1933.
95. Phillips-Fein, *Invisible Hands*, 25.
96. Garrett, *Salvos against the New Deal*, 118.
97. "Wall St. and Mulberry St.," *Business Week*, September 30, 1933.
98. "On Confidence," *Business Week*, June 16, 1934, 32.
99. Arthur M. Schlesinger Jr., *The Age of Roosevelt: The Coming of the New Deal*, 7th ed. (Boston: Houghton Mifflin Company, 1958), 398.

Chapter 3: A Two-Way Street

1. Kiplinger to Raymond Moley, November 23, 1966, Raymond Moley File, KA.
2. Moley to Kiplinger, July 21, 1934, MP.
3. Moley to Kiplinger, November 12, 1934, MP.
4. Kiplinger to Moley, August 3, 1934.
5. Moley to Kiplinger, November 7, 1966, Raymond Moley File, KA.
6. Kiplinger to Moley, August 3, 1934.
7. "Raymond Moley, Roosevelt Aide, Dies; Brain Trust Leader Coined 'New Deal,'" *New York Times*, February 19, 1975.
8. Raymond Moley, *Fundamental Facts for New Citizens* (Columbus: Ohio State Department of Education, 1922).
9. Raymond Moley, *After Seven Years* (New York: Harper & Brothers, 1939), 23. Another Roosevelt speechwriter, Samuel Rosenman, also claimed authorship of the term "New Deal." "Samuel I. Rosenman, 77, Dies; Coined New Deal for Roosevelt," *New York Times*, June 25, 1973.

10. Moley, *After Seven Years*, 72.
11. Moley, *After Seven Years*, 81.
12. Schlesinger described Moley as on the right and Tugwell as on the left. Arthur M. Schlesinger Jr., *The Age of Roosevelt: The Coming of the New Deal*, 7th ed. (Boston: Houghton Mifflin Company, 1958), 18.
13. Moley, *After Seven Years*, 155. Colin Gordon made a similar observation about the "essential conservativeness of the New Deal." Colin Gordon, *New Deals: Business, Labor and Politics in America, 1920–1935* (Cambridge: Cambridge University Press, 1994), 4.
14. Moley, *After Seven Years*, 151.
15. Moley, *After Seven Years*, 196.
16. Raymond Moley, *The First New Deal* (New York: Harcourt Brace & World, 1966), 516–17.
17. Kiplinger to Moley, November 26, 1935, MP.
18. *KWL*, December 3, 1932.
19. Moley to Kiplinger, December 5, 1932, MP.
20. Kiplinger to Moley, December 7, 1932, MP; *KWL*, December 7, 1932.
21. Moley, *After Seven Years*, 185.
22. See Gerald Berk, *Louis D. Brandeis and the Making of Regulated Competition, 1900–1932* (Cambridge: Cambridge University Press, 2009), 138; Bruce Murphy, *The Brandeis/Frankfurter Connection: The Secret Activities of Two Supreme Court Justices* (Oxford: Oxford University Press, 1982), 343.
23. Moley to Kiplinger, December 6, 1932, MP. Kiplinger credited the economist Constantine McGuire for the technical adviser proposal.
24. Laura Phillips Sawyer, "Trade Associations, State Building, and the Sherman Act: The U.S. Chamber of Commerce, 1912–25," in *Capital Gains: Business and Politics in Twentieth-Century America*, ed. Richard R. John and Kim Phillips-Fein (Philadelphia: University of Pennsylvania Press, 2017), 32.
25. Kiplinger to Herbert Hoover, July 10, 1936, Herbert Hoover Papers, Post-Presidential Correspondence, Herbert Hoover Presidential Library and Museum.
26. Franklin D. Roosevelt to Kiplinger, November 6, 1931.
27. Moley, *The First New Deal*, 229.
28. Moley, *After Seven Years*, 184.
29. "What's to Become of Us?" *Fortune*, December 1933, 120.
30. Franklin D. Roosevelt, "Commonwealth Club Address," San Francisco, September 23, 1932, https://teachingamericanhistory.org/library/document/commonwealth-club-address/.
31. Franklin D. Roosevelt, "Commonwealth Club Address," San Francisco, September 23, 1932, https://teachingamericanhistory.org/library/document/commonwealth-club-address/.
32. Moley, *After Seven Years*, 189.
33. Thomas W. Zeiler, "Tariff Policy—Hull's Revolution," *American Foreign Relations* (blog), undated, https://www.americanforeignrelations.com/O-W/Tariff-Policy-Hull-s-revolution.html.
34. Moley to Kiplinger, July 21, 1934.
35. Kiplinger to Moley, July 25, 1934, MP.
36. Kiplinger to Moley, August 3, 1934.
37. Moley to Kiplinger, November 12, 1934.

38. Kiplinger to Moley, May 16, 1934, MP.
39. Kiplinger to Moley, September 18, 1934.
40. Kiplinger to Moley, June 4, 1934, MP.
41. Kiplinger to Moley, July 2, 1934, MP.
42. For Kiplinger's praise of Richberg, see *KWL*, July 7, 1934; r for his praise of Hopkins, *KWL*, March 30, 1935.
43. Kiplinger to Moley, November 5, 1935. In a postscript to the letter, Kiplinger said he had interviewed various contacts about their perception of Moley's influence in the administration and all concluded he was still influential.
44. *KWL*, March 2, 1935.
45. Kiplinger to Moley, March 22, 1934, MP.
46. Kiplinger to Moley, June 4, 1934.
47. Kiplinger to Moley, January 6, 1934.
48. Kiplinger to Moley, January 6, 1934.
49. Kiplinger to Moley, August 3, 1934.
50. Kiplinger to Moley, September 13, 1934, MP.
51. Kiplinger to Moley, October 29, 1935.
52. *KWL*, September 14, 1935.
53. *KWL*, November 30, 1935.
54. Moley to Kiplinger, December 2, 1966, Raymond Moley File, KA.
55. Moley to Kiplinger, October 31, 1963, Raymond Moley File, KA.
56. Moley to Kiplinger, February 14, 1934.
57. Kiplinger to Moley, September 26, 1936, MP.
58. Kiplinger to Moley, July 20, 1934, MP.
59. Kiplinger to Moley, April 11, 1934.
60. Francis M. Stephenson, "Moley Quitting Brain Trust to Become Editor," *Medford Mail Tribune*, August 28, 1933, https://www.newspapers.com/clip/14889065/1933-08-28-moley-quitting-brain-trust/.
61. Moley, *The First New Deal*, 517.
62. Moley to Kiplinger, February 14, 1934, MP.
63. Kiplinger to Moley, February 6, 1934, MP.
64. Kiplinger to Moley, May 16, 1934.
65. Kiplinger to Moley, July 17, 1936, MP. In 1937 *News-Week* merged with the weekly journal *Today*, which had been founded in 1932 by Vincent Astor and W. Averell Harriman, who later would serve as governor of New York from 1955 to 1959.
66. Rexford Tugwell, *The Brains Trust* (New York: Viking, 1968), xxvii.
67. W. M. Kiplinger, "The Federal Family Budget," *Today*, March 31, 1933.
68. *KWL*, April 1, 1933.
69. *KWL*, July 15, 1933.
70. The reference was to the World Economic Conference in London, where Moley was a lead US negotiator. The conference fell into disarray after Roosevelt contradicted his own representatives on currency policy.
71. *KWL*, August 5, 1933.
72. *KWL*, November 4, 1933.
73. Kiplinger to Moley, May 16, 1934.
74. Moley, *After Seven Years*, 171. The references are to the economists John Maynard Keynes and Edwin W. Kemmerer, an architect of the Federal Reserve System in 1911.

Notes to Pages 105–111

75. Moley, *After Seven Years*, 171.
76. Donald A. Ritchie, *Reporting from Washington: The History of the Washington Press Corps* (New York: Oxford University Press, 2005), 2.
77. Moley to Kiplinger, September 25, 1936, Raymond Moley File, KA.
78. Moley's admiration for Nixon is evident in his 1959 correspondence. Moley to Kiplinger, August 21, 1959, Raymond Moley File, KA.
79. Richard Nixon, "Remarks on Presenting the Presidential Medal of Freedom to Eight Journalists," Washington, DC, April 22, 1970, https://www.presidency.ucsb.edu/documents/remarks-presenting-the-presidential-medal-freedom-eight-journalists.
80. Alfred M. Landon to Austin Kiplinger, October 22, 1971, KA. Landon also recalled the event in a June 21, 1954, letter to Willard Kiplinger, ser. 3, Alf Landon Collection, Correspondence, 1948–1987, Kansas Historical Society, https://www.kshs.org/archives/227124.
81. Kiplinger to Moley, October 29, 1935, MP.
82. Kiplinger to Moley, September 14, 1936, MP.
83. *KWL*, April 18, 1936.
84. *KWL*, July 25, 1936.
85. *KWL*, August 29, 1936.
86. *KWL*, June 13, 1936.
87. Kiplinger to Moley, September 26, 1936.
88. W. M. Kiplinger, "W.M.K. Autobiography, Unpublished," Washington, DC, 1960, chap. 14, 201, KA.
89. "Landon 'Best Choice' Says Kiplinger," *Boston American*, October 22, 1936.
90. "Landon 'Best Choice' Says Kiplinger."
91. "Landon Is Leading Digest Poll 2 to 1," *New York Times*, September 4, 1936.
92. *KWL*, October 31, 1936.
93. A close student of politics will note that the current electoral college total is 538 votes; Hawaii and Alaska had not yet been admitted into the union in 1936.
94. Kiplinger to Alf Landon, September 30, 1957, ser. 3, Alf Landon Collection, Correspondence, 1948–1987, Kansas Historical Society, https://www.kshs.org/archives/227124.
95. Alf Landon to Austin Kiplinger, October 22, 1971.
96. Alf Landon Collection, Correspondence, 1948–1987, Kansas Historical Society, https://www.kshs.org/archives/227124.
97. Kiplinger to Moley, September 26, 1936.
98. Kiplinger to Moley, February 16, 1934.
99. Elinor Morgenthau to Kiplinger, November 22, 1934, KA.
100. Kiplinger to Austin Kiplinger, May 3, 1963, KA.
101. Kiplinger to Henry Morgenthau Jr., September 21, 1936, KA.
102. Kiplinger to Moley, September 26, 1936.
103. W. M. Kiplinger, "This Is a Letter about 'Bias' in Writing," April 15, 1936, KA.
104. Oeveste Granducci, "Company History—Oeveste Granducci," October 13, 1977, KA.
105. George Kennedy, "Company History—George Kennedy," July 12, 1976, KA.
106. Kiplinger, "W.M.K. Autobiography," chap. 4, 6.

Chapter 4: Fetching Information and Guidance

1. This anecdote is drawn from Harold K. Wilder, "An Incident in Washington," undated, KA.
2. W. M. Kiplinger, "W.M.K. Autobiography, Unpublished," Washington, DC, 1960, chap. 3, 23.
3. Kiplinger, "W.M.K. Autobiography, ," chap. 3, 19–24. Meyer, then head of the War Finance Corporation, would become owner and publisher of the *Washington Post* in 1933.
4. Kathy Roberts Forde, "Discovering the Explanatory Report in American Newspapers," *Journalism Practice* 1, no. 2 (2007): 230.
5. Kathy Roberts Forde and Katherine A. Foss, "'The Facts—the Color!—The Facts': The Idea of a Report in American Print Culture, 1885–1910," *Book History* 15 (2012): 126.
6. Betty H. Winfield, "F.D.R. Wins (and Loses) Journalist Friends in the Rising Age of News Interpretation," *Journalism Quarterly* 64 (Winter 1987), 698–708.
7. Howard Penn Hudson, *Publishing Newsletters*, 3rd ed. (Rhinebeck, NY: H&M Publishers, 1997), 1.
8. John J. McCusker, "The Demise of Distance: The Business Press and the Origins of the Information Revolution in the Early Modern Atlantic World," *American Historical Review* 110, no. 2 (April 1, 2005): 295–321, 303.
9. Michael Palmer, "Global Financial News," in *The Globalization of News*, ed. O. Boyd-Barrett and T. Rantanen (London: Sage, 1998), 61.
10. Wayne Parsons, *The Power of the Financial Press* (New Brunswick: Rutgers University Press, 1990), 25.
11. Sidney Kobre, *Development of American Journalism* (Dubuque: W. C. Brown Co., 1969), 565; James D. Startt and William David Sloan, *Historical Methods in Mass Communication* (Northport, AK: Vision Press, 2003), 40.
12. Frank Luther Mott, *American Journalism—A History: 1690–1960*, 3rd ed. (New York: Macmillan, 1966), 732. See also Marion Tuttle Marzolf, *Civilizing Voices: American Press Criticism* (New York: Longman, 1991), 122.
13. Marzolf, *Civilizing Voices*, 128.
14. W. M. Kiplinger, "Interpret the News," *Journalism Bulletin* 13, no. 3 (1936): 294.
15. Kiplinger, "W.M.K. Autobiography," chap. 1, 6.
16. "Lessons of Leadership," *Nation's Business*, August 1966.
17. George Bryant, "Company History—George Bryant," October 4, 1976, KA.
18. Truman R. Temple, "Kiplinger's Daring Reporting Style Marks Top Journalistic Enterprise," *Washington Evening Star*, September 29, 1960.
19. Austin Kiplinger, "Notes for JWH Interview," April 18, 1977.
20. Marzolf, *Civilizing Voices*, 125.
21. Winfield, "F.D.R. Wins (and Loses) Journalist Friends," 706; Marzolf, *Civilizing Voices*, 123.
22. *KWL*, April 11, 1936.
23. *KWL*, April 25, 1936.
24. *KWL*, December 23, 1933.
25. *KWL*, July 13, 1935.
26. "Lessons of Leadership—Part XV—Keeping an Eye on Washington: A Conversation

with Willard M. Kiplinger, the Publisher of the Famed Washington Newsletter," *Nation's Business*, August 1966.
27. Matt J. Duffy, "Anonymous Sources: A Historical Review of the Norms Surrounding Their Use," *American Journalism* 31, no. 2 (2014): 244.
28. Janell Sims, "Bloomberg's Exec. Editor Focused on Transparency in Financial Reporting," Shorenstein Center on Media, Politics and Policy blog, October 1, 2013, https://shorensteincenter.org/laurie-hays/. Also see "Attribution," in *Associated Press Stylebook* (New York: Associated Press, 2020), https://www.apstylebook.com/ap_stylebook/attribution.
29. Matthew Winkler, *The Bloomberg Way: A Guide for Reporters and Editors*, 10th ed. (New York: Bloomberg LP, 1988), http://site.ebrary.com/id/10845589.
30. *KWL*, December 28, 1929.
31. Douglas A. Anderson, "Drew Pearson: A Name Synonymous with Libel Actions," *Journalism Quarterly* 56, no. 2 (June 1, 1979): 235–42.
32. *KWL*, December 23, 1933.
33. Kiplinger, "W.M.K. Autobiography," chap. 1, 7.
34. George Kennedy, "Company History—George Kennedy," July 12, 1976, KA.
35. Winfield, "F.D.R. Wins (and Loses) Journalist Friends," 705.
36. William G. McAdoo to Kiplinger, May 19, 1919, KA.
37. William G. McAdoo to Kiplinger, November 17, 1933, KA.
38. Franklin D. Roosevelt to Kiplinger, July 21, 1931, Letters from Prominent Men file, KA.
39. Kiplinger, "W.M.K. Autobiography," chap. 4, 39d.
40. Austin Kiplinger, Company History Interview—Austin Kiplinger," April 21, 1977, KA.
41. Kathleen Endres, "Newsletters, Newspapers Pamphlets," in *Journalism and Mass Communication*, vol. 1, ed. Rashmi Luthra (New York: United Nations Educational, Scientific and Cultural Organization, 2008), 90.
42. Jesse H. Neal, "A Review of Business Paper History," in *N. W. Ayer & Son Annual and Directory*, vol. 1 (Philadelphia, 1922), 1245.
43. Ferdinand Lundberg, "News-Letters: A Revolution in Journalism," *Harper's Magazine*, April 1940, 466.
44. Hudson, *Publishing Newsletters*, 1.
45. Endres, "Newsletters, Newspapers, Pamphlets."
46. *Oxbridge Directory of Newsletters*, National Mail Order Association, undated, https://web.archive.org/web/20210715222749/http://www.nmoa.org/catalog/newsletter_dir.asp. Endres observed that it is difficult to know how many newsletters are published because they are not required to register in any country. She cited a 2000 Newsletter and Electronic Publishing Association (NEPA) estimate of ten thousand subscription newsletters in the United States; more than two-thirds of those had been started in the 1980s. The most popular topics covered by newsletters are business, communication, computers/technology, health, investments, and international and legal issues. NEPA predicted continued growth of the medium, since readers especially value the specialized information provided by newsletters. Endres, "Newsletters, Newspapers, Pamphlets," 90.
47. Hudson, *Publishing Newsletters*, x. A 2013 survey of 1,300 investment newsletters estimated that they brought in $3.4 billion in revenues annually. See Scott Brown,

Jose Cao-Alvira, and Eric Powers, "Do Investment Newsletters Move Markets?" *Financial Management* 42, no. 2 (2013): 318.
48. Lundberg, "News-Letters," 464.
49. Lundberg, "News-Letters," 465; Hudson, *Publishing Newsletters*, 2.
50. Hudson, *Publishing Newsletters*, 6.
51. John Hazard, "Hazard Draft—KWE History—Unpublished," Washington, DC, May 1978, 40.
52. By 1940, Whaley-Eaton, Kiplinger, and the Research Institute controlled 90 percent of the circulation for business newsletters. Lundberg, "News-Letters," 466.
53. Lundberg, "News-Letters," 464; "Tipster News Service Flourish in Nation's Capital," *Chicago Tribune*, October 1933; "The Weekly News Service Letters Giving Washington Low-Downs," *Eastern Underwriter*, December 8, 1933.
54. *KWL*, December 23, 1933.
55. Lundberg, "News-Letters," 464, 465, 469.
56. Knight Kiplinger, telephone interview with the author, October 11, 2019.
57. Kiplinger to Eugene Black, January 13, 1934, KA.
58. Eugene R. Black to Kiplinger, January 23, 1934, KA.
59. Marriner Eccles to Kiplinger, December 11, 1936, KA.
60. Kiplinger to Marriner Eccles, December 20, 1936, KA.
61. Hudson, *Publishing Newsletters*, 1.
62. Evert Volkersz, "McBook: The Reader's Digest Condensed Books Franchise," *Publishing Research Quarterly* 11, no. 2 (Summer 1995): 52.
63. Lundberg, "News-Letters."
64. Lundberg, "News-Letters," 470.
65. Kiplinger in a 1949 *New York Times* article, cited by "The TJFR Group/MasterCard International Business News Luminaries of the Century," *TJFR Business News Reporter*, 2000.
66. Kiplinger, "W.M.K. Autobiography," chap. 9, 98.
67. Philip Napoli, *Audience Evolution* (New York: Columbia University Press, 2010).
68. Elihu Katz, and Paul Lazarsfeld, *Personal Influence* (New Brunswick, NJ: Transaction Publishers, 2006), 16.
69. Stanley J. Baran, and Dennis K. Davis, *Mass Communication Theory: Foundations, Ferment, and Future*, 7th ed. (Stamford, CT: Cengage, 2015), 200.
70. Napoli, *Audience Evolution*, 12.
71. Napoli, *Audience Evolution*, 12.
72. "After the NRA—the NRA?" *Fortune*, June 1934, 91.
73. *KWL*, April 22, 1933.
74. *KWL*, April 29, 1933.
75. Knight Kiplinger, telephone interview with the author, October 11, 2019.
76. "US Business Cycle Expansions and Contractions," National Bureau of Economic Research, accessed December 27, 2021, https://www.nber.org/cycles/cyclesmain.html.
77. *KWL*, August 2, 1930, Herbert Hoover Papers, Post-Presidential Correspondence, Herbert Hoover Presidential Library and Museum.
78. *KWL*, August 2, 1930.
79. Knight Kiplinger, telephone interview with the author, October 11, 2019.
80. Joel Whitaker, telephone interview with the author, February 14, 2020.
81. Rob Wells, *The Enforcers: How Little-Known Trade Reporters Exposed the Keating Five and Advanced Business Journalism* (Champaign: University of Illinois Press, 2019).

82. Paul Starr, *The Creation of the Media: Political Origins of Modern Communications* (New York: Perseus Books, 2004), 16.
83. Gloria Gómez-Diago, "Functionalist Theory," in *The SAGE International Encyclopedia of Mass Media and Society*, 2019, https://doi.org/10.4135/9781483375519.n260.
84. "Industrial Control Postscript," *KWL*, July 1, 1933.
85. *KWL*, July 22, 1933.
86. Talcott Parsons, "The Professions and Social Structure," *Social Forces* 17, no. 4 (May 1, 1939): 457–67.
87. Émile Durkheim, *The Division of Labor in Society*, trans. Lewis A. Coser (New York: Free Press, 1997), 39, 60, 108.
88. Harold D. Lasswell, "The Structure and Function of Communication in Society," in *The Communication of Ideas: A Series of Addresses*, ed. Lyman Bryson (New York: Institute for Religious and Social Studies, distributed by Harper, 1948), 37.
89. Ellis W. Hawley, *The New Deal and the Problem of Monopoly* (Princeton: Princeton University Press, 1966), 15.
90. *KWL*, February 18, 1933.
91. *KWL*, April 8, 1933.
92. "Industrial Control Postscript," *KWL*, June 10, 1933.
93. "Industrial Control Postscript," *KWL*, June 10, 1933.
94. *KWL*, December 23, 1933.
95. *KWL*, May 20, 1933.
96. "Industrial Control Postscript," *KWL*, July 1, 1933.
97. "Control of Industry," *Business Week*, May 10, 1933, 3.
98. "Regulating Recovery," *Business Week*, May 17, 1933, 1.
99. Both Kiplinger and the *New York Times* used this term in their 1932 coverage of business executives' anxiety over the New Deal regulations. See "Dictator' Is Urged as Recovery Need," *New York Times*, February 22, 1933; *KWL*, April 15, 1933.
100. Raymond Moley, "A Journalist's Journalist," *Ohio News*, August 21, 1967.
101. "Beside Still Waters," *Daily Worker*, February 8, 1935.
102. Earl Browder, "Report by Comrade Earl Browder for the Central Committee to the 8th National Convention, Communist Party, U. S. A," *Daily Worker*, April 14, 1934.
103. "The Barometer Points to Storm," *Producers News*, September 29, 1933, https://chroniclingamerica.loc.gov/.
104. "A Truce to Politics!" *Business Week*, June 9, 1934, 32.
105. Matthew Gentzkow, Edward L. Glaeser, and Claudia Goldin, "The Rise of the Fourth Estate: How Newspapers Became Informative and Why It Mattered," *National Bureau of Economic Research*, March 30, 2005, 25, 24.
106. "Statistical Abstract of the United States: 1926," US Department of Commerce, 1927, 760, https://www2.census.gov/library/publications/1927/compendia/statab/49ed/1926-12.pdf.
107. Mitchell Stephens, *A History of News*, 3rd ed. (New York: Oxford University Press, 2007).
108. John Heidenry, *Theirs Was the Kingdom: Lila And DeWitt Wallace and the Story of the Reader's Digest* (New York: W. W. Norton & Co., 1993), 42. Also see John Bainbridge, "Birth of an Aristocrat," *The New Yorker*, November 24, 1945, 38.
109. Walter Lippmann, *Public Opinion* (Charlottesville: University of Virginia American Studies Program, 2003), 8.
110. John Kobler, *Luce: His Time, Life, and Fortune* (New York: Doubleday & Co., 1968), 44.

111. Mott, *American Journalism*. *Reader's Digest* began carrying advertising in 1955. Mott, *American Journalism*, 833.
112. Ann Blair, "Information Overload's 2,300-Year-Old History," *Harvard Business Review*, March 14, 2011, https://hbr.org/2011/03/information-overloads-2300-yea.html.
113. "In 1255, the Dominican Vincent of Beauvais articulated eloquently the key ingredients of the feeling of overload which are still with us today: 'the multitude of books, the shortness of time and the slipperiness of memory.'" Blair, "Information Overload's 2,300-Year-Old History."
114. Heidenry, *Theirs Was the Kingdom*, 42.
115. "History of Publishing," in *Encyclopædia Britannica*, https://www.britannica.com/topic/publishing.
116. Kiplinger, "W.M.K. Autobiography," chap. 4, 35.
117. Heidenry, *Theirs Was the Kingdom*, 42.
118. Mott, *American Journalism*, 831; also Louis W. Liebovich, "American Dreamers: The Wallaces and *Reader's Digest*: An Insider's Story," *Journal of American History* 84, no. 2 (September 1997): 705.
119. W. M. Kiplinger, "Interpret the News," *Journalism Quarterly*, 13, no. 3 (1936), 290.
120. Knight Kiplinger, telephone interview with the author, July 12, 2019.
121. "Remarks of W. M. Kiplinger, Washington Business Writer, to American Association of Teachers of Journalism," Washington, DC, December 28, 1935.
122. Austin Kiplinger, "Notes for JWH Interview."
123. "The TJFR Group/MasterCard International Business News Luminaries of the Century."
124. A search in ProQuest for "Kiplinger" and "sweep line" and its variants produced one result, a passing reference in a 1993 *USA Today* article. An identical search in the database Academic Search Complete revealed two passing references in *Journal of Florida Studies* (2019) and *Time* (1953).
125. Jakob Nielsen, "How Users Read on the Web," NN/g Nielsen Norman Group blog, September 30, 1997, https://www.nngroup.com/articles/how-users-read-on-the-web/.
126. Arika Okrent, "The Listicle as Literary Form," *Uchicago Magazine*, Spring 2021, https://mag.uchicago.edu/arts-humanities/listicle-literary-form#.
127. Jared Spool, *Web Site Usability: A Designer's Guide* (Burlington, MA: Morgan Kaufmann, 1998), https://www.google.com/books/edition/Web_Site_Usability/zPl8e4W4dvMC?hl=en&gbpv=1&dq=Web+Site+Usability:+A+Designer%27s+Guide&pg=PR13&printsec=frontcover.

Chapter 5: A Battle with "Economic Royalists"

1. *KWL*, May 5, 1933.
2. *KWL*, June 17, 1933.
3. "Demand Business Discipline Itself," *New York Times*, May 4, 1933.
4. "Toward Stability," *Business Week*, May 10, 1933, 32.
5. Garet Garrett, *Salvos against the New Deal: Selections from the Saturday Evening Post, 1933–1940*, ed. Bruce Ramsey (Caldwell, ID: Caxton Press, 2002), 37.
6. "Industrial Control Postscript," *KWL*, October 21, 1933.

Notes to Pages 141–146

7. "The Next Labor Offensive," *Fortune*, January 1934, 61.
8. "Chamber for Change," *Business Week*, May 17, 1933, 3.
9. Arthur M. Schlesinger Jr., *The Age of Roosevelt: The Coming of the New Deal*, 7th ed. (Boston: Houghton Mifflin, 1958), 95.
10. Charles Merz, "Ten Vast Problems That Roosevelt Faces," *New York Times*, March 5, 1933.
11. William L. Silber, "Why Did FDR's Bank Holiday Succeed?" *Economic Policy Review*, Federal Reserve Bank of New York (July 2009): 19.
12. Raymond Moley, *After Seven Years* (New York: Harper & Brothers Publishers, 1939), 155.
13. *KWL*, January 21, 1933.
14. *KWL*, January 28, 1933.
15. *KWL*, February 4, 1933.
16. Silber, "Why Did FDR's Bank Holiday Succeed?" 21.
17. "Old Banks and New," *Business Week*, March 29, 1933. "Wire-pulling" refers to moving a puppet attached to wires, a metaphor for political influence.
18. "New Deal, New Money, New Banks," *Business Week*, March 15, 1933, 1.
19. "The Financial Markets," *Business Week*, January 4, 1933, 30.
20. "New Banks—Model T," *Business Week*, March 8, 1933, 5.
21. *KWL*, February 25, 1933.
22. "Relaxing Control," *New York Times*, March 9, 1933.
23. "The Banks Reopen," *Business Week*, March 22, 1933, 3.
24. *KWL*, March 10, 1933.
25. "Business as Usual," *New York Times*, March 7, 1933.
26. "New Deal, New Money, New Banks," *Business Week*, March 15, 1933, 1.
27. "New Deal Failing, Methodists Hold," *New York Times*, February 4, 1935.
28. Kim Phillips-Fein, *Invisible Hands: The Businessmen's Crusade against the New Deal* (New York: W. W. Norton, 2010), 19–21.
29. Garrett, *Salvos against the New Deal*, 38.
30. Phillips-Fein, *Invisible Hands*, 39.
31. Jouett Shouse, "No. 128 'The New Deal vs. Democracy,'" National Broadcasting Company, June 20, 1936. https://exploreuk.uky.edu/catalog/xt7wwp9t2q46_125#page/1/mode/1up.
32. "Business Leaders Appraise Future," *New York Times*, January 2, 1934.
33. Phillips-Fein, *Invisible Hands*, 19.
34. Raymond Moley, *The First New Deal* (New York: Harcourt Brace & World, 1966), 527.
35. *KWL*, November 10, 1934.
36. Two searches in March and April 2021 of the Kiplinger records failed to find any record of such correspondence. The personal papers contain letters from less prominent individuals during this same time period, however. Julie Shapiro, email to the author, April 18, 2021.
37. "58 Lawyers Hold Labor Act Invalid," *New York Times*, September 19, 1935.
38. Phillips-Fein, *Invisible Hands*, 28, 29, 36.
39. Grace Hutchins, *The Truth about the Liberty League* (New York: International Pamphlets, 1936), 20.
40. Kiplinger to Raymond Moley, November 27, 1934, MP.

41. Hinshaw later wrote a book profiling Hoover based on their thirty-five-year friendship. David Hinshaw to Raymond Moley, November 27, 1934, MP.
42. Raymond Moley to Kiplinger, December 6, 1934, MP.
43. *KWL*, April 29, 1933.
44. Graham J. White, *FDR and the Press* (Chicago: University of Chicago Press, 1979), 5.
45. *KWL*, July 8, 1933.
46. "Industrial Control Postscript," *KWL*, July 8, 1933.
47. *KWL*, July 29, 1933.
48. "Industrial Control Postscript," *KWL*, July 8, 1933.
49. *KWL*, July 15, 1933.
50. "Industrial Control Postscript," *KWL*, August 26, 1933.
51. *KWL*, August 19, 1933.
52. For examples of episodic critiques, see "This Business Week," *Business Week*, July 15, 1933.
53. "Convalescence," *Business Week*, June 10, 1933.
54. "NIRA's Teething Pains," *Business Week*, July 1, 1933, 3.
55. "Jobs," *Business Week*, June 2, 1934, 36.
56. "Auditing the New Deal," *Business Week*, July 21, 1934, 13.
57. "Labor—the Sore Point," *Business Week*, September 9, 1933, 5.
58. For example, see "The Labor Crisis," *Business Week*, October 7, 1933, 32.
59. "What's to Become of Us?" *Fortune*, December 1933, 29, 30, 118.
60. Garrett, *Salvos against the New Deal*, 34, 42, 30 29, 14.
61. *KWL*, October 21, 1933.
62. "Industrial Control Postscript," *KWL*, July 29, 1933.
63. Russell Owen, "Roosevelt Leads Attack on Three Fronts," *New York Times*, July 23, 1933.
64. R. L. Duffus, "Six Months of Roosevelt: Momentous Days," *New York Times*, September 3, 1933.
65. "Industrial Control Postscript," *KWL*, September 16, 1933.
66. *KWL*, September 9, 1933.
67. "Industrial Control Postscript," *KWL*, October 21, 1933.
68. *KWL*, November 4, 1933.
69. "Text of the Inaugural Address," *New York Times*, March 5, 1933.
70. "Mr. Roosevelt's Men," *Fortune*, April 1934, 95.
71. Peter Temin and Barry Eichengreen, "The Gold Standard and the Great Depression," *Contemporary European History* 9, no. 2 (July 2000): 207, 200–203.
72. "Washington Reads the Signs," *Business Week*, March 15, 1933.
73. "Ten Vast Issues That Confront Congress," *New York Times*, December 30, 1934.
74. "Bryan! Bryan!! Bryan!!! Bryan!!!" *Fortune*, January 1934; John L. Shover, "The Farmers' Holiday Association Strike, August 1932," *Agricultural History* 39, no. 4 (1965): 196–203.
75. Milton Friedman and Anna Schwartz, *Monetary History of the United States, 1867–1960* (Princeton: Princeton University Press, 1963), 462, 464.
76. "Franklin D. Roosevelt—Key Events," University of Virginia, Miller Center, blog, October 7, 2016, https://millercenter.org/president/franklin-d-roosevelt/key-events.
77. Friedman and Schwartz, *Monetary History*, 463.
78. "Chronological Survey of the Outstanding Financial Events of the Past Year," *New York Times*, January 2, 1934.

79. Harold Calleder, "Britain's Formula for Recovery—and Ours," *New York Times*, October 21, 1934.
80. "Recovery Awaits Pound-Dollar Tie, Flandin Assets," *New York Times*, December 24, 1934.
81. *KWL*, September 2, 1933.
82. *KWL*, April 22, 1933.
83. *KWL*, July 1, 1933.
84. ProQuest Historical Newspapers: *The New York Times*, search terms "dollar and devaluation and Roosevelt," April 1–August 15, 1933, https://www.proquest.com/search/1980300?accountid=8361.
85. "Franklin D. Roosevelt—Key Events."
86. Charles Merz, "Is Business Recovering?" *New York Times*, November 25, 1934.
87. *KWL*, July 8, 1933.
88. *KWL*, November 18, 1933.
89. John Maynard Keynes, "An Open Letter to President Roosevelt," *New York Times*, December 31, 1933.
90. *KWL*, July 22, 1933.
91. *KWL*, July 22, 1933.
92. "Industrial Control Postscript," *KWL*, August 19, 1933.
93. *KWL*, July 8, 1933.
94. *KWL*, August 5, 1933.
95. Austin Kiplinger, "Company History Interview—Austin Kiplinger," April 21, 1977, KA.
96. Kiplinger told Moley in September 1936 he feared Roosevelt could become a dictator. Kiplinger to Raymond Moley, September 26, 1936.
97. Kiplinger to Raymond Moley, April 6, 1936, MP.
98. Kiplinger to Moley, April 6, 1936.
99. William P. O'Neill, "As I See It," *The Times* (Munster, IN), April 28, 1936.
100. Raymond Moley, "Common Sense—1936 Model," presented at the National Association of Manufacturers, New York, NY, April 24, 1936, Raymond Moley Papers, Hoover Institution Library and Archives, Stanford, CA.
101. "Mr. Roosevelt's Men," *Fortune*, April 1934, 142.
102. W. M. Kiplinger, *Washington Is Like That* (New York: Harper & Brothers, 1942), 371.
103. Sender Garlin, *The Truth about Reader's Digest* (New York: Forum Publishers, 1943), 5.
104. John Heidenry, *Theirs Was the Kingdom: Lila And DeWitt Wallace and the Story of the Reader's Digest* (New York: W. W. Norton & Co., 1993), 131.
105. Garlin, *The Truth about Reader's Digest*, 26.
106. Kiplinger to Pearl Buck, October 1, 1942, KA.
107. *KWL*, February 11, 1933; *KWL*, April 1, 1933.
108. *KWL*, June 15, 1935.
109. *KWL*, March 31, 1934.
110. *KWL*, July 1, 1933.
111. *KWL*, March 30, 1935.
112. *KWL*, December 9, 1933.
113. "The Brain Trust," *Business Week*, March 22, 1933, 16.
114. "Wonder Boys of Washington," *Fortune*, July 1933, 20, 23, 19.
115. "Regimentation or Guidance?" *Business Week*, April 14, 1934, 12.

116. "The Brain Trust," *Business Week*, March 22, 1933, 17.
117. "Mr. Roosevelt's Men," *Fortune*, April 1934, 94, 99, 91.
118. *KWL*, August 26, 1933.
119. "Industrial Control Postscript," *KWL*, November 18, 1933.
120. "Industrial Control Postscript," *KWL*, August 19, 1933.
121. "General Motors Has 48% Sales Rise," *New York Times*, March 25, 1935.
122. "Industrial Control Postscript," *KWL*, September 2, 1933.
123. *KWL*, September 9, 1933.
124. *KWL*, September 16, 1933.
125. *KWL*, October 19, 1935.
126. Garrett, *Salvos against the New Deal*, 17.
127. "Subversive 'Junta' in Capital Charged," *New York Times*, November 22, 1935.
128. Phillips-Fein, *Invisible Hands*, 29.

Chapter 6: They SEEM Reasonable

1. "Triangle Shirtwaist Factory Fire," History.com (blog), March 23, 2020, https://www.history.com/topics/early-20th-century-us/triangle-shirtwaist-fire; History AFL-CIO, "Triangle Shirtwaist Fire," undated, https://aflcio.org/about/history/labor-history-events/triangle-shirtwaist-fire.
2. "US Inflation Calculator," 2008, https://www.usinflationcalculator.com/ (12 hours a day × 7 days = 84 hours a week).
3. AFL-CIO, "Triangle Shirtwaist Factory Fire."
4. J. Joseph Huthmacher, "Senator Robert F. Wagner and the Rise of Urban Liberalism," *American Jewish Historical Quarterly* 58, no. 3 (March 1969): 339.
5. Sam Roberts, "A New Verdict on Tammany Hall," *New York Times*, March 7, 2014.
6. "The American Federation of Labor," *Fortune*, December 1934, 82.
7. Arthur M. Schlesinger Jr., *The Age of Roosevelt: The Coming of the New Deal*, 7th ed. (Boston: Houghton Mifflin, 1958), 136.
8. Garet Garrett, *Salvos against the New Deal: Selections from the Saturday Evening Post, 1933–1940*, ed. Bruce Ramsey (Caldwell, ID: Caxton Press, 2002), 71.
9. The National Recovery Administration and the National Recovery Act share the same acronym, NRA. In this book I have made a careful distinction and use the acronym NRA when it is clear from the context whether it is referring to the governmental body or to the law. The National Industrial Recovery Act and National Recovery Act are the same and refer to the 1933 pillar of the First New Deal.
10. Louis Stark, "Union Labor Massing on Legislative Front," *New York Times*, April 26, 1935.
11. Philip Glende, "Labor Reporting and Its Critics in the CIO Years," *Journalism and Communication Monographs* 22, no. 1 (February 10, 2020): 5, 13, https://doi.org/10.1177/1522637919898270.
12. "The Next Labor Offensive," *Fortune*, January 1934, 58.
13. Schlesinger, *The Age of Roosevelt*, 90.
14. Kim Phillips-Fein, *Invisible Hands: The Businessmen's Crusade against the New Deal* (New York: W. W. Norton, 2010), 22.
15. Alan Dawley, *Struggles for Justice: Social Responsibility and the Liberal State* (Cambridge: Belknap Press of Harvard University Press, 1991), 298.

Notes to Pages 171-177

16. "The Next Labor Offensive," *Fortune*, January 1934, 58.
17. *KWL*, July 8, 1933.
18. Schlesinger, *The Age of Roosevelt*.
19. "Industrial Control Postscript," *KWL*, September 2, 1933.
20. Labor and Recovery, *Business Week*, October 14, 1933, 36.
21. R. L. Duffus, "Roosevelt's Two Years: Ten Epic Chapters," *New York Times*, March 3, 1935.
22. Anthony J. Badger, *The New Deal: The Depression Years, 1933-40* (Chicago: Ivan R. Dee, 2002), 126.
23. *KWL*, February 18, 1933.
24. *KWL*, February 18, 1933.
25. Arthur Krock, "'War Board' Proposed," *New York Times*, April 14, 1933.
26. *KWL*, April 29, 1933.
27. Badger, *The New Deal*, 80.
28. "Thirty Hours a Week," *Business Week*, April 19, 1933, 4.
29. "Industrial Control Postscript," *KWL*, December 2, 1933.
30. Ellis W. Hawley, *The New Deal and the Problem of Monopoly* (Princeton: Princeton University Press, 1966), 15.
31. Cabell Phillips, *From the Crash to the Blitz, 1929-1939* (New York: Macmillan, 1969), 216; David M. Kennedy, *Freedom from Fear: The American People in Depression and War, 1929-1945* (New York: Oxford University Press, 1999).
32. Phillips, *From the Crash to the Blitz*, 213, 217.
33. Marriner Eccles, *Beckoning Frontiers: Public and Personal Recollections*, ed. Sidney Hyman (New York: Alfred A. Knopf, 1951), 76.
34. Melvyn Dubofsky, *The State and Labor in Modern America* (Chapel Hill: University of North Carolina Press, 1994), 119.
35. Badger, *The New Deal*, 135.
36. Colin Gordon, *New Deals: Business, Labor and Politics in America, 1920-1935* (Cambridge: Cambridge University Press, 1994), 4, 92.
37. Schlesinger, *The Age of Roosevelt*, 136.
38. Dubofsky, *The State and Labor in Modern America*, 112.
39. "The American Federation of Labor," *Fortune*, December 1934, 80, 152.
40. "Recovery Setup," *Business Week*, June 10, 1933, 5.
41. "Weirton Fights," *Business Week*, December 23, 1933.
42. "Industrial Control Postscript," *KWL*, December 2, 1933.
43. "Stupidity of Labor Cause of Rejoicing." *American Guardian*. June 2, 1933.
44. "American Bankers Association showed its usual stupidity on matters of public and political relations by asking abandonment of deposit insurance at this late date. Bankers as credit technicians are all right: bankers as economic statesmen are questionable; bankers as judges of popular and political sentiment are total losses—more inept than any other single class of business men." *KWL*, September 16, 1933.
45. "The American Federation of Labor," *Fortune*, December 1934, 150, 85, 84.
46. "Industrial Control Postscript," *KWL*, June 17, 1933.
47. "Industrial Control Postscript," *KWL*, October 21, 1933.
48. "The American Federation of Labor," *Fortune*, December 1934, 85. For labor's misgivings about Perkins, see Dubofsky, *The State and Labor in Modern America*, 108.
49. "Labor and Recovery," *Business Week*, October 14, 1933, 32.

50. Dawley, *Struggles for Justice*; Rod Palmquist, "Labor's Great War on the Seattle Waterfront: A History of the 1934 Longshore Strike," Waterfront Workers History Project (blog), https://depts.washington.edu/dock/34strikehistory_intro.shtml.
51. Phillips-Fein, *Invisible Hands*, 20.
52. "Strikes Hurt A.F. of L.," *Business Week*, July 28, 1934, 7.
53. "Labor Puts on a Show," *Business Week*, April 6, 1935.
54. "Unions Get a Talking Point," *Business Week*, May 18, 1935.
55. "The American Federation of Labor," *Fortune*, December 1934, 85.
56. Schlesinger, *The Age of Roosevelt*, 150.
57. Dubofsky, *The State and Labor in Modern America*, 121.
58. Schlesinger, *The Age of Roosevelt*, 400.
59. Schlesinger, *The Age of Roosevelt*, 394, 151.
60. "New Deal Failing, Methodists Hold," *New York Times*, February 4, 1935.
61. *KWL*, June 10, 1933.
62. *KWL*, August 5, 1933.
63. James M. Beck, "The NRA Is Unconstitutional," *Fortune*, November 1933.
64. "Roosevelt Faces Test," *Business Week*, November 11, 1933, 5.
65. Phillips, *From the Crash to the Blitz*, 217.
66. "The Riddle of the Recovery," *Business Week*, October 14, 1933, 17.
67. "NRA Rebels Show Fight," *Business Week*, July 28, 1934, 10.
68. "The Labor Crisis," *Business Week*, October 7, 1933, 32.
69. "Strike Lull," *Business Week*, October 14, 1933, 8.
70. Dawley, *Struggles for Justice*, 373.
71. Franklin D. Roosevelt, "September 30, 1934: Fireside Chat 6 On Government and Capitalism," https://millercenter.org/the-presidency/presidential-speeches/september-30-1934-fireside-chat-6-government-and-capitalism.
72. "1935 Passage of the Wagner Act," National Labor Relations Board blog, undated, https://www.nlrb.gov/about-nlrb/who-we-are/our-history/1935-passage-of-the-wagner-act.
73. "Wagner Act," Roosevelt Institute blog, June 20, 2012, https://web.archive.org/web/20200103195955/https://rooseveltinstitute.org/wagner-act/.
74. Dubofsky, *The State and Labor in Modern America*, 116.
75. National Labor Relations Board, "Legislative History of the National Labor Relations Act," Washington, DC, 1949, 15, 17.
76. *KWL*, March 23, 1935.
77. Louis Stark, "Coal Strike Looms While Textile Leader Urges Defiance of Wage Cuts," *New York Times*, May 29, 1935; Louis Stark, "NRA End Enhances Labor Bill," *New York Times*, June 5, 1935.
78. *KWL*, May 25, 1935.
79. *KWL*, June 15, 1935.
80. *KWL*, October 12, 1935.
81. Grace Hutchins, *The Truth about the Liberty League* (New York: International Pamphlets, 1936), 1936.
82. "58 Lawyers Hold Labor Act Invalid," *New York Times*, September 19, 1935.
83. Phillips-Fein, *Invisible Hands*, 30.
84. "Lund for Changes in Recovery Bill," *New York Times*, May 18, 1933.
85. "Violations of Free Speech and Rights of Labor," US Senate Subcommittee of

the Committee on Education and Labor (1938), 14031. For details on the programs, see "The American Family Robinson," *Old Time Radio Catalog* (blog), 2001, https://www.otrcat.com/p/american-family-robinson#:~:text=The%20American%20Family%20Robinson%20was,around%20the%20country%20for%20free.

86. "Teeth for the Labor Board," *Business Week*, March 10, 1934.
87. John Hennen, "E. T. Weir, Employee Representation, and the Dimensions of Social Control: Weirton Steel, 1933–1937," *Labor Studies Journal* 26, no. 3 (2001): 30.
88. *KWL*, August 31, 1935.
89. *KWL*, September 28, 1935.
90. Richard R. John and Kim Phillips-Fein, eds., *Capital Gains: Business and Politics in Twentieth-Century America* (Philadelphia: University of Pennsylvania Press, 2017), 4.
91. "6-Hour Day," *Business Week*, May 10, 1933, 4.
92. "Platform Adopted by Young Republicans of the State," *New York Times*, June 23, 1935.
93. ProQuest search "Wagner Labor Relations" in New York Times Historical Newspapers, January 1, 1935–September 1, 1935. The author reviewed twenty-six articles for pro-and anti-Wagner Act emphasis. Of the twenty-six articles, eighteen were categorized.
94. "Underwear Firms Ask NRA Extension," *New York Times*, April 26, 1935.
95. "Publishers Fight New Curbs in Code," *New York Times*, April 25, 1935.
96. "The A.F. of L. Missed the Boat," *Business Week*, February 9, 1935.
97. "Trouble in Detroit," *Business Week*, February 8, 1933, 8.
98. "What About Labor," *Business Week*, July 15, 1933. 7.
99. "Recovery Trouble," *Business Week*, March 31, 1934, 1.
100. "Labor in Detroit," *Business Week*, March 24, 1934, 40.
101. "Washington Bulletin," *Business Week*, March 24, 1934, 1. For other examples of *Business Week*'s anti-union bias, see "the arrogant demands of organized labor" versus "concessions by employers" in "The Real Winner," March 31, 1934, and a report on the auto industry's response to labor disputes featuring the photo caption "'ON THE WARFRONT" in "Labor Showdown," March 24, 1934, 7.
102. *KWL*, March 17, 1934.
103. Frederick Roche, "Not a 'Jew Hater' Says Henry Ford," *Tulsa Daily World*, February 14, 1921.
104. Dawley, *Struggles for Justice*, 380.
105. *Schechter Poultry Corp. v. United States*, 295 U.S. 495 (1935) (US Supreme Court 1935).
106. *KWL*, January 12, 1935.
107. *KWL*, May 11, 1935.
108. *KWL*, March 23, 1935.
109. *KWL*, June 1, 1935.
110. *KWL*, June 8, 1935.
111. *KWL*, June 1, 1935.
112. *KWL*, November 30, 1935.
113. *KWL*, April 27, 1935.
114. *KWL*, June 8, 1935.
115. *KWL*, January 19, 1935.
116. *KWL*, August 31, 1935.
117. "Texts of Roosevelt Speeches in Three States," *New York Times*, October 30, 1936.

118. Raymond Moley, *The First New Deal* (New York: Harcourt Brace & World, 1966), 529.
119. Raymond Moley, *After Seven Years* (New York: Harper & Brothers Publishers, 1939), 289.
120. Moley, *The First New Deal*, 551, 548.
121. "The American Federation of Labor," *Fortune*, December 1934, 80.
122. Lewis became an ardent New Deal Democrat after 1933 and campaigned for Roosevelt in 1936. Schlesinger, *The Age of Roosevelt*, 138.
123. "The American Federation of Labor," 149–50.
124. Badger, *The New Deal: The Depression Years*, 133, 131; see also Schlesinger, *The Age of Roosevelt*, 395.
125. *KWL*, March 4, 1933.
126. *KWL*, October 12, 1935.
127. "Industrial Control Postscript" *KWL*, October 12, 1935.
128. *KWL*, November 28, 1936.
129. "'Confidential' News Agency Says All Talk of Wage Cuts," *Daily Worker*, April 30, 1931.
130. "Jobless Army to Grow, Says Secret Report," *Daily Worker*, January 21, 1932.
131. "Labor Militancy Pays," *Montana Labor News*, January 7, 1937, https://chroniclingamerica.loc.gov/.
132. "Secret Fascist Council Formed to Meet War and Deepening Crisis," *Daily Worker*, May 20, 1932.
133. "Text of Roosevelt Message on New Taxes," *New York Times*, June 20, 1935.
134. "Changes in The Tax Bill Forecast by Senators," *New York Times*, August 8, 1935.
135. *KWL*, June 29, 1935.
136. *KWL*, June 29, 1935.
137. *KWL*, June 29, 1935.
138. *KWL*, August 24, 1935.
139. Thomas K. McCraw, "With the Consent of the Governed: SEC's Formative Years," *Journal of Policy Analysis and Management* 1, no. 3 (Spring 1982): 361.
140. *KWL*, January 26, 1935.
141. *KWL*, November 10, 1934.
142. William M. Emmons, "Franklin D. Roosevelt, Electric Utilities, and the Power of Competition," *Journal of Economic History* 53, no. 4 (1993): 884.
143. Sarah Phillips, *This Land, This Nation: Conservation, Rural America, and the New Deal* (Cambridge: Cambridge University Press, 2007), 132.
144. Emmons, "Franklin D. Roosevelt, Electric Utilities," 880.
145. John Riggs, "Roosevelt's Drive to Break Up Utilities Brought Power to the People," *HistoryNet*, November 9, 2020, https://www.historynet.com/roosevelts-drive-to-break-up-utilities-brought-power-to-the-people.htm.
146. *KWL*, July 13, 1935.
147. *KWL*, July 6, 1935.
148. Riggs, "Roosevelt's Drive to Break Up Utilities."
149. "Message to Holding Companies," *Business Week*, March 16, 1935.
150. *KWL*, July 6, 1935.
151. "President Sees the Nation Developing All Its Power After Model of Tennessee," *New York Times*, November 19, 1934.

Notes to Pages 196–204

152. "The American Utility Soviet," *Business Week*, March 23, 1935, 36.
153. "Reform or Confiscation," *Business Week*, April 6, 1935, 48.
154. "Presidential Propaganda vs. Business Propaganda," *Business Week*, March 16, 1935.
155. *KWL*, August 31, 1935.
156. *KWL*, December 14, 1935.
157. *KWL*, August 31, 1935.
158. *KWL*, December 14, 1935.
159. Kiplinger, "W.M.K. Autobiography, Unpublished," Washington, DC, 1960, chap. 14, 202.

Chapter 7: The Promise of Independent Journalism

1. George Bryant, "Company History—George Bryant," October 4, 1976, KA.
2. Kiplinger to Raymond Moley, January 6, 1934.
3. Jane Mayer, *Dark Money: The Hidden History of the Billionaires behind the Rise of the Radical Right* (New York: Doubleday, 2016).
4. Aeron Davis, "Public Relations, Business News and the Reproduction of Corporate Elite Power," *Journalism* 1, no. 3 (December 1, 2000), 282–304.
5. Dean Starkman, *The Watchdog That Didn't Bark: The Financial Crisis and the Disappearance of Investigative Journalism* (New York: Columbia Journalism Review Books, 2014); Robert McChesney, "The Problem of Journalism: A Political Economic Contribution to an Explanation of the Crisis in Contemporary US Journalism," *Journalism Studies* 4, no. 3 (2003): 299–329; Gerald J. Baldasty, *The Commercialization of News in the Nineteenth Century* (Madison: University of Wisconsin Press, 1992).
6. Herbert Gans, *Deciding What's News: A Study of CBS Evening News, NBC Nightly News, Newsweek, and Time* (Evanston: Northwestern University Press, 1979), xxiii.
7. Marion Tuttle Marzolf, *Civilizing Voices: American Press Criticism* (New York: Longman, 1991), 107.
8. Austin Kiplinger, "Company History Interview—Austin Kiplinger," April 21, 1977, KA.
9. Austin Kiplinger, "Company History Interview."
10. Herbert L. Brown, "Company History Interview," October 14, 1976, KA.
11. Austin Kiplinger, "Company History Interview."
12. Truman R. Temple, "Kiplinger's Daring Reporting Style Marks Top Journalistic Enterprise," *Washington Evening Star*, September 29, 1960.
13. "It Started with Kip," *Newsweek*, August 21, 1967.
14. Mark Jurkowitz et al., "U.S. Media Polarization and the 2020 Election: A Nation Divided," January 2020, Pew Research Center, Washington, DC.
15. W. M. Kiplinger, "This Is a Letter about 'Bias' in Writing," April 15, 1936, KA.
16. Austin Kiplinger, "Company History Interview."
17. Margaret Rodgers, "Company History—Margaret Rodgers," July 10, 1976, KA.
18. Hazard made extensive comments about Kiplinger's personality and egoism in an interview with Lew Coit. Lew Garrison Coit, "Company History—Lew Garrison Coit," July 10, 1976, KA.
19. Yaron J. Zoller and Jeff Muldoon, "Coming Together after a Tragedy: How the S.S. Eastland Disaster of 1915 Affected Welfare Capitalism and Helped Shape the Hawthorne Studies," *Journal of Management History* 27, no. 2 (January 1, 2021): 230, 229.

20. *KWL*, January 26, 1935.
21. Bryant, "Company History."
22. Austin Kiplinger, "Company History Interview."
23. Brown, "Company History."
24. Austin Kiplinger, "Company History Interview."
25. "The TJFR Group/MasterCard International Business News Luminaries of the Century," *TJFR Business News Reporter* (2000): 43.
26. Austin Kiplinger, "Notes for JWH Interview," April 18, 1977.
27. Austin Kiplinger, "Company History Interview."

Index

accountability journalism, 130–31
Acheson, Dean, 161
After Seven Years (Moley), 105, 156–57
Agricultural Adjustment Act, 5
Alger, George W., 12
Almquist, Sally, 36, 62–63, 64
Amalgamated Association of Iron, Steel, and Tin Workers, 180
American Electric Railway Association, 78
American Enterprise Institute, 199
American Family Robinson, 183
American Federation of Labor (AFL), 15, 172, 174–77, 185–86; internal rifts in, 190–92
American Guardian, 176
American Lawyer, 18
American Liberty League, 15, 29, 138, 144–46, 168, 183, 185, 198–99
American Petroleum Institute, 19, 70
American Society of Newspaper Editors, 10, 21, 118
Annals of the American Academy of Political and Social Science, 22
anonymous sources, 118–21, 202–3
antimonopoly legislation, 76–77
anti-Semitism, 158–60
Associated Press, 4, 9, 10, 20, 32–33, 113–14, 199
associationalism, 7, 19, 67, 69–70, 71
Association of New York State Young Republican Clubs, 184
Astor, Vincent, 103
Aucoin, James, 46
Austin, Irene, 34
automobile industry, 77, 142, 150, 165, 178, 184, 185–86

Babson, Paul T., 35, 60, 126
Baltimore Sun, 53
bank holiday, Great Depression, 140–44

Baruch, Bernard, 52, 58, 141
Bay Tree Resort, 63–65
Beck, James M., 180
Berle, Adolph, Jr., 90
Bethlehem Steel, 173
Black, Eugene, 120, 125
Black, Hugo, 172
Black Lives Matter, 8
Blair, Ann, 136
Bloomberg Government, 205
Bloomberg News, 202, 204
The Bond Buyer, 18
Boom and Inflation Ahead (Kiplinger), 21, 40, 50
Boston Globe, 7, 24
Bourke-White, Margaret, 72
Brain Trust, 2, 13, 90, 160, 186
Brandeis, Lewis, 10–11, 13, 93
Briggs Manufacturing Company, 185
Brooke, Irv, 65
Browder, Earl, 23
Brown, Herb, 36, 200–201
"Brown Letter," 133, 191
Bryan, William Jennings, 140
Bryant, George, 32, 36, 65, 71, 116–17, 198, 205
Buck, Pearl, 160
Budd Manufacturing, 180
Buick, 185
Business and Legislation Report, 127
The Business Forum of the Air, 50
Business Intelligence Bureau, 122
business journalism, 16–18, 23, 46–49, 115–16, 200
Business Week, 27, 147, 160, 199, 206; on the bank holiday, 143; contribution to public discourse, 22; on currency and monetary policy, 152; on FDR's utility proposals, 196; on fights over the National Labor Board, 180; on Johnson, 55; on the

Business Week (continued)
  labor movement, 171, 175, 177–78, 185–86; on the National Recovery Act, 172, 180; on the New Deal, 133, 135, 148–49; on the Senate Banking Committee hearings of 1933, 85–87; on Tugwell, 161–62; on the US Chamber of Commerce, 16
Byrns, Joseph, 88, 97

Call-Bulletin, 87
capitalism: associationalism and, 69–70; changes in, after World War I, 74–76; democracy and, 8; Kiplinger's theory of modified, 14; managerial phase of, 18, 75; Moley and, 94–95; questions about future of, 13; re-envisioning the corporate executive and, 72; Senate Banking Committee hearings of 1933 and, 85–87; welfare, 76. *See also* laissez-faire economics
Carpenter, R. R. M., 145
Carter, Jimmy, 37
Caswell, Harold, 45
Celler, Emanuel, 160
Chandler, Alfred, 18, 77
Changing Times, 23, 40
Cherne, Leo M., 124
Ching, Cyrus, 174, 184
Christians, Clifford, 62
Christian Science Monitor, 21
Clapper, Raymond, 37, 58, 115, 120, 147
Clayton Antitrust Act, 13, 77
Cleveland News, 21
Clifford, Clark, 52
Club for Growth, 138
Cobb, Mary Louise, 44
Cohen, Nancy, 14, 22
Coit, Lew, 44, 64
Columbia Journalism Review, 51
Comfort, 136
Commercial and Financial Chronicle, 115
Commonwealth Club, 85, 95
Communist Party, 21, 23, 50–51, 191–92
Compton, Ann, 51
Congressional Quarterly, 138
Congressional Record, 22
Congress of Industrial Organizations, 189
Cook, Yates, 22

Cooke, Morris, 194
Corcoran, Thomas, 11, 43
corporate lobbying, 78
Cosmopolitan, 22
Coughlin, Charles, 158
COVID-19 pandemic, 8
Cox, James, 38
Crain's New York Business, 24
crowdsourcing by *The Kiplinger Washington Letter*, 126–29
Crusaders, 146–47
currency policy, 139–40, 151–52
Curtis, Raleigh T., 48

Daily Worker, 23, 50, 191–92
Dana, William Buck, 115
Darrow, Clarence, 98
Davis, Gerald, 75, 76
Davis, John W., 145
Dawley, Alan, 70, 177
Dennis, Everett, 206
Dennis Publishing, 23, 41, 58, 129
Dewey, Thomas, 21
Dickinson, Lester J., 165
Dubofsky, Melvyn, 178–79, 182
du Pont, Irénée, 29, 138, 144, 145
du Pont, Lammot, 144
du Pont, Pierre, 144
Durkheim, Émile, 131–32

Eaton, Henry. M., 123
Eccles, Marriner, 82, 120, 125, 173–74
The Economist, 115
Edmondson, Richard, 49
Eichengreen, Barry, 45, 152
E. I. du Pont de Nemours & Co., 77
Eisenhower, Dwight D., 111
electric utilities, regulation of, 193–96
Emergency Banking Act of 1933, 141
Emergency Relief Construction Act, 81
Emmons, William M., 195
Endres, Kathleen, 121–22
The Enforcers: How Little-Known Trade Reporters Exposed the Keating Five and Advanced Business Journalism (R. Wells), 17, 28, 200
Enforcers Thesis, 130–31, 204–6
Ethisphere, 63
explanatory journalism, 20–21

Farley, James, 89, 98, 104, 105
Federal City Council, 37, 52
Federal Communications Commission, 79
Federal Emergency Relief Administration, 98, 104
Federal Farm Board, 81
Federal Housing Administration, 79
Federal Reserve, 13, 45, 77, 82–83, 125, 128, 141, 143
Federal Trade Commission Act, 77
Filene, Edward, 42
Filene, Lincoln, 145
First New Deal, 27, 28; associationalism and, 19; big business as victor in, 132; FDR's conflict signals to labor movement in, 181; industry self-regulation and organization in, 15; Kiplinger's audience engagement regarding, 134, 205–6; *The Kiplinger Washington Letter* and, 204; Moley and, 94; National Industrial Recovery Act as centerpiece of, 93; *Schechter* decision as end of, 188; theory of modified capitalism in, 14. *See also* New Deal
Fisher Body, 185
Flandin, Pierre-Étienne, 153
Forbes, 135, 199
Ford, Gerald, 37
Ford, Henry, 142, 150, 184, 186, 204
Forde, Kathy Roberts, 115
Fortune, 17, 22, 27, 46, 72, 82, 115, 135, 206; on the AFL, 174–75, 177, 190; on amateurs in the FDR administration, 163–64; anti-Semitism and, 159; on business views of unrestrained competition, 140–41; on the evolving role of business in society, 77–78; on the FDR administration, 80, 84–85; on the labor movement, 171, 176, 178, 184; on leftist cabinet members, 160; on the New Deal, 147, 149; on Perkins, 177; survey of readers, 127–28; on Wagner and the National Industry Recovery Act, 167
Foss, Katherine, 115
Frank, Jerome, 91, 161
Frankfurter, Felix, 83, 161
Freedom Forum Media Studies Center, 206
Freidel, Frank, 70–71
Friedman, Milton, 45, 198

Fugger, Phillip Edward, 16
functionalist journalism, 17–18, 131–34
Fundamental Facts for New Citizens (Moley), 90
Funk, Isaac Kaufmann, 136

Galambos, Louis, 76
Galbraith, John Kenneth, 45, 47, 48
Gans, Herbert, 199
Garrett, Garet, 86, 140, 150, 165, 168
Garrison, Lloyd K., 179
Gaskill, Nelson B., 93
General Electric, 78, 173, 174
General Motors, 77, 165, 178, 184
General Theory of Employment, Interest and Money (Keynes), 82
Glende, Philip, 169
Gomber, William, 49
Goodrich Tire, 180
Goodyear Tire and Rubber Company, 138
Gordon, Colin, 77
Grady, Henry F., 97
Graham, Philip L., 37, 52
Granducci, Oeveste, 36–37, 111
Great Depression, 4–5, 12, 28–29, 66; associationalism and, 70; bank holiday, 1933, 140–44; rise in demand for business and economic news during, 44–46; Senate Banking Committee hearings of 1933 and, 85–87
Great Recession, 41, 62
Green, William, 191
Griffith, Robert, 75
Grimes, William, 198

Hadden, Briton, 115
Hall, Tammany, 167
Hamilton, David, 4
Harding, Warren, 69
Harper's, 123
Harriman, E. H., 173
Hawley, Ellis, 12, 69, 132
Hayek, Friedrich, 198
Hazard, John, 44, 203
H. C. Frick Company, 180
Hearst, William Randolph, 87
Heidenry, John, 135, 137
Herbert Hoover, Forgotten Progressive (J. H. Wilson), 68

Heritage Foundation, 199
Hinrichs, Ford, 65
Hinshaw, David, 146–47
Hitler, Adolph, 13, 56, 102
Hoover, Herbert, 5, 9, 15, 19, 28, 46, 47, 205; associationalism and, 70; changes in capitalism and business identity and, 74–76; Kiplinger's relationship with, 66–68, 72–73; regulatory worldview of, 68–71; relief programs under, 81; shipping scandal of, 73–74
Hope, Bob, 58
Hopkins, Harry, 98, 104
Houde Engineering Corporation, 180
Howard, Roy, 104
Howard University, 37
Hudson, Howard Penn, 123
Hudson Company, 185
Hull, Cordell, 9, 10, 37, 42, 88, 161, 201; relationship with Moley, 91–92, 96
Hume, Brit, 51
Hutchins, Grace, 146
Huthmacher, J. Joseph, 167

Independent Newsletter Association, 202
Indianapolis Times, 49
Industrial Control Reports, 53
The Industrial Discipline and the Governmental Arts (Tugwell), 83
information overload, 135–37
interpretive journalism, 113, 114–18
Interstate Commerce Act, 76

Jackson, Leslie, 34
John, Richard, 70, 75
Johnson, Hugh, 11, 129, 168, 199; automobile manufacturers and, 178; conflict with Kiplinger, 48, 52–56; fears of radicalism, 13; National Recovery Act and, 90, 98, 112–13, 173, 179
journalism: accountability, 130–31; anonymous sourcing in, 118–21, 202–3; business, 16–18, 23, 46–49, 115–16, 200; close reader engagement and crowdsourcing of information in, 26–27; coverage of the labor movement in the first hundred days of the FDR administration, 169; coverage of the New Deal, 147–51; Enforcers Thesis on, 130–31, 204–6; explanatory, 20–21; functionalist, 17–18, 131–34; during the Great Depression, 44–49; information explosion and, 135–37; interpretive, 113, 114–18; Kiplinger on political bias in, 110–11; objective, 7–8; ownership by, 200–201; regulatory evolution and, 78; role in democratic society, 7–8; role of newsletters in, 24–26; sweep line writing in, 137–38, 203; trust in, 201–3; watchdog, 130. See also newsletters; *specific publications*
Journalism Quarterly, 22, 116, 137
The Journalist, 115
Journal of Commerce, 43

Kalish, Max, 58
Katz, Elihu, 127
Keating, Charles, 200
Kennedy, George, 35, 37, 111
Kennedy, Joseph, 37, 98
Keynes, John Maynard, 82
Kiplinger, Austin, 26, 32, 156, 200, 205, 206; on Dennis Publishing, 41; real estate developments by, 59–60; relationship with Willard, 34–35, 37–39, 121; split with Willard, 43–44
Kiplinger, Bonnie, 34, 44, 58
Kiplinger, Clarence Gale, 32, 34, 59, 64
Kiplinger, Herman Miller, 32
Kiplinger, Jane Ann, 34
Kiplinger, Knight, 35, 38–39, 44, 58, 125, 129
Kiplinger, LaVerne Colwell, 34, 56–57, 59, 60–61
Kiplinger, Peter, 34
Kiplinger, Todd, 44
Kiplinger, Willard: ambition of, 32; associationalism and, 7, 19, 67, 71; attempt heal rifts in the FDR administration, 11; Bay Tree Resort and, 63–65; books by, 21–22, 40, 41, 50; on change in concept of liberalism in business, 14; conflicts with others, 42–43; conflict with Morgenthau, 108–10; the Crusaders and, 146–47; death of, 38–39; dispute with Johnson, 52–56; early years of, 32–39; on end of laissez-faire capitalism, 84; explaining the new order, 11–14; on explanatory journalism, 20–21; fear of failure of, 31; influence on public discourse, 22–23, 27, 49–52; interpretive journalism and,

Index

113, 114–18; involvement in community organizations, 37, 52; journalistic style of, 25, 199–200; legacies of, 198–200; as link between conservative business leaders and government regulators, 5; marriages and children of, 34–35; National Association of Manufacturers and, 156–58; on the New Deal, 79–80; New Deal debates and, 1–3; perfectionism of, 26, 35–36; as political actor, 9, 10; on political bias in journalism, 110–11; political philosophy of, 38; portrayal of Tugwell, 100–101; quiet social life of, 37–38; real estate holdings of, 58–60; re-envisioning the corporate executive, 72; relationship with Hoover, 66–68, 72–73; relationship with Landon, 106–8; relationship with Moley, 88–89, 92–94, 97–98, 198–99; relationship with Wilder, 112–13; specialized knowledge of finance and business of, 9; split with Austin, 43–44; sweep line writing developed by, 137–38, 203; trustworthiness of, 201–3; typewriter of, 30, 31; use of close reader engagement and crowdsourcing of information by, 26–27; wealth and generosity of, 25–28, 56–58, 65, 203–4; weekly reporting methods of, 119; work for the Associated Press, 32–33, 114, 199

Kiplinger Employees Profit Sharing Plan, 60–63

Kiplinger Foundation, 56, 57

Kiplinger Magazine, 23, 40, 43

Kiplinger's Family Buying Guide, 40

Kiplinger's Personal Finance, 23, 40, 129, 138, 206

Kiplinger Washington Agency, 39–41

The Kiplinger Washington Letter, 3–4, 5; anonymous sources used by, 118–21; anti-Semitism and, 159; on the bank holiday, 142–43; "Brown Letter," 133, 191; circulation of, 40, 123; Communist Party and, 23, 50–51, 191–92; coverage of the National Recovery Act, 171–73; coverage of the New Deal, 147–51; coverage of the Wagner Act, 182–83; criticism of Roper, 99; crowdsourcing by, 126–29; difference from trade journalism, 17; direct mail solicitation of, 40–41, 121; Enforcers Thesis and, 130–31, 204–6; as explanatory journalism, 20–21; FDR's subscription to, 120–21; functionalist role of, 16, 131–34; on government regulation as here to stay, 155–56; on the Hoover shipping scandal, 73–74; information overload and, 135–37; initial financing of, 33; interpretive role of, 116; on the labor movement, 169, 175–78; on Landon, 106–7; launch of, 10, 33–34; marketing strategy for, 124–26; as newsletter, 24–26, 40, 121–24; portrayal of Moley, 103–4; public sphere created by, 134–35; readership of, 14–15, 33–34; rise in demand for, during the Great Depression, 44–46; role of journalism in democratic society and, 7–8; sample of, 6; on the *Schechter Poultry Corp v. United States* decision, 187–88; on the stock market crash in 1929, 47–48; widespread influence of, 21–23; on the World Economic Conference, 153–55

Knight, Frank, 14, 84

Koch brothers, 138

Krock, Arthur, 120

labor movement, 80, 83, 87, 134; automobile industry and, 77, 142, 150, 165, 178, 184, 185–86; coverage of, in the first hundred days of the FDR administration, 169; internal rifts in, 190–92; *The Kiplinger Washington Letter* portrayals of, 175–78; labor market dynamics from the 1920s to the 1930s and, 170–71; Triangle Shirtwaist Factory fire and, 166–67

laissez-faire economics: associationalism and, 70; conservative business owners defending, 8; Kiplinger on, 164; liberalism and changes in, 75, 77; Moley on, 91–92; the New Deal and the end of, 5, 12, 14, 81–85. *See also* capitalism

Landis, James, 81, 161

Landon, Alf, 20, 106–8, 156–57

The Lantern, 32, 34

Lasswell, Harold, 132

Lazarsfeld, Paul, 127

Lewis, John L., 58, 174, 189, 191

liberalism, 75–76, 77, 86, 167

Liberty, 137

Lindley, Ernest K., 120

Lippmann, Walter, 136
Litchfield, P. W., 138
Literary Digest, 22, 108, 126, 136, 188
Littell's Living/Age, 136
Long, Huey, 154, 170, 193
Luce, Henry, 115, 136
Lund, Robert L., 183
Lundberg, Ferdinand, 122, 124

MacArthur, Douglas, 66
Mallon, Paul, 115
Marshall, Robert, 36
Mayer, Jane, 199
McAdoo, William Gibbs, 120
McCall's, 25
McCraw, Thomas, 77, 81, 194
McCusker, John, 115
McFadden Act, 39, 42, 201
McGuire, Constantine, 93, 94
Meany, George, 83
Mellon, Andrew, 85
Merton, Robert, 131
Meyer, Eugene, 114
Michelson, Charles, 53, 54–55
Mills, C. Wright, 169
Mills, Ogden, 90
Mitchell, Charles, 85
Moley, Raymond, 1–3, 9, 11, 27, 29, 43, 49, 83, 169; break with FDR, 105; capitalism and, 94–95; the Crusaders and, 146–47; Johnson and, 52, 54, 56; Kiplinger's advice to, 97–98; Kiplinger's cultivation of, as source, 92–94; *The Kiplinger Washington Letter* and, 3–4, 103–4; National Association of Manufacturers and, 157–58; political education of, 89–91; as political moderate, 91–92; relationship with Kiplinger, 88–89, 198–99; relations with media, 104–5; on the FDR's new political coalition and the Democratic Party, 189; tariff debate and, 95–97; *Today* magazine and, 101–3
Montana Labor News, 192
Morgan, J. P., 18, 75, 78, 85
Morgenthau, Henry, Jr., 9, 10, 82, 104, 108–10
Mott, Frank Luther, 44, 137

National Association of Manufacturers, 29, 70, 156–58, 180, 183, 198–99

National Bank of Commerce, 33, 118, 122–23
National Civic Federation, 70
National Industrial Recovery Act, 27–29, 182; automobile manufacturers and, 178; Brandeis and, 11; conservative opposition to, 180; criticism of, 147–51; industry self-regulation and, 15, 19; Johnson and, 53; Kiplinger's coverage of, 17, 133, 171–73; labor movement and, 80; laissez-faire capitalism countered by, 95; Moley's role in, 2, 5; purchasing power and, 173–74; FDR's mixed signals on, 178–81; *Schechter Poultry Corp v. United States* and, 186–88; Section 7(a), 174–75; Tugwell and, 83; Wagner and, 166; Wilder and, 112
National Labor Board, 178–81
National Labor Relations Act. *See* Wagner Act/National Labor Relations Act
National Labor Relations Board, 79, 87
National Mail Order Association, 122
National Press Club, 37, 98
National Press Foundation, 23, 51
National Recovery Administration, 10–11, 13, 15, 17, 48, 52, 112, 138
National Review, 105
National Thrift News, 130, 200
Nation's Business, 33
Neal, Jesse H., 122
neoliberalism, 19, 29, 69
New Deal, 1–7, 9–10, 12–13, 28, 68; American Liberty League and, 144–46; anti-Semitism and position to, 158–60; business backlash against, 14–16, 28–29, 138–39, 144–46, 183–85; claims about leftist influence on, 160–63; currency policy and gold standard under, 139–40, 151–52; discord within the FDR administration over, 147–48; electric utilities and, 193–96; end of laissez-faire and, 81–85; explained by Kiplinger to the business community, 13–14; goals of, 79–81; growing unpopularity of, 188–89; labor market dynamics and, 170–71; modified capitalism and, 14; negative press coverage of, 117–18; purchasing power and economic theory addressed by, 173–74; Revenue Act of 1935 and, 192–93. *See also* First New Deal; Second New Deal
New Freedom, 12, 13
New Nationalism, 12

Index

Newsletter on Newsletters, 130
newsletters, 24–26, 40, 121–24, 202. *See also* journalism
Newsweek, 7, 24, 25, 51, 138
New York Daily News, 48
The New Yorker, 135
New York Herald Tribune, 53, 104, 120
New York Post, 114
New York Stock Exchange, 85–87
New York Times, 27, 80, 120, 147, 199, 201, 203; on the 1929 stock market crash, 45–46; American Liberty League and, 146; on the bank holiday, 143; on the bull market, 48; on business opposition to the Wagner Act, 185; on currency and monetary policy, 154; on FDR's utilities proposals, 195–96; Kiplinger's obituary in, 33; Kiplinger's writing in, 21, 31, 42, 206; on the National Recovery Act, 172; on Wagner, 168; on the Wagner Act, 183
Niebuhr, Reinhold, 116
Nielsen, Jakob, 138
Nixon, Richard, 105
Norris-LaGuardia Act of 1932, 174
Noyes, Alexander D., 48

objective journalism, 7–8
Ohio State Journal, 9, 32
Okrent, Arika, 138
ownership by professional journalists, 200–201

Parsons, Talcott, 131
Parsons, Wayne, 23, 115
Pearson, Drew, 119
Perkins, Frances, 58, 104, 177, 179
Phillips, Cabell, 173
Phillips-Fein, Kim, 82, 83, 86, 145, 177
Politico Pro, 41, 205
populism, 189, 192
Porter, Sylvia, 206
Pratt, Joseph, 76
Producers News, 23
profit sharing, 60–63
Progressive Era, 12, 13; landmarks in regulation during, 76–78
Public Opinion (Lippman), 136
Public Utilities Holding Company, 194–95
purchasing power, 173–74

Pure Food and Drug Act, 78
Pyle, Ernie, 58

Quirt, John, 46–49

Railway Labor Act, 174
Ramsey, Bruce, 76
Raskob, John J., 145
Rayburn, Sam, 58, 97, 105
Reader's Digest, 126, 135, 136, 137, 158, 203; anti-Semitism and, 160
real estate holdings of Kiplinger, 58–60
Reciprocal Trade Agreement of 1934, 96
Reconstruction Finance Corporation, 81, 142
Reed, Earl F., 145, 146, 183
Reilly, Kevin S., 46, 72
Research Institute of America, 127
Reuter, Paul Julius, 115
Revenue Act of 1935, 192–93
Richberg, Donald, 98, 156, 179
Robinson, Frances, 54
Rockefeller, John D., 18, 75, 78
Rockwell, Norman, 57–58
Rodgers, Margaret, 34, 203
Roosevelt, Eleanor, 162
Roosevelt, Franklin D. (FDR), 1–5, 9, 12–13, 26, 79, 83, 120–21; associationalism and, 7, 19; cabinet of, 160–64; Kiplinger's writing shared with, 42–43; relationship with Moley, 90, 105; relationship with Wagner, 168; tax legislation, 1935, and, 192–93; World Economic Conference, 1933, and, 153–55. *See also* New Deal
Roosevelt, Theodore, 12, 76
Roper, Daniel C., 11, 99
Rorty, Malcolm, 93, 145
Rotary Club, 21, 124
Rural Electrification Administration, 194
Ruth, Carl D., 38
Ryerson, John, 5, 39, 44

Sachs, Alexander, 141
San Diego Union, 21
Saturday Evening Post, 22, 24–25, 34, 56, 86, 137, 147
Sawyer, Laura Phillips, 69
Sayre, Francis B., 96
Schechter Poultry Corp. v. United States, 186–88
Schlesinger, Arthur, Jr., 168, 179

Schwab, Charles M., 173
Scrap-Book, 136
Scribner's, 16, 21
Second New Deal, 29, 169, 196–97. *See also* New Deal
Section 7(a), National Industrial Recovery Act, 174–75
Securities Act of 1933, 80
Securities and Exchange Commission, 80–81, 98, 102, 145; public utilities and, 195
Securities Exchange Act, 80
Senate Banking Committee hearings, 1933, 85–87
Sherman Antitrust Act, 76
Shouse, Catherine Filene, 145
Shouse, Jouett, 145
Sidey, Hugh, 70–71
Sloan, Alfred P., Jr., 165, 184
Smith, Al, 138, 167
Smith, George David, 85
Smithsonian Institution, 58
socialism, 18, 190
Social Security Act, 166
Social Security Administration, 79
Society of Professional Journalists, 10
Spool, Jared, 138
Standard Oil, 76–77, 78, 184
Starr, Paul, 22, 130
statism, 70
Storm, Frederick A., 120
Strachan, Stan, 200
Studebaker, John, 51
sweep line writing, 137–38, 203
Sweet, William Ellery, 10, 42
Swope, Gerard, 145, 173, 174
Sylla, Richard Eugene, 85

Tampa Tribune, 21
Tarbell, Ida, 78
tariffs, 95–97
tax legislation, 1935, 192–93
Taylor, Myron, 174
Teagle, Walter C., 184
Tea Party, 29, 138
Television Digest, 202
Temin, Peter, 45, 152
Tennessee Valley Authority, 195
theSkimm, 24
Time, 22, 53, 115–16, 135, 136

Tocqueville, Alexis de, 69
Today, 21, 28, 54, 92, 101–3
Tomorrow, 51
trade associations, 165
trade policies, 95–97
transparency in journalism, 118–21, 202–3
Triangle Shirtwaist Factory fire, 166–67
True, James, 53
Truman, Harry, 21
Trump, Donald, 8, 29, 202
trust in journalism, 201–3
Tugwell, Rexford Guy, 11, 13, 18, 43, 83, 89, 90, 199; *Kiplinger Washington Letter* on, 100–101; leftist views of, 161–62

Underwear Institute, 185
United Mine Workers, 58, 174, 177, 178
United Negro College Fund, 37
United States Shipping Board, 73–74
United Textile Workers, 171
Urban League, 37
US Chamber of Commerce, 16, 19, 33, 51, 70, 80, 141, 165, 173
U.S. News & World Report, 7
US Rubber, 174, 184
US Steel, 174, 180

Vanderlip, Frank, 145

Wagnalls, Adam, 136
Wagner, Robert: labor relations and, 174; National Industrial Recovery Act and, 166, 167–68, 178–79; relationship with FDR, 168
Wagner Act/National Labor Relations Act, 27, 29, 80, 146, 166, 194; business opposition to, 183–85; introduction and FDR's endorsement of, 181–82; *The Kiplinger Washington Letter* coverage of, 182–83
Wallace, DeWitt, 136, 160
Wallace, Henry, 11, 51, 104, 161
Wallace, Lila, 160
Wall Street Journal, 7, 17, 24, 26, 47–49, 51, 65, 71, 198, 202
War Industries Board, 172, 173
Washington Evening Star, 37, 49, 53, 117, 202
Washington Is Like That (Kiplinger), 21, 50, 159, 206
Washington Post, 23, 24, 37, 52, 62–63

Index

watchdog journalism, 130
wealth and generosity of Kiplinger, 25–28, 56–58, 65, 203–4
Weinstein, James, 77
Weirton Steel, 168
welfare capitalism, 76
Wenn, J. Preston, 26
Westinghouse, 78
WETA-TV, 23, 37, 65
Whaley, Percival Huntington, 123
Whaley-Eaton Service Newsletter, 123, 127
Whitaker, Joel, 40, 130
Whitney, Richard, 85

Wietzel, W. E., 4
Wilder, Harold K., 112–13
Will, George, 23
Wilson, Joan Hoff, 68
Wilson, Woodrow, 8, 12–13, 32–33, 38, 42, 74, 76, 114
Women's Christian Temperance Union, 38
Woodin, William H., 86, 90, 91, 104
World Economic Conference, 153–55
World War I, 32, 70, 144

Young, Owen, 184
YouTube, 127

ROB WELLS is associate professor at the Philip Merrill College of Journalism at the University of Maryland. He is author of *The Enforcers: How Little-Known Trade Reporters Exposed the Keating Five and Advanced Business Journalism.* He earned a PhD in journalism studies in 2016 from the University of Maryland Philip Merrill College of Journalism and an MA in liberal studies in 2013 from St. John's College in Annapolis. He is the former deputy bureau chief of the *Wall Street Journal* Washington bureau, and prior to that, bureau chief of the Dow Jones Newswires Washington Bureau, and reporter for Bloomberg News, the Associated Press, and for small newspapers in California.